idea INDUSTRY

How to crack the advertising career code

D1533806

BRETT ROBBS University of Colorado at Boulder
DEBORAH MORRISON University of Oregon

EXECUTIVE EDITOR
Mary Warlick

EDITOR
Yash Egami

DESIGNER
Jennah Synnesvedt

© 2008 by One Club Publishing

First published in the United States
of America by:
One Club Publishing
21 E. 26th Street
New York, NY 10010
(212) 979-1900
www.oneclub.org

Distributed in the US
and Internationally by:
Rockport Publishers, a member
of Quayside Publishing Group
100 Cummings Center
Suite 406-L
Beverly, Massachusetts 01915-6101
Telephone: (978) 282-9590
Fax: (978) 283-2742
www.rockpub.com

ISBN-13: 978-0-929837-33-8
ISBN-10: 0-929837-33-9

10 9 8 7 6 5 4 3 2 1

To my students, whose creativity and insight make both advertising
and the world touched by its images just a little brighter.

BR

To talented and passionate students who taught me so much
as we became friends
and—always—to Dan, Alex, Sam + Max

DKM

Contents

THIS IS BIG

It's the beginning of your career in advertising. And it starts as you find mentors, inspiration, information, and ideas that lead you to what you want to be.

This, friends, is huge.

Whether you're in school, graduated, or considering a career change, your first mission is to understand the industry. Then, you need to figure out what the advertising industry needs from you. When you have that at the ready, you can start carving out a place as change agent and leader-in-training for a workplace that needs bright people with new ideas.

We've conducted over 100 interviews with the people who've gotten the jobs you want. We've talked to the gatekeepers and the big dogs. And we've collected thinking that shows where the industry is going, from people who lead the way.

We like to think this book can be part of the best career decision you've ever made.

As you decide whether you want to pursue that career in an advertising agency, of course, you need to know what it's like. Yes, you could save a few dollars and ask your parents or Uncle Charlie or a neighbor about it. But they can only tell you about one or two agencies at best. And—let's face it—the info might not be as smart as you'd like.

This book will let you hear from executives at many of the top agencies all across the country. They'll tell you what each career path in an advertising agency is all about from copywriting, art direction, and production to account service, account planning, and media. You'll discover how the departments come together to support one another and produce projects no single individual or department could pull off. And you'll see it's those very connections between people in different disciplines who are eager to hop fences and cross borders that make great ideas happen.

We collected updates on how interactive agencies are using new approaches to advertising. We looked at traditional agencies and noted how they're using innovative brand strategies for their clients and how they're changing their own organizations to reflect new thinking. We talked to folks who believe in the glory of the big idea, no matter what media it lives in.

No boring stuff, just real info you can use.

In fact, advertising is as far from boring as you can get. Every part of it is creative. After all, it's about ideas. Not only the ideas for the ads you see on TV, in magazines, and on the web, for example. But also insights about how consumers think, how they use media, and how brands can solve business problems. As Jeff Steinhour, Managing Partner and Director of Content Management at Crispin Porter + Bogusky, says, "If you love manufacturing cool ideas, it's a wonderful business to be in."

There's no better way to learn about advertising than from the people who live it every day. So we draw on their experiences to tell you all about the creativity, problem solving, art, and commerce that can make days at the agency a remarkable and meaningful adventure.

We take you to the workplaces and idea factories to show you what it took to create some of the advertising campaigns that you've probably seen and enjoyed. And we'll tell you about the interpersonal dynamics that make agency jobs both challenging and rewarding. We've collected these stories over the last couple of years of listening and weaving together the best advice possible.

In this industry, people and accounts move all the time—someone working in media at Crispin last week might be at an agency in Seattle or Philadelphia today. So consider this a window cut into the working lives of dozens of people that offers insight into their careers at one particular moment.

Giving you that insider's view of what the advertising business is all about will help you decide whether you want to pursue this profession. If you do, you can see what kinds of skills professionals say you'll need to bring to the table. And you'll come to understand how, in a world of war and politics and poverty, the advertising industry can help the world actually change for the better.

But you'll also get the "I need to know now!" part of starting a career. Like how to craft an effective résumé, how to be an effective part of a meeting, and how to handle the interview itself, including that crazy salary question.

We'll also help you think about very real questions concerning social responsibility and doing the right thing with your talents. The advertising industry needs you to be responsible, relevant, and ready to do good.

Advertising is evolving quickly. It's inventing media and becoming part of entertainment, gaming, podcasting, and blogging. Quite frankly, agencies need you. They need fresh, creative minds not tied to old ways of doing things, people eager to explore new media and new approaches who base all they do on strong ideas.

We're confident that this expert testimony is the best collection of advice and inspiration that could be gathered for people wanting to break into the advertising business. Right now, at the end of the first decade of the 21st century, you need information that is fresh and visionary. Those who've read the chapters and looked over the advice—graduating students and those out in their first year of job-hunting—pronounce it "life-changing" and "the best collection of usable advice to explain what this career is all about."

So we hope you'll explore with the idea that big things are about to happen to you. We want to prepare you for that. We believe this little book will give you a slight edge, one that can make a difference in your job search and help you launch your own highly successful advertising career.

Then we'll call on you for the next big wave of inspiring stories. That's how it works.

Brett Robbs
University of Colorado at Boulder

Deborah Morrison
University of Oregon

Razor-sharp strategies, brilliant media plans, pre- and post-measurement, focus groups, econometric media models, consumer connection touch-points, and whatever other marketing hooha exists out there mean absolutely nothing without a great, engaging creative idea at the other end.

David Baldwin
Former Executive Creative Director
McKinney
Durham, North Carolina

AND SO WE BEGIN WITH THE IMPORTANT STUFF: taxidermy, that Ferris Bueller scene in the middle of a Chicago parade, mad scientists, playing pool in that cool pizza parlor, cultural engineers, and changing the world. It's all inspiration for the ideas that will flip and spin and transform into wonderful messages.

This advertising gig is about making ideas come to life.

Although the entire advertising industry is a creative playground, we're going to talk here about the shorthand, easy definition of creative professionals: the people who think up and execute advertising and branding ideas on a daily basis. These folks have creativity officially written into a job description and a career plan.

Creatives — advertising writers and art directors and designers — can lead a wonderful life. They are deputized in the industry to take strategy and make it sing. They are asked to be poetic about ketchup and appliances and tennis shoes while being given the opportunity to help create empires for big brands and great issues. They travel, they meet famous people, and many become famous themselves along the way. They must attend to the logical — deadlines, reports, budgets, clients who want satisfaction — and to the fanciful — *What if we used a blimp? How many monkeys does it take to change a light bulb? What does October taste like?*

In truth, creatives carry a substantial load of the success story of the agency and the industry; when we think advertising, we think of the beautiful — or the not-so-beautiful — ads that proliferate in our culture.

> **This is a job that pays you not only to sit around and think of ideas for print and TV spots but also gives you serious money to produce them. It's a job that pays you to not only sit around and think of ideas for print and TV spots but also television shows, movies, short films, video games, hit songs, concerts, magazines, books, clothing lines, furniture, toys, software, websites, and anything else that can express a brand idea. And finally, it's a job that lets you do all this while sporting shorts and flip-flops.**
>
> *William Gelner, Executive Creative Director, 180, Los Angeles*

And it's not a regular kind of 9-to-5 job. It's a way of life. Creatives are pushed to work a near 24/7 existence inside their heads. They let their brains go boldly where others have not, taking risks and asking *what if?* as regularly as they guzzle coffee. In the best cases, they are even given permission to fail; that is, not all of their ideas are expected to make the cut. In the rough-and-tumble world of professional creativity that means maybe one idea out of a hundred might make it to a client meeting.

Writers and art directors work and play and win awards in the business by virtue of how well they can imagine and bring their best ideas to life in a hectic environment. In fact, the job is so much fun that one young writer, who spent a month filming in South Africa during his first year out and won a bucket of awards for his work, now wonders why he ever contemplated law school.

Since the goal is imaginative and provocative work, you should study the best. Consider how it ticks and who made it work that way. Here's a great example of engaging work that connects with an audience and was awarded the 2007 One Show Best of Show: Tate Tracks. Fallon, London created this multimedia campaign for London's Tate Modern museum, targeting 16-24 year olds who didn't use the facility. It was a year-long promotion involving established musicians who composed exclusive tracks inspired by their favorite works of art on display at the Tate. It used posters, postcards, radio, packaging, street media, and PR. It created buzz. It made a difference.

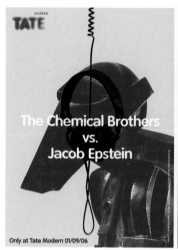

And it grew from a collaboration of creatives and account people and planners who pushed the boundaries of what advertising can be. That's the work you should aspire to.

If you're feeling the magic, then read on. We'll walk you through what the creative industry is, what type of preparation and training you'll need, whom you should connect with, and why — with just a few smart pieces — your portfolio needs to show work that inspires someone else. That ability to create great work is what will set you apart and begin your career.

Writers and Art Directors

Let's start with the basics. Copywriters and art directors (CWs and ADs) work individually and in paired teams. They use gut instinct and mix that with insights given to them by account planners, media planners, and account executives, and then they turn the whole thing into a beautifully crafted idea that connects to someone. Creative directors usually select the people on their creative team, sometimes hiring teams and sometimes combining groups of writers and art directors for the right synergy. If the agency is large enough and the creative director needs a hand, a creative manager will be the gatekeeper to get the right talent through the door and viewed by agency creative leaders.

A Little History to Let You Know How We Got Here

Back in the early days of advertising, writers wrote and art directors designed and visualized, with no mingling between the two job descriptions. They worked separately and didn't talk much even when working on the same account. In fact, creatives weren't always considered that much of a talent base but rather were looked at as producers of necessary content. Bill Bernbach, advertising creative hero and founder of Doyle Dane Bernbach (DDB) in the late 1940s, was a gifted writer and a brilliant manager. He knew that his best ideas happened when he sat in the office and talked with art director pal Paul Rand (now a One Club Hall-of-Famer just like Bernbach), and they solved the problem together.

Bernbach Knew What It Took to Create Meaningful Work

Bernbach was inspired. His agency reinvented how creatives work by teaming the two parts of the creative endeavor. The creative team concept was born from that, and it changed the way the industry used its talented creative base. Stellar advertising became a reality, even marking that time and the advertising aura created by that shop with the enduring label, "creative revolution."

The revolution was really about people and how they work. It's now a given: Creatives work in teams — unlike any other industry except maybe for cops in patrol cars like Starsky & Hutch — and a team's ability to work in sync becomes vitally important to the success of the process. We expect great work from the right people and partnerships.

The Get It Factor

Writers and art directors build careers on their ideas. And the ideas come before the type treatment, before the smart headline, before the cool alternative media. Idea is king. No, wait, idea is emperor.

Now, writers often solve problems visually or with no words at all; art directors and designers sometimes write headlines and taglines and find the right words to fulfill the strategy. Sometimes two writers or two art directors make things happen depending on agency size and culture. And in some agencies, art directors and designers — traditionally classified in a world all their own — now see more overlap in the way they work and in the language they use to grow and describe their craft. You'll hear their titles often used interchangeably, though their focus and process is often a bit different.

The important thing to know: Writers and art directors are, above all else, idea people. Adrian Alexander, a writer at Crispin Porter + Bogusky (Crispin) in Boulder, sums it up this way: "How does my job differ from an art director's? In the beginning of the process, there is absolutely no difference. Only later when we get into crafting and production stages do the blurred lines come into focus. You're not necessarily a great creative because you can write headlines and think up cool visuals. You come up with that stuff because you're a great idea person. That's the key."

It comes down to this: No matter the pairing or the job title, two brains offer a powerful synergistic approach to solving problems.

How It All Gets Done

How a project moves from assignment to finished product varies by account, agency size, and type of agency. Basically, the process works something like we explain here. But beware, every agency works differently. Many pride themselves on their own organizational and process structure. So use this as an example of what might be.

Writer Adrian Alexander works another late night at Crispin in Boulder. Long hours, hectic schedule, millions of ideas are part of the job description.

Writers and art directors report to an associate creative director (ACD) and creative director (CD) who have moved up the agency food chain to manage the creative process and finished product. That creative director is assigned the task of orchestrating the direction of creative work for the group or the agency, depending on his or her level and title.

So, an assignment might come through the creative director for a print campaign, a radio script, or a viral branding approach. It might be for collateral (coasters? booklets? point of purchase?) or out-of-home posters or that online project that the client bought. At some agencies, juniors can even be assigned a TV or video project fairly quickly. There may also be those unexpected requests for your ideas on a short brand film or a set of posters for a pet agency project or event. Focus on the prospect of making great ideas and then decide how those ideas live in different media.

You should know: Now that interactive is no longer considered a "new media" option and just about every agency is pushing for an online presence, there's a distinct possibility that your creative director will throw a digital project your way no matter the agency you're in. It might even be an assignment that calls for an integrated approach to all of the media choices mentioned above. Once again, it depends on how the agency assigns work and how nimbly teams move from making ideas to finding the right medium for the brand message.

After being briefed on the assignment by a CD or strategy team, the job for the writer and art director is to find a concept both can love. They might work together to come up with this, and they might also spend some time working apart. They might go to other meetings or play a game of pool at the pizza place across the street.

"After the briefing, when it's time to put something on paper, I usually don headphones, listen to mindless music, and get down and dirty with my notebook," explains Andrea Minze, a young writer at GSD&M in Austin. "After an hour or so of focus, I'm ready to cruise the halls and find my art director so we can give and take ideas."

Whatever the technique, the partners eventually meet and talk through the possibilities. When they're happy with the directions they've mapped out, it's time to start hammering: headlines, scripts, taglines, and slogans. A writer might go through pages and hours finding the right stuff and sharing that with the art director.

Maybe the art director looks up and says: "Wait! Read that line again. That had a beautiful rhythm." And they think about fine-tuning and layering on type ideas, layout possibilities, or pacing for telling a story on the screen.

Maybe the writer says: "You know the visual concept here has to feel like those carnival posters at the turn-of-the-century." Negotiations, synergy, compromise. About then, it's time to go figure it out, even send some email back and forth to get the details down.

From there, the art director will often turn the concepts the team likes best into rough layouts for presentation. These roughs are more tentative and ready to be explained to a CD who is sure to suggest ways to fine tune the concepts but also may ask to see more approaches or may even have the team start over completely. In a large agency, work approved by an ACD will still need to be approved by more senior managers. Once again, there is sure to be feedback and more revisions.

Not every idea presented makes it out of the agency. In fact, the ratio of ideas produced to work shown the client may be 100-to-1. Agencies want to work to bring down that ratio to something seemingly more efficient. The smarter you get at making the quantity/quality mix work in your favor, the more invaluable you become.

Once the team gets the necessary approvals, roughs grow to comps: Comprehensive layouts, computer work with art/illustrations/photos that really grow the idea. Once these would have been hand-drawn, but these days they're usually a slicker set of computer-generated comps produced by the art director. Some agencies present these to the client on foamcore board to be held or posted in the presentation room, while others use Keynote or PowerPoint. In either scenario, the ideas have to be explained and sold to the client.

Creative meetings happen as concepts are being built. Writer Rex McCubbin at The Martin Agency gets feedback from Senior VP CD Joe Alexander on ideas for the JFK Museum.

Pitching Ideas to Overlords and Clients

Brian Shembeda is a creative director and kickass art director at Arnold in Boston. His take on the process: "The computer comp/layout is the black hole of any AD's time. If I have 72 hours until the presentation, I will work on the layout for 71 hours and 59 minutes before sprinting to the printer and arriving four minutes late to the meeting. This is the AD's revenge because the writer usually performs the complicated song and dance for a hostile crowd of account people/clients in the presentation, only to have the AD arrive bearing gifts." Again, there are sure to be revisions.

Clients will at best want minor changes and sometimes — in the most dastardly scenario — they might kill all of the work and demand to see fresh approaches. But generally, after a few nips and tucks the client is happy, and the work is at last ready to go into production.

If it's a video or film project, both the writer and art director will be involved in casting calls, go on shoots, and watch rushes at the production house. For print work, the art director will work closely with art buyers, illustrators, photographers, and producers. All of this might take a week or a couple of months, depending on the project. For interactive, the ramp up works faster, and the process takes on its own life — one different from that of traditional media. Creative directors will be in on all of this production watch, some hovering close by, some having a hands-off "get it done" attitude.

Finding the Rhythm

Overall, writers and art directors have much to do together and individually to complete the campaign. In terms of time spent executing ideas, art directors probably put more hours in after the idea has been approved. Then again, depending on the team, the agency, the client, and the deadline, the whole process might have a different rhythm.

No matter the rhythm, the workload can be heavy. Former Lowe Worldwide Vice President for Creative Services Betsy Yamazaki offers some perspective on working hard in your first few months: "A new junior team I hired was so busy that the writer actually asked my permission 'if it might possibly be okay' to schedule some personal plans on a Saturday or Sunday at the end of the following month. Gotta love that."

This Team Thing

Although the entire process is certainly team-oriented (and that means everyone on an account — including the client — trusting and working with everyone else), the real partnership is between the writer and art director assigned to bring life to the work. At a small shop, there might be a couple of teams. At a large agency, there might be dozens of teams working on different aspects of one brand and on all of the agency's other work as well.

Tomer Ciubotaru, a writer at Taxi New York, remembers how in his first week his CD smiled and said: "Hmmm...that's an interesting line..... bring me four more pages full of lines like this one. And can you do it in the next hour? We have a client meeting at four. Thanks!"

And remember, for such a huge industry, the creative world is relatively small. You'll find all sorts of relationships — former partners and co-workers, *I used to work with him and he's a real* ____ (insert good or bad descriptor here) sort of connections. People move around, move up the ladder, take on new responsibilities. As they do, they bring with them a network. You'll use yours a million times over the course of your career.

The advice you get often sticks with you. Founder and Creative Director Glenn Cole of Santa Monica's 72andSunny (he and Art Director John Boiler started this fast-track agency after a few high octane years at Wieden + Kennedy in Portland) believes the best advice he ever received was to surround yourself with people who are better than you are. He explains that the remarkable Wieden + Kennedy (W+K) writer Evelyn Monroe "advised me to 'work with a great art director' and the renowned art director Charlotte Moore advised me to 'work with a great writer'." Work with people who push you to be absolutely the greatest you can be, he says. A partner should be someone who makes you do your best work.

Growing a team takes all the relationship mojo of a marriage or at least a long engagement. Peter Rosch and John Hobbs, who were executive creative directors at Lowe New York until 2006, have been partners for years. They're now freelance and have also jumped into the directing game, but they still base ideas of success on their mutual respect for each other.

"Not a day goes by that I don't thank my lucky stars to have him as my partner and friend. And it is important," Rosch explains in a recent blog entry. "Working with someone that you don't quite mesh with makes life miserable. I say life because it is more than work. In this business you see your partner a lot, more than your friends, spouse, girlfriend or boyfriend. I'd put it at roughly 70 percent of the hours in a week."

---

5 Ideas on Growing a Team
Writer Dustin Ballard and Art Director Jason Ambrose formed a dynamite team at Crispin Porter + Bogusky in Miami. They were named one of *Adweek's* young creative teams to watch in 2004.

1 • Chasing Rabbits. I just had a 45-minute discussion with my partner Jason about palindromes. Jason wondered why the word "palindrome" itself was not a palindrome. He suggested "palinilap" while I preferred "wordrow." Jason brought up the fact that everyone's name can be palindromified (mine being Dustinitsud Ballardrallab and Jason's being Jasonosaj Ambrosesorbma).

We theorized that there's probably a language in Africa devised entirely of palindromes but nobody in the Western world has ever picked up on it.

Jason and I have these conversations constantly. Last week it was about taxidermy. I can't tell you exactly what triggers them. The one today started as a brainstorm at Starbucks. And like 99 percent of our conversations, it never led to a brilliant ad idea. This is what we call chasing rabbits.

For us, advertising is a battle between staying on strategy and venturing away. Too much focus on the brief and you haven't gone anywhere. Too much venturing, and you're forever lost in La-La Land chasing taxidermed rabbits.

2 • Schizophrenia. I work best in silence. Jason works best listening to Waylon Jennings. I'm a morning person. Jason's a night owl. And yet we spend 80 hours a week together. It would be a recipe for disaster if we didn't have a common goal: Making ads we're proud to show our friends. And so we compromise. I've learned to work while listening to *Luckenbach Texas*, and he's learned to work in abandoned conference rooms. Sometimes we work late; sometimes we show up early. When you fuse two brains, you're inevitably going to have mild schizophrenia. Don't fight it; learn to love it.

3 • Using your New Brain. Jason and I taught a brainstorming class once at Miami Ad School. There was one student who had a real knack for explaining in detail why someone else's idea wouldn't work. Whenever he spoke, something amazing happened: Nothing. Crickets chirping, tumbleweeds blowing. You could feel the creative flow being sucked out the door. That's when Jason and I realized something we'd been doing all along as a team: Listening.

Any idea we've ever made started as a pathetic, embarrassing, half-baked thing. If you and your partner haven't created an environment where you're comfortable pitching those "bad" ideas out there, you'll never get on base. So listen to your partner. Treat every idea as a Gold Pencil in the rough. Take a swing, and see what happens.

4 • Hunger. We were never given a brief for our first TV spot. We weren't assigned to it. We were told it was "under control." But we worked on it anyway, squeezed a spot through, and two years later we've produced 16 more spots for the same client. Be hungry. Be curious. Be humble. The rest will fall into place. (But don't get too hungry or you'll end up like Jason standing in your boxers at a taco stand in Tijuana).

5 • Formula for Success. Jason and I have a theory called the Law of Decreasing Exponential Success. It goes like this: 1 in 10 of our ideas is worth putting on paper. Of those, 1 in 10 is worth showing our creative director. Then 1 in 10 of those makes it to the client, and 1 in 10 of those is actually published. Therefore, 9,999 in 10,000 ideas have no direct bearing on anything. In summary:

$$S = x/10{,}000$$

Of course, success is inversely related to sleep deprivation, the number of teams working on the assignment, and the number of clients seeing your work. Assuming your creative director's mood fluctuates roughly along a sine wave, the actual formula for success is this:

$$S = f(0/24) \{\sin y(x/10,000)\} \, dx \, / \, c{*}t$$

This is a fun career. While your friends are crunching numbers, you and your partner are getting paid to draw humanoid hot dogs in a sketchbook. Never forget that.

To have a productive partnership, you have to trust and push each other. You have to have your partner's back while she has yours. You have to know the two of you will make something better than if just one was working solo.

Finding a partner you can work with beautifully is vital. For juniors, the partner experience can have ups and downs. Sometimes, a good partnership begins in school, two creatives who click and send their books out as a partnered offering. Most of the time, writers and art directors go out solo.

At the agency point-of-entry — the hiring moment with a creative manager or creative director — a writer and an art director often will be thrown together without much ceremony and told to hit the ground running.

"That's worked both ways for me," says one art director from New York with a few years of experience. "At the first agency I worked at, we were thrown together, and nothing was done to let us get to know each other or find out each other's style. It was 'here, work on this, and get it done.' It was an awful experience." Awful, she says, because their styles of working through the concepting process and of presenting their work were so vastly different. Awful, because they didn't hit it off as friends or colleagues. "We didn't match on any level. In fact, we parted ways and vowed never to talk to each other again." Such is the way of some partnerships.

> **Let me emphasize how important your partner will be. She/he will be your partner-in-crime, a Harley to your Davidson, a yin to your yang, a Thelma to your Louise. A good partner is the difference between gold and a foolish waste of time.**
> *Beth Ryan, Writer, BBH, Singapore*

But other times, creative directors and creative managers will take time to help a new hire choose the right partner and nurture a good working relationship. That same art director who had the bad experience says her next agency was totally different. "The creative manager asked me to look through some books and choose two or three people to help interview to be my partner. She empowered me to choose the right person," she explains with a very different tone than she had about the first experience. "It was wonderful. And I found this guy straight out of art school who was phenomenal. We clicked right away and have been making great stuff for a couple of years now." She adds that their success is due to a creative manager who really knows how to nurture talent.

Whether it works or not generally comes down to liking and trust. "When the trust is there," notes Mike Heid, an award-winning writer at Peter A. Mayer in New Orleans, "you can talk about the most recent John Cusack movie for half an hour without worrying about the campaign you're concepting. That's where the great ideas come from...John Cusack and trust."

And Then There's Working with All the Other People Who Help Make It Happen

To get the job done, creatives work with a long list of agency folks. They work with account planners. They work with account people and brand managers. They work shoulder-to-shoulder with producers, buyers, and traffic experts for print and video. As media selection grows a stronger relationship with creative execution, some agencies have media and creative people making decisions together. The relationships creatives maintain with key players in each of these areas end up affecting the work, the quality, even the possibility of great ideas.

Some creatives say account planners are their best friends. Their approach to strategy and insight can jumpstart ideas and make the work better. The same goes for partnering with a media planner, especially these days when new media is driving more ideas. A good account manager can also help creatives understand why something isn't working or even suggest a strategic tweak that can make an idea stronger. In short, the most nimble of agencies use that synergy between areas to facilitate terrific ideas.

But it's not just agency colleagues you'll find yourself becoming tight with. Making things happen also entails pulling in people you'd never have dreamed you'd have as a partner. Vince Cook, a creative director at Leo Burnett in Chicago, had a simple, beautiful idea for a billboard sundial for McDonald's. Important note: It had to work.

"I've got to give so much credit to the engineer we worked with. He plotted, graphed, took GPS readings, built a CAD animation and shadow patterns before I even did the final layout," says Cook. The billboard won many awards and a lot of press for Cook and the agency.

And maybe some of the most important folks to work with smoothly will be clients. Even in your first few months, you could have major contact with the

people paying the bills. You might present in the new business pitch; you might be there for the briefing meetings; you might be the guy given the task of talking through first ideas. Depending on the size of the agency and the client, you could be the person the client counts on to come through with the killer idea.

"I've been surprised by how stubborn, unpredictable, demanding, and sometimes very smart the client can be," says one first year art director in a small shop in Manhattan. "They might change gears unpredictably after two months of approvals and revisions. It can be frustrating. But if you really have a partnership with the client and a good team of people at the agency to support you, you can make it work."

He adds: "Never think your creative work is what makes everything work. A couple of dozen people along the way turn good ideas into gold. Make sure you are the one who acknowledges that at every turn." And many times, he says, the client should get those kudos loud and clear.

Working with many people to produce something of value usually means meetings. And Arnold's Shembeda claims meetings are time bombs.

"I hate meetings. They're the worst part of my day. I'm not talking about creative presentations but the meetings to tell us client changes. We have meetings to 'set-up' meetings for meetings before the meeting. Fifteen-minute meetings. Half-hour meetings. Lunch meetings — pizza helps, but cold sandwiches and potato chips decrease participation by at least 62 percent, and don't get me started on wraps. Brainstorm meetings (the word 'session' is not fooling anyone). Quick meetings. Big meetings. Small meetings. Meetings of the minds. 'A few minutes of your valuable time' meetings. Kick-off meetings. Wrap-up meetings. Always a meeting lurking somewhere to take you away from work. I can't help but feel the time we spend in meetings would be better spent creating. Shouldn't we all have a get-together to talk about all these meetings? Meetings. I hate 'em."

And so, a word about how to do meetings and keep your sanity.

---

5 Great Tips for Creatives—Especially Juniors— to Make the Most of Meeting Time

Best advice from creative directors, headhunters, and those who've played the game well.

1 • Be on time. It's a simple thing, but few people actually pay attention to it. By doing this you show respect to everyone in the room. Remember: Some of the folks might be in a position to dole out the next great project, and they'll note that you're ready. And, big deal: Know everyone's name. If you walk in five minutes early and know names, you've started with the right tools.

2 • Come prepared. If you're a writer, bring your copy deck — your PowerPoint or printed collection of work and strategy — and any earlier versions that are relevant. If you're an AD, bring a copy of the boards. This seems like a duh moment, but you'd be surprised how many times folks just don't bring the resources they're supposed to.

3 • Listen to what everyone has to say. There's an art to this. It means eye contact. It means taking notes like you haven't taken since sophomore year's chemistry final review. Since everyone talks and few remember what's said, this is your chance to pull it together.

4 • Know what you're selling and who you're selling it to. Project confidence. Love your work, but be able to take feedback and suggestions. Start by explaining the strategic, smart grounding for what you've done. When you've built the foundation, then offer the work. But don't over explain or offer too many caveats. Best way to learn: Ask to watch some of the masters in your office sell their work. Study and learn.

5 • Understand the assignment at the end of the meeting. Have verbal agreement about what each person will do. Most importantly, know turnaround time for your piece of the puzzle. Walk out with a thank you and an agenda.

What Agency Is Right for You?

A major part of your career decision tree has to be dedicated to deciding what type of agency you want to work for. Ask yourself that important question. Most first responses come back as: Not sure, all I know is that I want a job, and I want to do great work and...

But in all honesty, preparing yourself well for the job hunt means that you become a walking encyclopedia of best work, great agencies, and names of smart creatives. To do that, you need to consider basic details of agency size and mission, and who's doing what where. You need to read about the greats and pour through the trades.

You have to be the smartest kid on the block when it comes to knowing who did what, which agencies are ruling the universe, and why one place has potential for next year and another one might not.

Size Matters

How large an agency is can usually predict how it behaves organizationally, where approval processes happen, who engages with the client, which creatives work on which accounts, and — importantly — what you'll be paid after a while.

Larger agencies have offices in places you might expect: London, New York, Chicago, San Francisco, Beijing, Mumbai, and on around the globe. And their staffs are deep in structure (junior writers turn into writers, who turn into senior writers, who turn into associate creative directors, who turn into...). Size also means stability and deep resources from larger clients. Bonus: Maybe there's a spectacular smaller group in a large agency acting as a small agency. The downside can be the impersonal nature of working on the 18th floor of a 34-floor office or never getting to meet the client or higher-ups in the agency.

Smaller agencies — maybe you're looking at a 30-person shop — have a tendency to be more nimble, and the boundaries for job titles and responsibilities are more ambiguous. The good news is that many small agencies usually get more radical work approved. You'll also probably work more closely with the client and be mentored by the visionary guy who started the place. And all that says you'll learn a huge amount. The bad news is that when small agencies lose a client they often have to cut staff. After all, they can't keep everyone if half of their income disappears.

Still, small agencies can maintain global power. Strawberry Frog has offices in Manhattan, Amsterdam, and Tokyo. Open Intelligence, a branding strategic shop, has four employees, one in London, one in Amsterdam, one in Sydney, and one in New York. In fact, Amsterdam seems to be the European mecca for smaller U.S. and British agencies, and the offices are full of young professionals who carry on their luggage so they'll be nimble at a moment's notice.

Terrific small agencies are all over the place, a few people bound together to do good work. This ability to have multiple small offices and still keep overhead low takes away the rules as to what accounts the agency can pitch, how the work flows, and how they're understood in the advertising culture.

The key factor when looking at agency size: Can this place give me a chance to grow my talent and make the work better?

Leaders and Mentors Wanted

Small or large, much of that agency decision comes down to the next big issue: Leadership. A small agency with a founder not ready to take risks or be a real change agent probably will do cautious, low-energy work. Larger agencies that are driven by profit and a "this is the way we've always done it" mentality will often be stultifyingly boring and produce mediocre work. Leadership determines all of these courses. A great executive creative director will make a great agency by making sure the work and the talent and the resources are dedicated to that. Sometimes new leadership is brought in to turn the tide and create a new feel and perspective for the agency itself.

"Anytime I speak to students I encourage them to learn a lot about the creative director they're going to work for, before taking the job. They should look at the work that creative director has been responsible for, even ask to see it during the interview," notes freelance director Rosch.

"My first mentor at my first job was the founder of the agency," says one art director who started his career at a small shop in North Carolina. "He took the time to teach me how to do exceptional work, while he made the major decisions of which clients we wanted to pursue and how we could stay small and healthy. He gave me the tools I needed to have a great career."

How the Agency Sees Itself

A third issue to consider is how the agency sees its mission. Is it a branding agency? A design-oriented shop? Has it jumped full force into the digital realm? Does it have a reputation for producing great broadcast or unexpected new media approaches or does it offer classically beautiful print work as its reason for being? Does it produce strong work across the media spectrum?

Geography Also Matters

Finally, you'll want to consider region. Terrific work is being produced at smart agencies all over the globe. But you do have to ferret out the cultural and community vibe of the place where that agency lives. Manhattan, obviously, is huge for advertising careers. So are Minneapolis and Chicago and San Francisco. But we're also looking at Boulder, Colorado and Austin, Texas, and Salt Lake City and Seattle and Portland and Atlanta and Dallas and North Carolina as magnets. It's happening everywhere. Look for it, and plan your roadtrip accordingly.

But whatever the path and wherever you end up, work hard. "To be honest, there is no one right way to do it. But I've come to think that outside of a few shops, there really isn't anywhere you shouldn't start," explains Rosch. "Once you're in, do the best job you can. Work like crazy. Meet anyone and everyone at every ad function you can. There's a good chance you'll meet the person who gets you your next job or lead or even hires you."

In ten years, Rosch has worked as an art director, then a writer at large agencies and smaller ones, including Young & Rubicam, J. Walter Thompson, and BBH with a stint at Cartoon Network stuck in there also. Then he was named executive creative director at Lowe. Now he and his partner are freelance directors, ready for the next chapter of being creative.

What About the First Few Days?

There's such a wide continuum of work you might be doing in your first week or your first year that there's no one great story that captures it all. With that in mind, let's look at different views of those first few days in the saddle.

Wexley's Bryan Chackel produced a 35-foot long bus wrap during his first week on the job. Fun stuff, he says, and a great way to learn.

Bryan Chackel is an art director at Wexley School for Girls in Seattle, a small ten-person agency dedicated to smart creative content. He jumped from school to a great internship there and made himself invaluable.

My first job in the first week was for Washington Mutual. This bus I designed traveled around Southern California informing first-time home buyers about buying a house and getting the right loan. I couldn't have asked for a more daunting project. Not only did I have to organize the photo shoot (something I had really no experience doing) for the bus wrap, but I also had to build a 35-foot long Astroturf welcome mat, including a decorative flower accent. On top of this, there was a full size for-sale sign, a mailbox, and a white picket fence surrounding the welcome mat. The best part came about halfway through this project when I realized that I could be thrown a demand like, "Hey, can you create a mailbox and for-sale sign for the bus and send it to so-and-so by noon?" and I could say, "Sure, anything else?" And I have to also say, seeing the final product actually out there and seeing it getting reactions was pretty amazing, too. That's something I really love about working here, seeing the reaction of people to our work (the what-the-hell? factor). It's pretty awesome.

Andrea Minze is a writer at GSD&M in Austin. She writes, she draws, she does crazy voices, and she plays guitar in a girl band. She is smart and funny and mixes work and play well.

It seems like there are so many crazy moments in your first few months. But a few months after I was hired, I wrote a Super Bowl spot. It survived most of the red tape, and it seemed like our CDs really liked it. We were given some time to polish before they went in to present to the big-wigs. It was right up to the last minute that we reworked it; then they took the script into the meeting. Somewhere between my hand-off of the script and their butts hitting the chair, they decided I should be the one to present it. This hour wouldn't have been so crazy had I actually been in my office when they came to relay the news. My art director and I had gone across the street to the bookstore to concept, and my phone ran out of juice. Everyone was in a frenzy trying to find us. We walked back over, and the second I hit the door I was whisked into this meeting — all eyes on me to act out the spot. There was no room for nervousness; I just had to do it. It was great. It was crazy. When I got out of the meeting I was like — what the f*** just happened?

GSD&M Writer Andrea Minze proofs designs with the AT&T team including NFL greats past and present, Deion Sanders and Roy Williams.

Writer Matt Zaifert had two first days within a span of six months. His first job was at a cool agency in lower Manhattan. After a few months, he moved over to a writer's job at BBDO, New York in a position with more responsibility. The first week at both jobs gave him something to report.

JOB #1: So after months and months of waiting, hoping, wishing, praying for a job — it's time for my first day. I'm going to a hot young shop in New York City that's getting great press in all the trade pubs. The office is in a trendy warehouse with tons of stainless steel and glass. This is what an ad agency should be. Everyone is young, good-looking, and relaxed. Meanwhile, I'm grossly overdressed — wearing khakis and a button-down — and scared shitless. Will they discover I'm a hack on the first day? I had months to work on my student book, crafting every line exactly how I wanted it to read. Now, I'd be expected to crank out headlines in a few hours and complete ads in days, if that. Am I really good enough to make a living doing this?

After about an hour I'm taken to a desk and set up with my own computer. My CD swings by to say hello and tells me just to hang out for the day. The people in my cubicle area don't say a word to me, and because I'm too much of a wuss to introduce myself, I just sit there for the next few hours, checking my email and reading espn.com. Once I see other people start to leave at around 6:30, I grab my bag, and my first day is officially in the books. Pretty uneventful. Yawn. The next morning I'm expecting more of the same. However, when I get in I'm introduced to my partner and told that we're going to be briefed on an assignment in a half hour. My partner is the girl that has been at the agency basically since it opened a couple of years ago. She's the most popular girl there. Hands down. I latch on to her like an older sister and am now introduced to everyone in sight. We get briefed on a print and radio assignment, and I'm starting to feel official. Time to go to work. I write pages and pages of headlines and copy for this seemingly small assignment and show them to my CD. He checks the few he likes, and just like that I wrote my first professional print ad. By the end of the week, I was juggling three different assignments and really felt like a valued member of the team.

Then I changed jobs soon thereafter...so, Job #2: First day. Take two. This time I'm going to one of the "big name" agencies. It's been around forever and has hundreds and hundreds and hundreds of employees. A little wiser this time, I decide to leave the khakis at home and go for the jeans instead. I meet at main reception for an orientation, bright and early. I'm not as scared as I thought I'd be and am actually pretty relaxed. After the obligatory orientation talk of how to fill out time sheets and such, I'm taken to my cubicle. I'm impressed...it's pretty big. In usual fashion, my CD swings by, welcomes me, and instructs me to hang out for the day. Fast forward to midweek, and I'm working on radio and print. Another mid-level writer is working on the same assignment, so I know I've got to come with my best stuff. Flip through annuals and listen to the Radio Mercury Awards 2000-2005 most of Wednesday. Start writing on Thursday through early Friday morning. By lunchtime Friday I'm in my CD's office presenting 16 scripts for one :60 radio spot. If nothing else, the sheer amount of work should impress him right? A few scripts actually survive and are presented to the client later that afternoon. And just in time for the happy ending, the client actually selects one of my scripts. In my first week, I sell a radio spot.

David Roth, Writer, and Shaun Bruce, Art Director, were hired as a junior team at Amalgamated in New York straight out of school. In their first year, they were named as the team to watch by *Boards Magazine*.

Three wonderful things about our first week:
1. Getting assigned to work on TV spots for Ben & Jerry's Ice Cream.
2. Having Ben & Jerry's come in and make us hot fudge sundaes with Chocolate Chip Cookie Dough Ice Cream to inspire us.
3. Earning the nicknames "Hot Dog" and "Scotch" which catch on, which means we've instantly become invaluable resources.

Since then, they've set about to become a hot team in the crazy world of advertising.

It's Not Just About Your Portfolio: The Other Important Stuff

We'll discuss actual portfolio building in the next section. At this point — before we get into what you'll produce — let's take a look at how you view the world and what you need to bring to that creative process in terms of brains and heart. Much has been written about what it takes to be creative. Researchers suggest that creative personalities in general have a great capacity for risk-taking, for seeing the world in childlike (not childish) fashion, and have a strong capacity for finding order in chaotic surroundings. They are playful, motivated, and more likely to question the status quo.

Ah, the personality traits of the great advertising creative. How do you explain incessant attention to detail, passionate investment in the process, living the quirky existence, and soaking up culture like a blotter? Different advice grows from different quarters.

Crispin Executive Creative Director Andrew Keller — winner of every advertising creative award on the planet — sees the great creative as being "a mad scientist" ready to create monsters and explosions and chaos as well as solve the problem.

If newcomers can listen and work hard, they'll be in the top 20 percent of the industry from the start. It takes that kind of humility and commitment to be successful.
Glenn Cole, Creative Director + Founder, 72andSunny, Santa Monica

Scott Z Burns — a renowned writer, creative director, director, and producer for the last two decades, who now works on feature films and documentaries — adds warrior to the list. "You must have a warrior's mentality. You must be able to create from strength and defend your ideas voraciously." Burns won a 2007 Oscar for his work as a producer on *An Inconvenient Truth*. His warrior mentality forged in advertising is a huge asset as he moves into the thought leader ranks of the film industry.

Sometimes what is needed is the ability to understand that it's not about you but about something bigger. Hadji Williams, author of *Knock the Hustle* and a longtime copywriter and Chicago marketing consultant, explains that young talent needs something very basic for success. "It's about Humility. Honesty. Morals," he says. "I like humble kids. Lots of kids get arrogant—they think they know everything. So they don't push themselves as hard as they could or should." To him, honesty must be the heart of building a career to counteract all the noise and poison out there already.

Art Director Kelly Colchin at DDB, San Francisco believes you also need to be a collector. "I collect everything that is beautiful or interesting or has a color or texture I've never seen before. Not ads, but stuff. I have a wonderful collection of stuff." You should possess a love of learning and that beautiful characteristic called intellectual curiosity. And that means collecting ideas, voices, bits of humanity that can inform your work.

Creative guru and GSD&M Executive Creative Director Luke Sullivan keeps it real: "Don't whine. People don't want to work with whiners." You must be persistent without losing faith. Character becomes real in the fourth or fifth try for a solution. It also takes persistence to work and re-work your book as you get feedback from people who tell you it's not ready yet. And it will take perseverance to remember criticism isn't aimed at you personally; it's focused on your ads and what you need to do to get your book ready.

And absolutely in your first years in the business, the go-to guy attitude is vital. "Energy and enthusiasm are tools," says Arnold's Shembeda. "Or maybe they're weapons. Enthusiasm is contagious. It affects clients, creative directors, co-workers and most of the time in a very positive way."

Warren Berger, advertising journalist, the editor-at-large of The One Club's *one. a magazine*, and author of *Advertising Today*, *No Opportunities Wasted*, and *Hoopla*, has covered agencies and their creative evolution for a dozen years. "The motto is: Live well, work better. There's a connection between how we work and how we live," he says. "Live an interesting life, and it will come through in your work." In fact, your list of who you are and what you do should make people want to meet and work with you. Russell Davies, the legendary planner and blogger, has some advice on doing just that.

How to Be Interesting
Russell Davies, Planner + Planning Blog Guru
Founder, Open Inteligence, London
Read more of Russell's wisdom on russelldavies.typepad.com

1 • Take at least one picture everyday. Post it to Flickr. You should carry a camera with you. A phonecam will do. The act of carrying a camera and always keeping an eye out for a picture to take changes the way you look at the world. It makes you notice more things. It keeps you tuned in.

Posting it to Flickr (or other photosharing sites) means that you're sharing it. It's in public. This will make you think a little harder about what you shoot, and it might draw you into conversation about your pictures.

2 • Start a blog. Write at least one sentence every week. It's easy to knock blogging as a kind of journalism of the banal, but in some ways that's its strength. Bloggers don't go out and investigate things (mostly); they're not in exciting or glamorous places; they're not given a story but have to build one out of the everyday lives they lead. And this makes them good at noticing things,

things that others might not have seen. Being a blogger and feeling the need to write about stuff makes you pay attention to more things, makes you go out and see more stuff, makes you carry a notebook, keeps you tuned in to the world.

3 • Keep a scrapbook. I've talked about this before. It's good. Do it.

4 • Every week, read a magazine you've never read before. Interesting people are interested in all sorts of things. That means they explore all kinds of worlds; they go places they wouldn't expect to like and work out what's good and interesting there. An easy way to do this is with magazines. Specialist magazines let you explore the solar system of human activities from your armchair. Try it; it's fantastic.

5 • Once a month interview someone for 20 minutes. Work out how to make them interesting. Podcast it. Again, being interesting is about being interested. Interviewing is about making the other person the star and finding out what they know or think that's interesting. Could be anyone: a friend, a colleague, a stranger, anyone. Find out what's compelling about them. Interviewing stops you butting in too much and forces you to listen. Good thing to practice. (And it's worth noticing the people who are good at it.) Podcasting is sharing. Sharing is something you must get used to.

6 • Collect something. It could be anything. It could be pictures of things. But become an expert in something unexpected and unregarded. Develop a passion. Learn how to communicate that to other people without scaring them off. Find the other few people who share your interest. Learn how to be useful in that community.

7 • Once a week sit in a coffee-shop or cafe for an hour and listen to other people's conversations. Take notes. Blog about it. (Carefully). Take little dips in other people's lives. Listen to their speech patterns and their concerns. Try and get them down on paper. (Don't let them see. Try not to get beaten up.) Don't force it; don't hop from table to table in search of better eavesdropping, just bask in the conversations that come your way.

8 • Every month write 50 words about one piece of visual art, one piece of writing, one piece of music, and one piece of film or TV. Do other art forms if you can. Blog about it.

If you want to work in a creative business (and before long most businesses will be creative businesses), you'll have to get used to having a point of view on artistic stuff. Even if it's not very artistic. You'll have to be comfortable with expressing an opinion on things you don't know how to make or do, like music or writing. You get better at that through practice. And through sharing what you've written.

9 • Make something. Do something with your hands. Create something from nothing. It could be knots; it could be whittling, Lego, cake or knitting. Take some time to get outside your head. Ideally, make something you have no idea how to do. People love people who can make things. Making's the new thinking. Share your things on your blog, or, if you're brilliant, maybe you can share them on etsy.

10 • Read. Great places to start:
Understanding Comics by Scott McCloud
The Mezzanine by Nicholson Baker
The Visual Display of Quantitative Information by Edward Tufte

All these books are good for their own reasons, but they're also good examples of people who are really interested in stuff that others think of as banal and who explain it in a way that makes you share their passion. That's good.

And that's it.

Finally, Crispin's Keller offers advice about generosity. "Always say 'we' when talking about your ideas," he says. "This is a team expedition, not an individual journey." And once again we learn lessons on how to play nice in order to be successful.

Humility, curiosity, wild abandon, intellect, enthusiasm, a sense of humor, the ability to get along well with others, persistence, a strong work ethic. What else do you need?

Beyond Obligation in All You Do

Maybe it's about who needs you. The advertising world needs new talent ready to change things. It needs you to help garner the respect it deserves for good work produced. The honest truth is that it needs you to help make the world a better place to live. That means your inner do-gooder is present on the first day of your career.

We're not talking about being a Pollyanna or regulating your work to only "nice" messages. Being creative means you look for ideas in all places. But, using optimism and insight to develop messages that make the world better is an inspiring way to make a living. It can also be incredibly challenging to find relevant, marketable messages that change brands and people. For examples of inspiration, find the work that does it well. Think Dove's Real Women campaign from Ogilvy & Mather. Think Liberty Mutual's campaign based on Responsibility from Hill| Holliday in Boston. Think the Truth campaign from Crispin in Miami and Arnold in Boston. Or dozens of other strong messages that add something to the culture.

According to so many of the advertising leaders we spoke to, the best way to make better advertising is to incorporate a sense of "beyond obligation" when you craft messages for the culture. Not just in pro bono and not-for-profit work but in the way you approach all work.

Over and over, the thread of something bigger than advertising came through in interviews. John Boiler of 72andSunny says it plainly: "What you have as a starting point is your sense of self, your sense of making the world better." Do good to make good. It's a career strategy.

Crafting Work that Makes You Proud

Genworth Financial 100+ Campaign, Rachel Howald
Founder + Creative Director, Howald & Kalam, New York City

The centenarian campaign for Genworth Financial grew from a desire to make a positive statement about the Genworth Financial brand and its product offerings. Plus — in a provocative way — we wanted to make a positive statement about the potential for a long and healthy life. Almost every other insurance and financial services provider in this crowded market is clamoring to tell baby boomers, "You can be a young 65." But Genworth Financial chose to take a more optimistic approach that said, "Hey, 65 is young. You could live a long and healthy life. Plan for it."

Born of a truth about the aging population in the U.S. (of healthy couples age 65, there's a 50 percent chance that one of them will live to at least 91 and a 25 percent chance that one will live to at least 96)*, the campaign presented both an extraordinary opportunity and a unique challenge.

Using real centenarians and simple, elegant black and white portraiture made the work stand out in both still and moving media. But finding the right centenarians and making the vision a reality proved more difficult.

The director, Wally Pfister, had a tremendous track record as an Oscar-nominated cinematographer and documentarian. But this was his first opportunity to take the long overdue leap from DP to director. Ahmer Kalam, my art director partner, and I had worked with Wally on previous spots. We had confidence not only in his abilities as a gifted director but also in his interviewing skills, kindness, patience, and empathy toward the centenarians. While we didn't know who or what we would be shooting, we had absolute confidence in Wally's ability to make it both reverential and visually stunning.

Nationwide casting techniques included using casting agents who specialized in real people casting, Internet research, consultation with organizations that represent the elderly, and coordination with academic researchers in the field of gerontology. All of those efforts led to a small pool of viable candidates.

We then boarded planes and headed out across the country. Within the first 72 hours of casting, Ahmer, Wally, and I met with eight to ten candidates in Seattle, Phoenix, Prescott, Sun City, Loma Linda, Palm Springs, Los Angeles, and New York. On-camera interviews lasting 30-45 minutes gave us an opportunity to learn more about the people and their lives, both past and present. The first two spots were shot in Indio, California and Prescott, Arizona. They featured Roberta Smith, the granddaughter of a slave, and Rosie Ross, a musician who still plays weekly gigs in a band every Friday night. The message for the brand was simple and strong and conveyed not only the importance of planning in a world where a long and healthy future awaits but also product specific benefits relevant to particular Genworth offerings.

What began as simply a strong concept and visual style — with no idea of who, what, where, or when spots and print ads would be shot — turned into an experience that represents the best of a client-agency relationship. Partnerships were key. Were it not for the client's faith in the idea and trust in the agency to make it happen (and our trust in the director and photographer), it would have been simply another good idea that never saw the light of day. Because the agency and client were able to collaborate throughout the entire process, the work could evolve in real time. Scripts could be written, changed, rewritten, and revised as necessary on location while consulting the team and client. The result of all of these efforts was not only a unique, arresting campaign that communicated a clear, strong brand message but also an uplifting experience for all of us that was life-affirming. And how often do you hear those words in the advertising business?

*source: Ibbotson & Associates

Preparing Yourself

In the '80s, training programs for young creatives were standard fare. You got a first job, got further training in the culture of that agency, looked around for a good partner, and then gradually entered the pace of agency life. That was before mergers, new technology, and booms and busts eliminated such luxuries. Now, training programs are rare. More likely, training consists of a meeting or "let's see if this works" internship before you start.

So today, the learning curve has to be much faster. There is no time for extensive on-the-job-training. Junior writers have to walk in ready to work and be well-versed enough in the ways of concepting, partnering, and producing that work can happen fast. They have to be writers and thinkers extraordinaire. Junior art directors need to be schooled in design, type, images, and color. Plus they must be able to make ideas happen fast.

You have to be able to hit the ground running. And that requires preparation. But there are more ways to ready yourself than you may think.

Education and How to Use It

You have a great set of choices in terms of learning about advertising to ready yourself for the industry. You might study anthropology as an undergrad, then either take a Master's degree in advertising at a university or move on to a good portfolio school. Or maybe you learn advertising as an undergrad in a communication or advertising department and jump straight into the industry. You might even start out as a stockbroker in a high-powered office and get the yearning to do great writing that pays well. Still another option is the genius mode of quitting school in the 6th grade, working for a few years as a savant, then putting together a raw, glorious portfolio that stuns the industry. All are possibilities.

To be honest, to work in creative, it's less about degrees, programs, GPAs, majors, and courses than it is about your ability to act creatively within the culture and present your work well. But it is important to prepare. University advertising programs and portfolio schools offer a strong foundation for understanding how it all gets put together.

But courses and programs and advertising majors cannot ensure you'll create a strong portfolio. And they will not guarantee that you'll be intellectually curious enough to poke and prod ideas into smart content. That comes from you and something outside of advertising.

Jelly Helm, W+K's Executive Creative Director and Director of the successful 12 program, has a saying: It's not about what it's about.

So true for studying advertising creativity: To be ready, better to study a conglomeration of your grandparents' love letters, Shakespeare, Ferris Bueller's passion in that great parade scene, and a smattering of Japanese anime and Southern Baptist sermons. Or, name your own collection of life, literary, and cultural lessons. And be able to translate that into insightful ideas for connecting with people.

In short, all of the "other" courses you take in art, history, mass media, and sociology, for example, may be much more advantageous to your career than you could ever dream — more advantageous than studying advertising books and awards annuals. That said, strong conceptual creative courses mixed with classes in media, strategy, and campaigns certainly readies you for the industry.

The Get It Factor

Best advice heard over and over again: Keep an idea book or journal. Observe. Archive. Collect. Get your thoughts and passion down in a book you keep with you wherever you go. It's not a diary; it's a collection of words and images and possibilities for all the work you'll do.

Photoshop, Illustrator, InDesign, Flash, and Quark are all important as a knowledge base. But they shouldn't be the intellectual base from which you build your work. "Use computer programs as you would pencil and paper... they're just tools, and your work shouldn't be about them. It should be about your ideas and concepts," says Richard Wilde, Director of Advertising at the School of Visual Arts in New York.

But to sell all of this knowledge and potential and talent means you have to show exactly how your brain works. That's where your portfolio comes in.

Portfolio Building 101

Finally. Let's talk about your ticket to the industry. You have to be great. You have to ready and enthusiastic and smart.

Your portfolio — your book — has to be killer. It is your collection of brand relevant work executed in campaigns and one-shots and great content that shows how you think.

Everyone we spoke to agrees on that. It should reflect you — your thinking, your ability to solve problems, your sense of humor and priorities, your passion for work well done, your attention to details. Maybe your book includes carefully selected art and photos and haiku that you do as a passionate pursuit or maybe there's a video you shot about an issue that's meaningful to you.

The big caveat: It all has to be smart and show how you think to solve prob-lems. Relevant professional creative content shouldn't be solely traditional advertising. "It really doesn't matter to me as long as the content is killer," says

Rosch. "And for me killer content is work that makes me extremely jealous. I see lots of books with solid thinking, carefully crafted art direction, humorous content. But I rarely see an idea that I wish I had done. And ultimately that is how I gauge an idea."

All of these ideas used to reside in a big black case, an actual portfolio. Not any more. In fact, more of it lives on a computer, on a site or a blog, and in an evolving set of mini-books — smaller collections that can be changed easily and sent out without being returned — than in a portfolio carryall. Conventional wisdom says your portfolio or mini-book contains 15 to 20 well-edited pieces, your résumé and contact information.

"Definitely have a website where I can look at your work quickly," says one creative director who sees 100 books a month. "And if you get to the interview stage, you might want to have something for me to hold and something new for me to look at online. If you send me PDFs, make sure I can open them and they're easy to navigate."

"Whether the book is online or hard copy," says Rachel Howald, Executive Creative Director of Howald & Kalam, "I want to be able to go through it quickly. It impresses me when you have work that is well-edited and well-presented and that you understand I have maybe five minutes to spend looking."

If you break these guidelines, you'd better break them well. "The best book I've ever seen was a writer's book. It was a far cry from the traditional ad school mini-book sendout. There were even hand-drawn black-and-white roughs in it," says Mary Knight, Executive Creative Director at DraftFCB in Seattle. "But be careful. If you present work in that raw form, there had better be ideas that have never been seen before. Lots of books are strong. Only a few are like this one...ideas I would never think of in a thousand years."

If the strange presentation on napkins and handwritten copy has genius ideas, you're golden. If they're run-of-the-mill ideas, you just look stupid. The lesson in that becomes showing your work takes a personal style and the ability to translate that style to others.

The Get It Factor

A portfolio should be digital, either as a website or blog or collections of PDFs. It should also live as hard copy for interviews and creative directors who prefer to hold something as they look at work. Most important in preparing how your book will be viewed: Be flexible, know what your favorite agency wants to see.

But it's the work that matters most, much more than the form you present it in. The collection should be ever-evolving. And your job is to make sure it's ready to be seen by the right people.

"Before I open a book, I think, 'I hope this has something inside that I've never seen before and I never would have thought of myself in a thousand years,'" explains Knight. And she's not alone. The best in the business say each time they look at a portfolio, they're hoping it will be the one that is so different they will have to get that person in the office immediately.

5 Great Ways to Check Out the Creative Competition

Looking at good work should be inspirational. Viewing other junior books gives you an idea of where you should be steering your own collection. Beware: It's good to be very judgmental about what you view. Just because it's out there doesn't mean it's perfect.

1 • Check out university program and portfolio program websites. Most have collections of student work, faculty bios, and a good sense of their industry network. Each also has good work they show as representative of their program.

2 • Look at award-winning student work on The One Club site (oneclub.org) in the College Competition and Client Pitch Competition sections under Education. You can see how judges ranked the work. You can also check out how your competition pitched their ideas to clients and judges.

3 • Competitions for student work abound. Check out Lurzer's *Archive* Magazine, *CMYK* Magazine, Cannes Young Lions, and the Addys for collections of award-winning student work.

4 • Larger agencies have creative managers attached to their creative departments. These managers serve as human resources folks for hiring and managing writers and art directors on a larger scale. Often these offices will look at books, offer some feedback and general resources, and be able to show you good work they've hired in the past.

5 • Some talent representatives and headhunters across the country are dedicated to representing strong junior talent. If they agree to take you on, they'll be able to show you other work of the caliber they represent. Talent managers and headhunters don't charge you for their connections; agencies pay them for bringing in the best talent. See 5 Great Tips from Talent Manager Dany Lennon in this chapter for more info on this topic.

That means it's really simple to get the job of your dreams. All you have to do is impress people with radically different, thoroughly insightful ideas. You have to be able to find products and brands worthy of your attention, think through a strategy and insights, execute to those, and produce the work smartly.

So the issue becomes: How does your book show your brain and your ability?

You'll want to go deep. The more thought and depth your solutions show, the more likely you are to separate yourself from the pack. And the media you use to embody your ideas and solve the problem may be almost as important as the ideas themselves. The days of portfolios filled with three ad print campaigns are gone.

Zach Canfield, the creative watchdog at Goodby, Silverstein & Partners, reviews 50 books a day looking for the right ones for his agency. What he wants are "ideas that are different. Maybe there's some traditional print thinking in there, but it better be better than good. And at least a couple of the campaigns should really blow out to see what the idea can do in many different media. And absolutely, we are looking to juniors coming in to show us interactive." That's whether you consider yourself a digital expert or not, he says, "because you have to show that you understand how ideas work in that realm."

In fact, ask Rex McCubbin, a writer at The Martin Agency in Richmond, Virginia, about the opportunity to include interactive work in your portfolio, and she'll tell you it's just that: An opportunity. "The best part ... is the IDEAS... you don't just write headlines, you dream up websites and content and all sorts of other games and platforms....I love it and I'll never do strictly traditional work again."

Jesus Ramirez, Creative Director at Cartel Creativo in San Antonio, underlines another key point — the ability to connect with audiences that are unlike yourself. In many of the portfolios Ramirez sees, "the young writer or art director is oblivious to the customer and makes ads for him/herself.... There's no real heart or understanding" of the Latino market. And it applies to other markets as well.

The Get It Factor
Your book should show you can think and talk to different people, not just your own demographic. Your ability to understand a range of people, cultures, ages and perspectives is important.

Putting the Finish on a Collection of Work
A few practical suggestions were offered up repeatedly. Have 15 to 20 pieces with quality trumping quantity. Use lesser known brands with a mix of good media. Don't laminate anything because that nice plastic polish sends a signal that you think it's as good as it can be. And don't add anything for a product or brand that already has great advertising. As one headhunter says, "Why in the world would you show me anything for Mini or Nike? All that says is you're dumber than a post."

Then there's that interesting subjectivity thing: What goes over well at one agency or in one office, might not be liked in the next. Your job is to take all the advice, the feedback, even the smiles and make sense of them. Keep changing your book so it remains fresh. Keep reminding yourself that this is your ticket.

5 Great Tips for Making a Strong Book

Greatest advice from all we talked to: It's the idea that counts the most. After that...

1 • Choose interesting products, brands, and issues to include in your collection. Don't pick brands and products that already have a strong message and identity; instead, find a few that you feel good about and that offer a blank or uninteresting slate for you to reconfigure.

2 • Remember there should be a mixture of advertising ideas and strong conceptual work you've produced. Old news: Six print campaigns and a couple of one-shots. New approach: Give yourself the freedom to create branding campaigns in multimedia, interesting approaches to media and audience. Add some other relevant fodder — maybe a documentary or branding film, a brand book that inspires thinking about the brand, comics, a blog that's interesting — and you're creating your own template for what a book should be.

3 • Be a craftsman. Care about the ideas, the language, the design, the type, and the medium. Look at the binding. Make sure there are no typos or missing pieces. Loving the details shows you care.

4 • Work with a partner and a community. You can't do this in a vacuum. And a support group for helping you grow your ideas can exist online, at a Friday morning coffee, or in a class.

5 • You're never done. Even when you start sending it out. Even when you land that first job. Your book should evolve as long as you're in the business.

But what about portfolio tips specifically for writers and art directors? Ian Cohen is the creative director of Wexley School for Girls in Seattle and a strong writer himself. For writers, his advice is simple: Don't just write. Don't just put a headline on the ad. Learn when to write. "A headline should be something that is truly amazing or intriguing or educational for the reader. If it's not amazing, it's not good enough."

Freelance creative director and writer Kathy Hepinstall — who penned the smart Nike for Women campaign of 2005, which won a Kelly Award — believes that writers should understand and respond to rhythm. "Everything is on a rhythm. Write that way so that the natural sound of the language comes through." Whether it's a headline or a tag or an outdoor board, care about the language.

If you're an art director, you'll want to ask yourself if you're designing to a great idea? Are you paying homage to concept? Is your type immaculate? Is the ad, website, or poster really thought out? Are your designs different on each campaign, each showing off a different skill or technique? For McCann-Erickson Art Director Julio Olvera, it's also more important than ever for art directors to be able to demonstrate their design skills in everything from shopping bags and retail design to magazine layouts for in-store publications.

I Get It. Now What Do I Do?

Let's begin with overall strategy for the job hunt. Understand your target and make a plan. This should happen as you find that you're at a good point to actually show work. Don't show your book formally when it's still in very tentative stages, when you know the whole thing will have to change. A good rule-of-thumb is to send it out only after a few informal reviews and classroom critiques where you're given basic feedback that lets you know you're headed in the right direction.

First, researching your top ten agencies is a must. Understand who they are and why you want to work for them. Read up on the history of the places. Know who their major players are and what accounts they've recently been awarded or lost. If you read the trades with any regularity, you'll know what accounts are in review and where they may be going. You should be ready to send work as soon as you hear that one of your top agencies has been awarded a major new account.

Second, find the right person to talk to. Larger agencies have creative managers, a person dedicated to bringing in writers and art directors at different levels and nurturing the agency talent. They will oversee recruitment, review portfolios, and understand who the up-and-comers are in the industry.

Calls to agencies should result in the name of the creative manager or creative director who looks at portfolios. Make sure you have the name spelled correctly, get the title right, and have a strong sense of that person's role in the agency. This is a professional conversation, so be smart.

Third, decide on the form your book should take for that person. Will you send a mini-book with a note? Do you email pdfs of your work and then make a phone call? Your plan has to include how you'll send work to each prospective employer and what you'll do to follow-up.

Important to the plan: Keep notes. Have a notebook where you keep a running list of whom your book was sent to, what response (if any) you've gotten, and what you did as follow-up.

Make a Plan, then Deal with the Details

Tell Mom not to buy that suit. Lots of parents want to buy the traditional "interview suit" as you graduate and start the search. Tell them to hold off. Most creatives aren't going to be looking for you to come in a Brooks Brothers ensemble or the typical Wall Street business look. Instead, look smart in something that's respectful but cool. Tone down the jewelry. Don't wear the holey jeans. Make sure there's not midriff or too much of any one body area showing. Give yourself a look that is confident, professional, even hip without being overbearing or too crazy.

Show who you are on a good day. As one creative manager in Chicago said to us, "I don't want to think about your clothes during the interview. I want to think about how smart your book is. I want to think about how I can put you to work yesterday."

Strategic thinking also comes into play when you're sending your book out for review. Rethink your book and its contents every time you send it out. After all, you can't send the same book to a hot creative boutique that you'd send to a much larger agency. Different agencies have different styles and different kinds of problems to solve.

This award-winning print campaign for Nike Women is a writer's piece with beautiful design. Written by Kathy Hepinstall. Art directed by Mira Kaddoura.

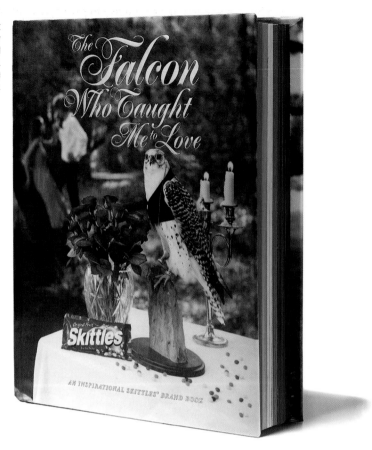

"One thing I did wrong when I was starting out was hesitating to change my book," says Matt Barber, a writer who landed his first job out of school at Strawberry Frog in New York. "I made a ton of excuses for not doing so, from not having the right software to telling myself that the people who really liked my book as it was were the people I really wanted to work for. The bottom line is this: When you change your book, you have a good reason to go back and see people. I suggest making tons of changes and personalized versions for places you really like and for the people who told you to change it."

Remember, there are people out there who can connect you with the right people in the industry. Some of this is done through networking and knowing someone who knows someone. That type of job lead is invaluable. So ask each person you talk to for the names of other people you can show your book to. Five contacts can quickly become 70.

And if there's someone you really want to talk to but you don't have a referral, don't hesitate to cold call people. Even important people. Generally, they'll try to be helpful because they remember that someone helped them get their start.

And if they are too busy to see you, they are likely to pass you along to someone else in the agency.

5 Rules for Working with a Talent Rep

Dany Lennon
Founder
The Creative Register

1 • Research your talent rep. Know who she is, what she's about, her reputation, her modus operandi, the type of agencies she works with, the type of people she represents. The more you know, the more you'll understand whether or not she's the right fit for you long term.

2 • Tell her about you. Make sure you meet that talent representative knowing who you are and what you're about, too. Give her a sense of your perspective, goals, strengths, weaknesses, and personality insights. Everything helps to develop the relationship with that person. You'll want her to take an interest in you that's deeper than your portfolio. Plus, listen! Hear everything and anything she has to say.

3 • Make sure you walk into that talent representative's office having done your homework on the industry. With so much info available to you online, there's no excuse whatsoever for anyone to not have researched companies that they find interesting and ultimately would kill to work at. This will give your talent rep a sense of your ambition and drive. Not to mention your commitment to working just as hard as he'll be working for you.

4 • Never 'cheat' on your talent rep. Cheating is simply not telling him where you're going to interview, what you're doing with other talent reps or headhunters. If you've commissioned a talent representative to give you 'entrée' to his roster of contacts and knowledge, then you must demonstrate respect, honesty, and trust. He should know at all times if you're meeting with anyone that he's provided the introduction for or with someone you arranged. This gives the talent representative the option to NOT represent you if he's the 'exclusive' type, i.e., someone who contractually agrees to be your sole representative.

5 • Be appreciative and humble. Make sure you thank your talent representative for everything that she's doing for you. As noted, this is a long term relationship, and the last thing you need is to have a talent manager that thinks you're wasting her time.

Big opportunities also grow from using a headhunter or talent representative to show your work around to the right people. Most talent reps are very selective about working with juniors; they prefer to represent the senior and CD levels. But many are open to representing a very talented junior who might want to see further options in the industry. You don't have to pay for these services. The agency pays a finder's fee. But there are some definite points of etiquette you must attend to when working with a headhunter or rep.

One last reminder: Don't give up, and don't worry that your parents don't understand. "Be ready for that part," says one writer, "because this industry is different than what most parents have experienced in their own job hunting."

The Résumé

Unlike most job-hunting résumés, the ones for writers and art directors shouldn't be super formal. Take the template in all résumé-writing workshops then let it get friendlier without being gimmicky or over-designed.

"Whatever you do, don't list your knowledge of Word and Excel as a selling point. I would much rather know where you've traveled, that you like to read Shakespeare and the *Weekly World News*, or that you have a passion for collecting old maps or feather boas. Show that you're interesting," observes one creative manager.

Sometimes it's the wonderful extras listed that help the most. Maybe you studied abroad and have a line about Oxford or taking a pastry class in Paris. Dustin Ballard says the line on his résumé about playing violin jumped out at the people interviewing him at Crispin. He got a job there as a writer and played fiddle in the agency rock band.

The Get It Factor

Your résumé doesn't need gimmicks. Instead, it should have a clean design, offer a focused look at what you've done and how you think, and be a strong connector to your portfolio. Keep it simple. Your goal should be to make that creative director say, "We have to get this kid before someone else does."

AtmosphereBBDO's Kate Lummus reports that her internship in Hillary Clinton's office was always a topic people wanted to know about when she was looking for that first job. "The Clinton internship definitely helped me get in the door at agencies," she says. "I never would have thought so, but people saw that one line on my résumé and called me in to talk about it. In fact, I went on several interviews where that's all people wanted to talk about. And once they liked me and got to know me, they took a look at my book and liked the package. I have been so grateful it's on there."

And remember, the résumé needs to make important information easy to find. Make sure to indicate the specific position you're applying for. Never say you're open to anything. Give your contact information: name, address, phone number, email, and web address if you have one. And don't come across as an ad nerd. Give some hobbies and past experiences that show that you have interests beyond advertising.

The Interview

Find-a-job books and résumé workshops will talk about the informational interview as a role-playing technique. Make no mistake: Neither your informal "would you look at my book?" meeting nor the "would you come in for an interview with our creative director?" request from the agency are information-al interviews. Both are very real and very important to your cause. So that traditional job-hunting term just doesn't apply here.

Your request for someone to look at your book is a gateway to getting feed-back, building a relationship with that person and that agency, and a method for you to see what kind of organization and personality the agency has. "We always try to make time to look at someone's book and help. We've been there," is the general attitude from most writers and art directors. Ask for 15 minutes and you'll usually get 45. But use the time wisely: Take notes, ask questions, be polite.

If you've been asked to come in for an interview after the agency has seen your book, you're in a good position. It may be that they're so interested they've flown you in for the interview. Or, it may be they've expressed interest and asked that when you're in the city, please come in and talk.

Your job is to come in knowing about the agency and asking the right ques-tions. Even more, you should bring in new work to add to that they've already seen. They also want to see someone who is able to discuss good advertising, explain and defend their own work (without being defensive), and who is enthusiastic about the experience.

"The interview for me is a chemistry check: Do I think they'll complement our culture? Do I feel the same spark from the person that I felt from the book? Are they a good fit with out projects and clients?" explains DraftFCB's Knight. "And in my experience, most people don't blow it in the interview; they blow it in the idea stage."

It's okay to be nervous, but you still have to be ready to explain your work and approach. "Many students seem to think that being nervous is a deadly sin in an interview. For the record, I'd like to say that EVERY entry-level candidate has at least a slight case of nerves when they sit down at my table," says Yamazaki who looks at about 200 entry-level books each year through portfolio reviews and books coming in to her office. "But let's say we've got two great books and only one job open. The losing candidate is the one who can't articulate anything sensible about the work."

What If Your Book Just Isn't Good Enough Yet?

What if you get a bad review? Kara Taylor, Vice President and Creative Manager at Leo Burnett in Chicago, talks about the honesty of telling someone they simply aren't ready yet. "It's hard, but we need to tell them the truth. If it's their concepts that aren't right, we need explain to them why. When someone's ideas are really off the mark, we like to show portfolios of entry-level candidates that we've hired so they understand our standards. When they see the difference and perk up, it's a good sign. When they are defensive and angry, it's much more difficult to encourage them. In either case, they need to get back to work."

"If all else fails and you can't land a job in the business," Rosch suggests you take a break, get some perspective. "Go do something else for awhile, give your book a break, and try again later. Advertising isn't going anywhere, and you might be better off rescuing polar bears for a year or two." You can always jump back in with a fresh perspective and better ideas.

The Follow-Up

You've sent your book out to key places. You've been through portfolio reviews. You've networked and talked and listened and taken notes. You've been through the anxiety of the big interview. Now what?

Consider being gracious and appreciative, just like your mother and etiquette advisor told you to be some years ago. A few ideas from the pros:

- Handwrite a thank-you note with a real message of gratitude. It's a great way to start.
- Send work you've tweaked back within the week to show you listened to advice, and used it to improve your work.
- Send a handmade or memorable postcard so it arrives every week on the same day for a number of weeks. Each time it reminds the recipient who you are, that you're still looking, and that you value their time.
- Call or mail a card to people you've interviewed with announcing that you've gotten a job and that you appreciate their help. Folks in this industry have a long memory; when you're nice, you'll be remembered.
- Write a congratulatory note to those who took time with you. Maybe they won an award. Maybe they were written up in a trade pub or were named to a special project or board. Maybe you heard they changed jobs or wrote a book. Congratulate them.

Keyword: Perseverance

At times, the whole journey will feel like it's not worth it. You'll be frustrated and down. You may even reach out to friends and tell them your troubles.

Crispin's Alexander made the move with the agency from Miami to new digs in Boulder, Colorado. His job at one of the premiere agencies of the decade is awesome, he says. But things weren't always so great. His first job right out of school with an agency in the Southwest was a bad match. The agency did work he didn't respect, and it turned out that some key folks there weren't the leaders he'd hoped for. He quit. He looked around for another position. He traveled. He felt discouraged.

But then, in one of those beautiful strokes of luck and talent, he sent his book to Crispin on a whim. They called. He went to Miami. And now he lives happily ever after. In the Boulder office.

But he never would've made it there without believing in himself and taking the time to send that portfolio out one more time.

Best advice for juniors building a book: Look for collections of work you respect and consider the idea and strategy used. To see this animated student piece from the Zinkproject in Madrid, go to oneclub.org and click on the 2007 student competiton showcase.

Salaries and Nailing It

Maybe you get the call. Maybe it's time to talk salary and do the dance of negotiation and ask about where your desk will be.

A few guidelines: First, salaries for juniors ebb and flow with agency size, the economy, and the region of the country you're in. Junior writers and art directors can expect anywhere from $20K to $60K, depending on all of those factors. And that may change tomorrow. Senior creatives get more, usually determined by what they've accomplished and what they ask for. After a few years, some creative directors attain rock star status and can command up to $250,000, and maybe more for someone on the A-list. Those people you're reading about who do consistently great work and run creative empires? Maybe above half a million to too many zeroes.

But you're at the starting point. Now it's about opportunity, not money. A $25,000 offer from a terrific agency might be better than $40,000 from a mediocre one. Maybe you take the lower offer from the hot shop. Do amazing work for six months. Ask for a six-month review. Have stuff to prove that you're invaluable, that you've tackled every project with wit and insight. Explain to them you know the janitorial staff as well as the President of the agency because you're there at all hours. Then you can ask for a raise with confidence.

It all comes down — one more time — to your ideas and how you use them.

Or maybe they'll ask you to intern for a few months while everyone sees how the fit between you and the agency feels. Good agencies are doing that frequently these days, often with good results for both agency and creative. One important note: Most places pay interns during this time.

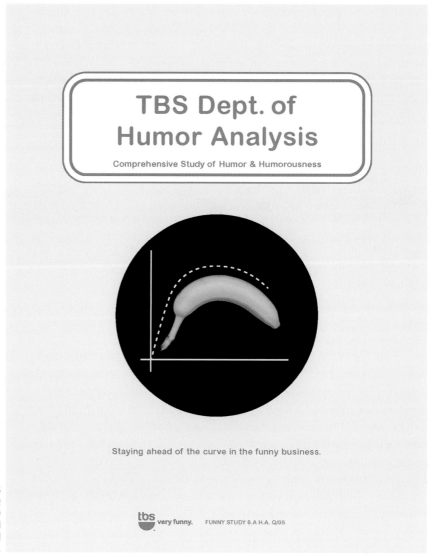

TBS Dept. of Humor Analysis

Comprehensive Study of Humor & Humorousness

Staying ahead of the curve in the funny business.

tbs **very funny.**   FUNNY STUDY 6.A H.A. Q/05

Small or large agency? Creatives who work for smaller agencies realize the opportunity for interesting projects, like this TBS Humor Booklet concepted and produced by Mother New York. It won a Gold Pencil for Design at the 2006 One Show.

Writer Matt Heath took an internship/trial period at JWT in New York on the basis of videos he'd written with a partner. "I also had some great captions for New Yorker cartoons and a couple of quick campaigns," he explains. But it was enough to convince them that his style was JWT-worthy. In his first week, he wrote scripts; he concepted; he worked long hours. After a three-month stint with a lot of work produced, he got an offer from 72andSunny in Santa Monica and hasn't looked back.

Staying Inspired
Once you have that job, then what? How do you keep the edge?

There are dozens of good books on how to keep your creativity honed and your ideation process revved up before you get a job and after.

But we do need to address the reality of staying inspired over the long haul. How do you stay ready to work and rework your book? How do you keep the pace up after you get that first job? How do you keep ideas coming? When ideas are your professional lifeblood, you must find ways to nurture and protect your strongest asset.

Rossana Bardales, Group Creative Director at Mother, London, has won every award and then some. She started out in New York at award-winning shops like Cliff Freeman & Partners, then went to London for the next exciting chapter of her career. For her, London is part of the inspiration. To be inspired, "I only work in places where I'm surrounded by the best creative talent," she says. "I don't want to work in a place that is too comfortable. I want to work in a place where I'm sitting on the edge of my seat, where I know that the person sitting next to me could possibly be writing the next Grand Prix for Cannes or next short film at Sundance or starting up the next top band."

Danny Gregory, Creative Director at McGarryBowen in New York and author of *Creative License*, uses sketchbooks and journaling to keep inspired for life, not just advertising. His ideas for staying creative are inspiring by themselves.

Writer Matt Heath finds the best couch to work through his first scripts at JWT during a summer stint in the New York City office.

Staying Creative
Danny Gregory, Creative Director/McGarry Bowen
See Danny's approach to drawing
and life on www.dannygregory.com

Good advertising begins by capturing people's attention; for that you need to be novel and clear, drawing from the broadest possible references to create never-before-seen syntheses.

Good advertising provides a POV you can relate to. To create that effectively, you need to be a dimensional human being, not just an ad nerd. You need to know how people feel, how they are persuaded, what they yearn for, how to speak in terms they like.

Where do you get that first grain of sand to drop into one's creative oyster?

Where do you find inspiration?

I'd urge you to look far afield. Sure, the most recent One Show annual, issue of *Creativity* and Cannes show reel are all full of great ideas. But I think the best work draws from sources way beyond the confines of advertising.

A FEW IDEAS FOR INSPIRATION:

Look at what graphic designers are doing; they seem to draw such diverse ideas into the way they solve problems. Great resource: aiga.org has lots of great links and profiles. I also like to look at the work of individual design studios like Sagmeister or Pentagram or Cahan.

Spend time at the newsstand. Don't just look at design and advertising trade pubs. Look at comic books, at magazines for skateboarders, craft books, literary zines, fashion magazines, shelter books like *Wallpaper* and *World of Interiors*, and art magazines from *Art Forum* to *Juxtapoz*. Study their use of type, layout, exposition, photography, illustration, humor, shock.

Watch TV, all sorts of TV. Watch movies, all sorts of movies. Read books, all sorts of books. Listen to music, scour the web ... you get the idea. Try to experience everything the readers of your ads will see. And then some.

Don't spend all your time working. Live. Make friends (and not just people in advertising, please!). Have dinner parties. Shop. Nap. Hang out. Learn jokes. Travel when you can. See how people around the world communicate, how they make things, how they express themselves.

Draw. Whether you're an art director or a writer, facility with a pencil — even stick figures! — will help you express your ideas to partners, bosses, clients , photographers, and directors. It will also help you see the world more clearly and will expand your creativity.

Make your own art. Don't reserve your creativity for paying clients. Express yourself in little films, drawings, short stories, poems, websites, pranks, crafts, cooking, tattoos, clothes.

The very best advertising usually doesn't feel like advertising. It feels like life. So make sure you have a life before you try to create an ad.

It's important to know that advertising creativity often gives way to other outlets. Writers and art directors often find themselves working in other genres outside of work — writing novels, screenplays, art, or directing — and becoming quite successful in a second creative career. This isn't necessarily instead of or in spite of advertising.

More likely, it's another illuminating outlet for all of the ideas and possibilities they nurture. In other words, nurturing your talent for advertising doesn't stop with headlines and designing pages. It often leads to other substantial creative opportunities. What a great career!

Don't spend too much time sitting back and staring at your accomplishments. The joy is in the creating. So keep doing it over and over again. Don't stress on how much you are getting compensated. Or the number of awards you have won. Just keep crafting communications and everything will fall into place.

Robert Rasmussen, Executive Creative Director, R/GA New York

Rosch sums it up this way: "Read about politics, science, movie stars, biochemistry, oceanography, conspiracy theories. Limit the YouTube. Take up kayaking, open an art gallery, design jewelry, cook, organize community events, write for a magazine that has nothing to do with advertising, eat at dives, go to countries that other people think are dangerous, and I don't know? Maybe go to the gym. I had someone ask me recently how there could possibly be time for outside interests when the general rule is: Get a job in the business and crush yourself trying to do great ads. My answer in two parts: There is always time if you make the time, and anyone who thinks otherwise isn't somebody you want to work for."

So much for limiting your horizons.

It is a lot less about scheduling, timelines, organization, and management. It is really about thinking and solving problems. That's a pretty cool thing.

Alan Snitow
Vice President
Group Planning Director
SS+K
New York City

Account
planning

ACCOUNT PLANNERS WILL TELL YOU THEY HAVE THE BEST JOB IN THE AGENCY—
and maybe in the whole world. But if you ask 20 planners what they've worked on in the last 48 hours, you'll get 20 different answers. In fact, there's no "typical day" for a planner — no same old, same old. Planners love to solve problems, and in ad agencies they get paid to tackle an unending stream of varied and interesting challenges:

- pouring over stacks of data looking for a business opportunity everyone else has missed
- interviewing consumers to find out how they really feel about the product
- morphing a business strategy into a creative strategy
- guiding the creative team through the lives of consumers
- brainstorming new media approaches to maximize a tiny budget
- analyzing cultural trends to understand the implications for the client's business

Planning isn't a job for those who favor routine or want everything to proceed in a linear fashion. "There is a lack of respect for order," says Britton Taylor, Strategic Planner at Wieden + Kennedy (W+K). "I haven't seen too many planners with clean desks." He's right. Jeffrey Blish, Partner and Director of Planning for Deutsch LA, admits it is often difficult to see the floor in his office. Adriann Cocker, another Deutsch planner, has shelves of cow figurines adorning her office.

But don't let the piles of paper, unusual artwork, or odd paraphernalia fool you. Amidst the chaos lies a keen creative intellect, and it really is controlled chaos. It's illustrative of a key characteristic of planners: They have strong left brain and right brain skills — highly creative and highly analytic. They understand sales figures, trend data, and popular culture. And they can see the relationship between all three. Insight is the magic link.

This insight *aha!* moment is also a creative act, the result of seeing things from a new perspective. It might be an insight into how a consumer understands the brand, how the brand can be extended, or how to communicate about the brand. Whether it's a creative, strategic, or research problem, planners need to look at it from multiple points of view and develop an insight that leads to a solution.

Planners didn't invent the notion of insights. The truth is that great agencies have always been good at them even if they didn't use the planning label. Leo Burnett tapped into rugged individualism with the Marlboro man; and N.W. Ayer & Son linked DeBeers diamonds with eternity. Account planners also don't have a stranglehold on insight within an agency. If it's a good idea, it doesn't matter which department it came from. But the planner's job is to ensure that insights are more than personal and idiosyncratic and that they connect with the brand in a way that will drive the client's business.

Planning—Then and Now:
More than "The Voice of the Consumer"

Like many other innovations, account planning was launched by viewing a problem as an opportunity. In the late 1960s, Stanley Pollitt of Boase Massimi Pollitt in London felt that agencies weren't really in touch with consumers. Research approaches were often highly formulaic and sometimes seemed to work against breakthrough creative work. Pollitt wanted research that helped him understand buying behavior more deeply so the agency could make even better ads. Enter account planning.

In contrast to traditional agency researchers, account planners have ongoing involvement with the project. They view research as a means to an end (a breakthrough insight) rather than primarily for measurement and validation. They also use research to both provoke and satisfy their curiosity.

Jay Chiat, advertising luminary and One Club Hall of Famer, was instrumental in bringing account planning across the pond to the U.S.

Jay Chiat, one of the founders of Chiat\Day (now known as TBWA\Chiat\Day) imported account planning to the United States in the 1980s. Many, if not most, of the first generation of planners in the United States came from the United Kingdom. Now you no longer need to have a British accent to be a planner. Today, almost all of the major agencies in the United States and most regional ones have account planning in one form or another.

Originally touted as "the voice of the consumer," the American approach to planning drew heavily on research expertise. The planner was responsible for understanding consumer research and writing a creative brief that would inspire the creative teams to brilliant executions. In this early version, the day-to-day activity of the planner emphasized creative strategy and development, i.e., the message the ad needed to communicate in order to stir the consumer to action.

Smarter Brands, Smarter Consumers:
The Planning Mission Grows

With the development of increasingly sophisticated brands and shifts in agency structure and revenue streams, planning evolved to a broader strategic role. It also became more involved in the client's marketing and business. As Earl Cox, Director of Strategic Planning for The Martin Agency in Richmond, Virginia, notes, "Planning goes from a very creative-centric kind of planning that helps the creatives get smart about the target to an approach that is much more business-centric, marketing-centric, client-centric."

It's all a matter of agency culture. So you need to know that there are many versions of planning, and no single definition covers the range of planning activities. The variety of job titles reflects this evolution: account planner, brand planner, strategic planner, strategist, universal planner, and even cognitive anthropologist.

In most agencies, planners are still responsible for understanding and synthesizing research and writing a creative brief. However, they also help maintain
the brand relationship across a variety of marketing communication channels,
meaning they could be involved in everything from the national television
campaign to details like employee uniforms.

> **As the relative importance of pure 'advertising' diminishes in business,
> marketing, and culture, planners are increasingly applying their skills beyond
> advertising and are thinking about all aspects of brands, life, and stuff.**
>
> *Russell Davies, Planning Guru and Consummate Blogger*
> *russelldavies.typepad.com, Principal, Open Intelligence, London*

That's another thing about planners: They're a part of the whole process. "Most
planners get a real kick out of seeing their insight come to life in something
tangible," says Cox. "So it isn't just that they bring the insights but that they
help engineer how they are applied."

It's the opportunity to be involved in every stage of the work that also appeals to
planners like Deutsch's Blish: "I love advertising. I love working with the
creative department. I couldn't do what I do without them. You get to see the
ideas manifest in TV ads, print ads, stuff on the web, outdoor, in dealerships or
restaurants. You have all sorts of opportunities to really influence what the
brand stands for in the world."

It's this total involvement that separates planners from brand consultants who
develop insights and then move on to other projects before their insights begin
to be turned into print ads and TV spots. So as you consider possible jobs in
this area, you'll want to think about how much of the process you want to be
connected with. That will help you determine, for example, whether you'd
rather be a planner or a brand consultant.

Different Agencies, Different Kinds of Planning

The role of the planner will vary by the size and culture of the agency, the
nature of the clients, and the type of project. Generally, smaller agencies and
those founded by and with planners have most successfully integrated planning into the agency structure.

SS+K's Snitow points out that the change to a planning-centric culture isn't
automatic. "In some of the younger shops, there has never been a time when
planning wasn't there. But in a lot of older blue-chip Madison Avenue agencies,
they may have changed the name on the door but not the people or the
processes. It takes a long time to turn around a big ship culturally."

A major part of your pre-career job is to know agencies and their approaches.
That will bring you closer to finding the work you really want to do at the place

where you really want to do it. But remember: This business changes quickly. Agencies change, accounts are won and lost, and people move around. According to a 2007 survey by account planner Heather LeFevre of The Martin Agency, even though 93 percent of the planners who responded love their jobs, more than one-third expect to change jobs within a year. Good news: This is great for networking. Because folks move around so much, after a few years you'll know people in agencies across the country.

What Planners Do and Who They Work With

Planners are jugglers and multi-taskers. Whether they work on a single brand or several different accounts, most planners will be dealing with a variety of projects all going on simultaneously. But the projects are usually all in different stages: business strategy development, creative development, media strategy development, or campaign evaluation. "You just hope they aren't all hot at the same time," says W+K's Taylor. "That's when things get really nuts." And when planners must multitask in amazing ways.

In short, planners work with every part of the agency — account management, creative, and media. They help put together the business strategy, develop the creative brief, and provide insights into how consumers use media. But what does all of that involve? And would you like it? The following sections will help you decide.

How Planners Work with Account Management

Consumer insight is only useful if it works for the client's business. So the planner must understand that business. How does the client's company make money? What challenges does it face? How can advertising contribute? What problems can't be solved by advertising?

"Ultimately it has to be about sales and share gain," states Neil Saunders, Senior Vice President, Planning Director at Leo Burnett in Chicago. "At the end of the day, we've got to sell product. I can't figure out a relevant consumer insight if I don't understand the client's business."

Planners work closely with account management to determine the brand position and communications strategy. Account executives have a deep knowledge of the client's business. That knowledge is shared with the planner who pairs it with an understanding of the consumer to identify the strongest points of connection between the consumer and the brand. During strategy development, planning activities range from analyzing existing research and overseeing new research to identifying an insight and writing a communication strategy that may be directed at both employees and consumers.

So in this career you'll need to be creative, focused, strategic, organized, and able to communicate smartly with your audience.

Here's an Example to Explain It

There is no better example of how planning must get inside and understand a client's business than the work the Los Angeles office of TBWA\Chiat\Day did for Pedigree dog food. Planner Kathleen Kindle was asked to help Pedigree clarify its core brand identity.

Pedigree's employees were dog owners who loved their dogs. But Kindle discovered that some days it was easier for them to slip into a corporate mentality than to keep dogs first and foremost. That helped her realize that before Pedigree could rally around its dog food and promote it effectively, it would first need to make its internal identity of "being about dogs" more apparent in every part of the company.

To help the company believe differently and be even more focused on the idea that "everything we do is for the dog," Kindle set up disruption workshops in eight cities around the world, which were attended by both the agency and company executives. Disruption workshops, developed by TBWA\Chiat\Day President Jean-Marie Dru, identify the unstated assumptions about how to do business that keep a company from being more innovative. The experience clearly helped Pedigree solidify its identity as a company made up of dog lovers, not just dog owners.

Employees from the delivery dock to the boardroom got the idea in a big way. They put pictures of their dogs on their ID badges and business cards. They launched doggy insurance policies and health plans and dog-friendly offices. The Pedigree Café in Paris welcomes dogs and their human companions.

Only after the whole company was fully on board did they begin advertising to consumers. The agency discovered that no one was really celebrating the role of dogs in peoples' lives. Kindle explains: "We realized we needed to address people as dog lovers and not just as dog owners. The relationship isn't just about buying food." Not surprisingly, good ads came out of good planning. The series of ads arising from this insight no doubt contributed to *Adweek* naming TBWA\Chiat\Day Agency of the Year in 2004.

How Planners Work with Creative

For many planners, the opportunity to work closely with the creative team and see the strategy come to life is one of the most exciting aspects of their work. "One of the coolest parts of the job," says W+K's Taylor, "is actually seeing the whole process through from start to finish and collaborating to get good ads."

The most important part of that process may be the writing of the creative brief. That's the document that writers and art directors use to guide their creation of the advertising. Developing it is definitely more art than science. "If there isn't creative thinking in the strategy, you can't expect creative thinking back in the execution," SS+K's Snitow points out. "Not only should it be written in a creative way — succinct, smart, and inspiring — but the strategy also needs to be creative."

Of course, in writing the brief, a planner doesn't have to go it alone. In fact, it's usually a collaborative process with lots of give and take between planners and creatives. Michael Doody, who is a brand strategy director at New York's Kirshenbaum Bond + Partners (KBP), firmly believes that the best work comes from partnerships between "planners who think creatively and creatives with brilliant strategic minds."

The Get It Factor

Account planners — a.k.a. strategists, engagement specialists, brand planners — craft the creative brief that will guide the creative team to do great work. They are thinkers, writers, researchers, and artists. And they inspire great work.

One way to think of the brief and the creative work it leads to is to understand advertising as a form of storytelling. The planner has to figure out what the target is like and what kind of story will touch the audience, and the creative team needs to figure out how to tell that story in an engaging way.

Every agency has its own version of the creative brief. Ultimately, these briefs all distill the relevant information down to a few key points: the problem to be solved, a profile of the target, and the message (main idea) that the audience will find most compelling.

The Creative Brief and the Target Profile

After conducting research and getting a handle on what the target is like as a person, the planner must communicate that understanding to both the writer and art director. Otherwise, they will not be able to develop ads that connect with the audience.

> **A good creative brief often requires a leap of faith. Research alone rarely tells you exactly what will inspire consumers.**
> *Earl Cox, Director of Strategic Planning, The Martin Agency, Richmond*

But planners can't just pass out a stack of research reports. Creative people are, well, creative. So planners have to communicate with them in ways they'll be able to relate to. In short, they have to make their briefings creative as well. And that's part of the fun.

When W+K's Taylor was still at Goodby, Silverstein & Partners (Goodby), he needed to demonstrate an understanding of the 21-to-27-year-old male beer drinker. To bring that perspective to life for the creative team, he conducted and videotaped in home research in the style of MTV's *Cribs*.

"We had people who live alone, those who live with a bunch of roommates, and we had people who live with their parents. It was kind of funny to have the *Cribs*-style with a 23 year old who lives with his parents. But they knew the show, and they were into it," Taylor explains. "So, we'd be walking through his house and the guy would say, 'Here's my Dad.' And we went into his room and listened to him play his guitar. He showed us his favorite Guns N' Roses t-shirt and the food in the refrigerator that he never eats because he says he never eats at home. We talked about what beer he drinks."

Making that video, says Taylor, was not only fun, it was also "a lot more interesting to watch than just snippets of a focus group. It helped the creative team get in the mindset of the audience and understand how these guys really live."

The Creative Brief and the Message

Before the creative team can develop advertising, they also need to know what that advertising should say. The brief the planners write identifies that message. Here's how the planners at Crispin Porter + Bogusky (Crispin) went about identifying that message for Google.

Google presented the agency with an interesting problem: They receive more than 1500 applications a day — many more than they can handle. And far too

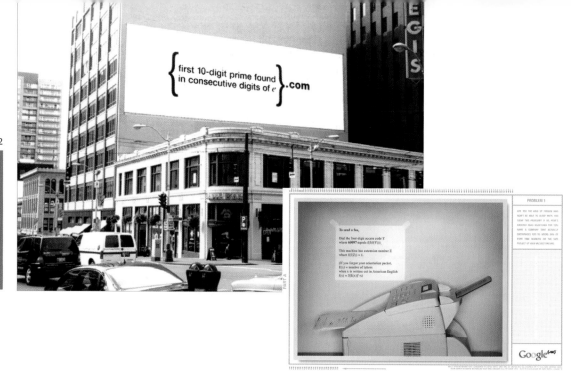

few of those applicants are truly qualified for the positions they desire (less than one-half of one percent).

For Google, sorting through all the applications eats up valuable time. So they challenged Crispin to generate more qualified leads. Planners set out to discover an insight or truth about qualified applicants and then used that to develop the message.

After hours spent analyzing survey results, interviewing engineers, and hanging out in campus computer labs late at night, Tom Birk, Director of Cultural and Cognitive Studies at Crispin, and Jamie Webb, Cognitive Anthropologist, kept coming back to the fact that computer engineering superstars aren't motivated by monetary rewards like big cars, big houses, or big salaries; they simply love big challenges — solving seemingly impossible tasks. They spend their free time playing chess, solving logic problems, and playing video games. They expect equally challenging tasks from their work.

The key insight? Computer engineers love solving problems — the bigger the better. So the main message to the creative team was to make getting in the door and getting an interview at Google the ultimate challenge.

The ads the creative team developed based on that strategy recruited prospects through a series of challenging problems. If they were able to solve the problems successfully (and thereby demonstrate they were a qualified candidate), they were directed to the Google Labs page that invited them to submit a résumé. The campaign produced over 2400 pre-qualified leads and over $830,000 worth of free press coverage. Definitely a success story.

Once a campaign like the one for Google has been approved and has run, planners may then be involved in designing research to track the consumer's reaction. Gathering that sort of information can help reinforce the client's buy-in and also help the creative team develop additional ideas for the campaign.

How Planners Work with Media

Planners don't just work with account and creative people anymore. With media options exploding, planners are much more involved in media decisions than ever before. Obviously, it's no longer a matter of just deciding between print and television.

Today, there are technology-driven media opportunities like mobile phones, blogs, podcasting, and online viral marketing. Due to the variety of media options, account planners are increasingly included in channel and communication planning. And their briefs now often include insights about how the target spends their time and how media fits into their lives.

That sort of work requires a keen understanding not only of the media consumers use but also when and how they interact with it. Karen Goulet, Director of Ignition, OMD West in Los Angeles explains: "For a working woman, we have to understand if the message will work best in a magazine that she reads after 10 p.m. when she's relaxed and it's her downtime, or if messaging in the work environment is more effective. So we really have to understand her life, what motivates her, and how to connect with her." There is no standard procedure for who figures this out. Most often, it is a collaborative effort.

Annie Sarabia, Media Planner at MindShare Interaction in New York, notes that one of her first-year realizations was the relationship between a good media department and the planning department: "I think the media planner and account planner should be best friends. The best ideas for media and creative often come from great insights account planners provide."

Here's more good news about opportunities in this field: It's not just media departments within traditional advertising agencies that need insights from planners. Many large agencies have spun off their media departments into freestanding, independent media services companies like OMD, which work both for clients and a variety of advertising agencies.

These giant media services companies may not always call the position "account planning," but they are all looking for people to help them understand consumers and how they use all of these new media options. That means more planning jobs and career opportunities for you.

How Insight Happens

As you've just seen, planners work with account service, creative, and media. The insight that leads to the main message can come from anyone or anywhere: the client's archives, a remark during a meeting (see the story about California cheese), a stray comment during a consumer interview or focus group, an observation of consumer behavior, or even a unique product feature.

How Happy Cows Were Born: The Insight Behind California Cheese

When Deutsch LA was developing the brief for Real California Cheese, the challenge was to get people to look for it when they shopped. That wasn't easy. After all, cheese is cheese, and cows are cows. There were no rational attributes or claims to build the strategy around.

The *aha!* moment came when the entire team – account management, creatives, planners, and media – were sitting around the conference table trying to figure out what to do. Eventually, they began to think about playing off the idea of California pride. As Jeffrey Blish remembers it, "That got us into the idea that life is better in California, which led one of the creative guys to say 'if life is better in California, then even the cows are happier here.' The minute someone said that we knew that was it. If the cows are happier, they must make great milk. Great milk makes great cheese – and there was our irrational reason to believe. Once the idea that cows are happier too was on the table, the campaign just took off from there."

That insight was at the heart of the brief that helped the creative team come up with the line: "Great Cheese comes from Happy Cows. Happy Cows come from California." Over the years the ads have won numerous awards, and the cows have become so popular that the Real California Cheese website sells "Happy Cow" merchandise nationwide. To see the latest TV spots and the integrated approach to the message, check out: www.RealCaliforniaCheese.com. Not only is the work great creatively, but it is also smart business. California is on target to become the nation's leading producer of cheese.

However, the insight generally grows out of research. Planners use both qualitative research (the kind that involves interviewing or observing people) and quantitative (the kind that uses surveys and numbers).

But there is a fundamental difference between being a researcher and a planner. According to The Martin Agency's Cox, "Most researchers choose to stop at reporting the facts and information. They don't try to speculate on what it means. Planners need to get beyond the facts and make decisions about what the information means and determine an effective strategy. A good creative brief often requires a leap of faith. Research alone rarely tells you exactly what will inspire consumers."

Conducting Qualitative Research

Because qualitative approaches are better at getting at the emotional aspects of the consumer experience, planners tend to be more hands-on with these approaches — particularly standard focus groups and individual interviews. After all, they pride themselves on their ability to help consumers articulate things they don't think about or have words for.

For example, when KBP worked with AdoptUsKids and The Ad Council to increase interest in the adoption of foster children, they conducted research to get a better handle on the problem and an insight into the target.

The breakthrough insight came when an adoptive mom recalled how a friend approached her in a supermarket and remarked that she was a saint for adopting a child out of the foster system. Her adopted son immediately piped up with, "She's not a saint; she's my mom."

The boy's comment crystallized the agency's thinking about a key idea: "You don't have to be perfect to be an adoptive parent." KBP realized that potential parents needed permission to believe that adoption required patience and love, but not perfection. The agency delivered that idea in the creative brief this way:

> You don't need to be a super-parent.
> You don't need a three-bedroom house on a hill.
> If you have a bit of patience and a heart that beats a little faster when you see a child in need, then you're probably up for the task.
> Our kids might demand some extra attention, but all they really want is somewhere to call home.
> Someone to call mom or dad.
> Someone who's not only willing to be there for them today but tomorrow as well.
>
> You don't have to be perfect to be a parent.

Fielding Quantitative Research

Planners also need to understand quantitative approaches. Generally, an independent research house is hired to do the nitty-gritty work of quantitative research (finding the right people, administering a survey, and tabulating the responses). But planners may be intimately involved in developing the survey questions and interpreting the answers.

Interpreting the Research Findings

Obviously, everything hinges on obtaining good information from the qualitative and quantitative research. But that's just the first step. When the planner sits down and begins to analyze the data, that's when "the magic starts to happen," says Burnett's Saunders. "Good planners have an ability to take the same data that everyone else is looking at and see it in a new way. And that's remarkable."

To see the data in fresh ways, planners must be able to get beneath the surface and discover underlying patterns and unexpected connections between disparate pieces of data. Some say it's a matter of "mixing and matching," of "taking an idea from here and putting it over there." Regardless of how planners go about it, almost everyone interviewed describes the end result as "magic," "an epiphany," and as "more art than science."

Clearly, planning is as much a creative act as coming up with the idea for a great television commercial. But for planners the moment of insight is only the first step in the process. That insight must also be relevant and strategically sound. Examining the insight to make sure it has those qualities is the point where art meets logic.

And it's that need to involve the whole self, to use both the analytical and creative parts of the mind, that makes planning so challenging and so rewarding.

Getting Started: What an Assistant Planner Does

Now you know what a planner does. But what will you do when you're just starting out? And what's that first job even called?

There are a slew of titles for that entry-level job: "account planning coordinator," "assistant account planner," and "junior planner" are among the most common titles. You might even see more conceptual titles such as cultural anthropologist or insight maven. For convenience, it's referred to here as "assistant planner."

Alyson Heller, Assistant Account Planner at Fallon in Minneapolis, had an *aha!* moment while reading the account planning website before she applied for an internship. "I thought 'that's me.' I couldn't believe I would get paid to do this. I love digging and figuring out exactly who our target is and what motivates them."

Her current work fuels this passion. "It's fun to pull together all these different resources — some of the numbers, the research data — and combine that with more qualitative stuff like profiles that psychologists have done as well as some of our own experience with these people. It's really fun to see how that information all comes together."

Darcey Kramer, Assistant Planner at Denver's Integer Group, thinks of planning as the account-side parallel to being an art director. "You have this freedom to think outside-the-box. You get to have these big ideas and see overarching values, but you don't have to figure out exactly how to do it. That's where the creatives are brilliant. They figure out how to communicate it."

Like Heller, she's enthusiastic about her job: "I like to see what inspires people, what makes them tick, how they think about things, and why they do things. I like to see how the mind works — not so much psychology but more anthropology. How cultures are involved. How other people do things. It's kind of ridiculous how pumped I am to go and do interviews. There is nothing more exciting to me. There's nothing cooler than knowing 'why do you do that?'"

For Kramer, a "typical" day can include any of the following — and then some:
• locating and coordinating the logistics for videotaping in-home interviews in another state
• accompanying consumers on a trip to a retail store to hear them talk through the process of selecting hair coloring
• pulling statistics to support key recommendations, e.g., the number of single family households in a particular market, sales tracking data, etc.
• synthesizing data from multiple sources on color and flavor trends.

It's detail work, but it's also important. There's also a creative aspect to these tasks: "It's like a 'choose your own adventure' book," says Kramer. "I decide where I'm going first — Lexus Nexus, WGSN (Worth Global Style Network), Google, and what path to follow. I am constantly thinking and re-evaluating where I stand, how I am thinking about things, and how other people might be thinking about the same thing and then making connections between the information and how people behave."

However, neither Heller nor Kramer is pulling this all together alone. Assistant planners are the quintessential apprentices paired with more senior planners to observe and learn. Very few agencies have formal training programs in account planning; most do, however, periodically gather the planners together to share information and techniques.

"Training is really training on the job and really a kind of mentoring by a senior planner. It tends to be *ad hoc* as the need arises," claims John Thorpe, Goodby's

Director of Brand Strategy. Nonetheless, Thorpe indicates his agency will periodically host sessions on such things as presentation skills, moderator skills, or writing the creative brief.

Initially, the work is almost all behind-the-scenes with little client and consumer contact. "They have to suck it up is the usual sort of advice," says Thorpe. "A lot of it is grunt work. They work with a senior planner and do a lot of shadowing to begin with." Kramer refers to her shadowing as being "the Integer stunt woman. I do some of the behind the scenes stuff that makes them look really good."

But she is quick to point out the value of grunt work. "You produce work for other people to take to meetings. So there isn't much client contact at first. But all the behind-the-scenes stuff is still part of planning," says Kramer. "You start to understand the resources better and how much it costs and how long it takes and what kind of information you need. That's really helpful the first time you have to do a project yourself."

As they gain understanding of planning, assistant planners are eased into a more visible role. They might observe a few interviews, be given a stack of discussion guides from other research efforts, and then be asked to create the first draft of a guide for an upcoming project.

Initial consumer interviews are apt to be person-on-the-street interviews to help add texture to a creative briefing or a client presentation. After they have attended several focus groups, "bit by bit they will be encouraged to conduct focus groups," says Thorpe.

But a junior planner is not a minion to an all-mighty senior planner. Deutsch's Blish points out, "It's not hierarchal in a political sense. Obviously, some people have more experience than others and different titles. But if we have a new business pitch and we are sitting in a conference room trying to figure out what to do, the ideas come from anywhere and anybody. The learning goes both ways." A brilliant insight can come from anyone, and sometimes the assistant's fresh perspective is just what the account needs.

Still, the assistant's job primarily involves providing support for more senior people. Coordinating those time consuming but essential details provides an opportunity to practice and master the key aspects of the planner's job: collecting information, drawing conclusions, making strategic recommendations, and working with creative teams. Since most agencies no longer have training programs, this opportunity to learn on the job is critical.

Here's the career takeaway: The faster you learn, the faster you advance.

Building Your Career One Little Insight at a Time

Newly minted undergrads are hired as planning assistants or coordinators — and, every now and then, as entry-level planners. When assistants are promoted to planners — generally after a year or two — they are given their own (usually smaller) accounts. As with other areas in the agency, you "move up" by being given larger, more prestigious pieces of business.

A planner usually moves to a senior planning position within two to three years, but there is no magic timeline. The opportunity for advancement can vary by the size of the agency, the activity level of various accounts, employee turnover, and the success of new business pitches.

"One of the things that is nice about advertising is that it is a meritocracy. If you are good at it, you can be successful and move up the ladder," says SS+K's Snitow. "Many agencies have really young planning directors. There are great planning agencies where the head of planning is 34 years old or 32. It's not that rare. So you can move up really quickly."

The wider your range of experience and expertise, the more valuable you are to the agency. Sometimes it is better to be a junior planner on an important account than to be a senior planner on a stale account.

Senior planners work as the sole or lead planner on several key accounts in addition to supervising junior planners. Planners also move up by acquiring new experiences on different kinds of accounts. As KBP's Doody explains it, "If you don't feel like you are learning new stuff and still having fun, then it might be time for a new account, a new agency, or maybe even a new career."

In general, advertising is a very young business. You work long hours, often with very tight deadlines. It's crazy fun, but it can also be exhausting year after year. In truth, you'll find that most of the "gray hairs" in an agency are either owners or senior management.

Ultimately, it's possible for a highly experienced planner to become the director of account planning or its equivalent. But because there is usually only one such executive at an agency, in order to continue building a career, many senior planners leave the agency and move on to brand consultancies, research and marketing firms, or the client side.

Such movement is not only due to limited room at the top but also to the kinds of changes that are reshaping the advertising industry as boundaries blur between advertising and other forms of marketing communication.

In fact, there are lots of opportunities for planners after agency life. "One of the coolest things about this job is that you can apply it anywhere. It's about life," says Doody. "I don't know what I want to do next, but I certainly want to be as excited about it as I am about what I do now."

What Makes a Good Planner: "I'll Know It When I See It"

Everyone may want a planner to walk through the door with finely honed research skills and deep experience in marketing strategy. But agencies know they can't expect that from most entry-level candidates. Instead, they look for people who have the potential to develop those skills.

Part of that potential involves having a degree of comfort with numbers and basic business knowledge. Some of that knowledge can be picked up easily. Candidates, however, do need to have at least an interest in and, hopefully, a basic understanding of business and branding. Without that, notes Burnett's Saunders, "you don't have the framework to evaluate whether an insight will contribute to the client's bottom line."

But don't worry; nobody is expecting you to have a business degree. In fact, there is a perception at many agencies that those with business degrees, especially MBAs, are trained to think too linearly. "They assume there is a right way to do it, and it is all very black and white," says Saunders. "It's not a green light, red light deal. Advertising works with ideas, not formulas." Being able to work with numbers is just as important. Although planners are far more practiced in conducting focus groups, one-on-one interviews, and other kinds of qualitative research, they can't be afraid of quantitative approaches and the numbers they involve.

Quant is actually quite fascinating and will give a young person a real edge over the competition for jobs. Good quant is based on a well thought out hypothesis, and when the resulting cross tabulations land on your desk (or desktop), your hypothesis is either right or wrong. It's a bit like watching a slot machine stop...either the numbers (or cherries) line up or they don't.

Cheryl Greene, Chief Strategy Officer, Deutsch, New York

"It's not that you have to be a quant jockey or a data grinder," notes Goodby's Thorpe. So, you don't need to be a stats wiz. But you do need an appreciation for the kinds of information that statistical approaches yield.

Big news: You can't be the sort of person who says, "I don't do math." You need to be willing to interpret the numbers. So if your brain automatically shuts down when you see a column of figures, this isn't the field for you.

Characteristics of a Planner: There's No Magic Check List

If necessary, an agency can train you to moderate focus groups or read research reports, but they can't conjure up a natural way of being in the world. As W+K's

Taylor points out, "A few can make the crossover from management or pure research, but it is difficult to mold someone if they don't have the right disposition innately." He adds, "I think that it's a default career for many. Maybe you were in a band before; maybe you studied philosophy. But you were passionate about something, and you bring that richness of perspective to planning."

In short, there is no substitute for simply living an aware, engaged, and inquisitive life, plus having a passion for great advertising.

As you might suspect, there is no magic checklist for what makes a good planner, and the overall description can seem rather daunting. Deutsch's Adriann Cocker easily rattles off an impressive list of characteristics: "intuitive, curious, empathetic, analytic, persuasive, creative, with an actual love of advertising. A formal education does not always help. Many are 40 going on 16." And, she adds, "Attitude and confidence are as important as intellect."

Give or take a word or two, it's about the same list you'll hear from any planning director. And they all say, "I'll know it when I see it." You won't see all those attributes profiled below, but you can make the connections yourself.

Curious

"Good planners are naturally curious and naturally strategic," says Crispin's Birk. "They never lose the sense of curiosity, and they just get better strategically with more experience."

Planners like the idea of getting inside people's heads because they find people inherently interesting. They're curious about how a barista in a coffee shop assesses each customer who walks in the door or what educational choices look like from the perspective of a middle-aged Latina versus a Baptist preacher.

"There is still a bit of child-like curiosity that seems to remain in planners long after they are children," says The Martin Agency's Cox. Fallon's Heller refers to it as a "genetic need to find out more." And it's not idle curiosity either because it's rooted in passion, in what Birk calls "a kind of bulldog determination to dig down and understand what makes things tick."

The planner's curiosity also remains ultimately respectful when it comes to consumers. You may not always agree with the consumer's worldview, but you do have to respect and appreciate it (the empathy part). If that doesn't come naturally, you're apt to miss important information because of your own biases.

Creative Intellect

Planners are creative and non-linear thinkers but not creative team wannabes. They find links between the brand, something a consumer said, and a cultural observation. And there's a thrill in magically connecting all of those dots to find a new solution (the creative aspect). But they also have an ability to boil all the complexity down into a single key idea (the analytic aspect).

A planner is able to weave a coherent story from what others see as only stray threads — not because they make up stuff but because they make connections that others may not see. It's about being an expansive big-picture-thinker who also pays attention to detail when it really matters.

"It is the combination of a very academic bent with common sense," says Deutsch's Greene. "For the planning piece, you have to be able to read academic stuff that wasn't made for popular consumption. You have to dig. You have to like things that are kind of leading edge. So it is a funny combination. Some of it is common sense, but you also need a very sharp intellect."

Culturally Savvy

You'll find planners are street smart as well as book smart. They pay attention to trends, cultural and social. The best planners are also passionate about culture — not culture as in high culture (you know, opera, MOMA, fine wine, and gourmet food) — but culture as in what's going on in the world, what's in and what's out.

"The people you meet in agencies tend to be really interesting people who are in touch with what is going on," says SS+K's Snitow. "You will always be the cool uncle if you work in advertising because you are going to know who the bands are, what the cool toys are, and you're going to know what the news is and who the celebrities are. You are just in touch with stuff going on in the world in a way that you aren't in corporate America."

Trendspotting is big business these days. Being culturally savvy is not the same as trendspotting. But by the time the trend shows up in *Newsweek* or *Time*, planners have already known about it for at least a year or two. While they may not be the ones to spot the trend initially, they can tell you *why* it is happening and what it means for their clients.

"Being savvy is being able to apply what you know," says KBP's Doody. "You can buy all kinds of information. It's more important to be able to use it."

Long distance teamwork is part of the 21st century agency. Here, Crispin creatives in Boulder are briefed by planners in the Miami office

Persuasive Communicators

Strong communication skills are essential. A planner must be able to go from a morning presentation to the top executives of a *Fortune 500* company to an evening in a bowling alley talking to serious league bowlers about their lives.

As The Martin Agency's Cox puts it, "Planners really have three audiences: the end consumer, the client, and the creative team. So one of the things I look for is for people to be a bit of a chameleon. Planners are a bit like closet actors.

They need to be able to excite creative people but also command the respect of our clients and be able to talk business."

As a planner, you'll also need to be able to seize a room's attention. Or as Goodby's Thorpe says, you must "have some kind of force of personality that makes others want to hear what you've got to say. Because like it or not, often the role of the planner is to get up amongst a bunch of people you may not necessarily know and say something some people aren't going to want to listen to. That's a hard trick to pull off."

Planners also need to be willing to take a stand and fight for an idea. That, too, requires confidence and a presence. "We always have to have a point of view when we go into the room," notes KBP's Doody. "Great planning is about more than just coming up with new ideas. It's about believing enough in what you say that you don't water it down just because someone challenges you. We need to stand up for good work."

In fact, planners defend not only their strategies but the creative, too. As Doody explains: "What makes one ad different than the other ad? What makes one strategy different than the other one? If we don't care, then the client can just put them on the table and pick one as if they are all equal. But they're not. If we believe one is truly better, then we owe it to our clients to tell them that."

Distinctive "Interesting People"
"The great planners that I've known have always had something wrong with them — an edge, a nervous tic, just something a bit off kilter that distinguishes them from the account folk," says W+K's Taylor. Planners aren't borderline bughouse, but they do have a slightly different perspective on the world. For example, if you grow up bi-racial in a white community or as an Army brat who lived in six different countries before the age of 12, you also tend to have a heightened awareness of people and culture. You notice things other people don't, and planning is a place where that is valued.

More than one of the planners interviewed for this chapter claimed a sense of relief when they discovered planning. SS+K's Snitow refers to it as "an epiphany moment." Here is a creative place where people with the combination of right brain and left brain interests and skills can fit in.

One planner who wished to remain anonymous described planners as "geeks with personalities and really good social skills. You are too analytic to be a really good creative and not detailed enough to be an account person. Plus all that project management stuff would make me insane. Planning is the right fit."

After a year as a planner, Fallon's Heller says finding "people here like me" was one of the biggest and most pleasant surprises: "It was pretty exciting to find this group of people. I never knew I would have this much fun."

Being interesting is so important in this industry that we discuss it in other places. Creative strategist, planner, and idea guru Russell Davies of London offered a list of ways to be interesting that we shared with you in the Creative Chapter. Read it again, and see why it works from any perspective.

Preparing to Be a Planner: Lots of Ways to Get There

There's no standard path to becoming a planner. Each person just seems to find their own way there. Until a few years ago, there were no educational programs designed to prepare people for account planning careers. So most senior planners didn't take a direct route.

Deutsch's Greene, for example, credits several years of full-time motherhood before getting an MBA as a critical part of her preparation. "I really understood what life was like in an American suburb," she notes, "and that is where a lot of consumers live." Both Julie Liss of TBWA\Chiat\Day in Los Angeles and Crispin's Birk came to planning from backgrounds that nurtured their creative and analytical sides. Liss got a degree in statistics and then did improv at Second City. Birk taught college and worked in print and TV production.

Today, with a number of undergraduate and graduate programs providing some preparation, many larger agencies have begun looking for candidates who have an educational background in planning or a related area or compatible career experience.

Rye Clifton came out of the Miami Ad School. W+K's Taylor originally had a strong interest in science before falling in love with film as well as creative writing — again that mixture of both left and right brain activities. After doing a stint as a seventh grade teacher, he decided to sign up for the planning program at the VCU AdCenter.

Building My Personal Brand
Rye Clifton, Account Planner, The Richards Group, Dallas

In retrospect, everything makes a lot of sense... but along the way, I wasn't quite sure where I was heading. In high school, my strongest classes were math and physics. So in college I thought I should focus on business.

Somewhere along the way, however, my left and right brain needed some balance, and I signed up for some advertising classes. By the time I graduated, I had switched to advertising and minored in English with a focus in creative writing. More importantly, I had found the perfect mix of rhyme and reason, creativity meshed with numbers and analysis: account planning.

I first learned of planning while attending summer school in London. For a month, I was in the heart of planning. SMU in London allowed me to meet some of the greatest planners at the top planning agencies in the world. The first planner I met was Russell Davies at Wieden + Kennedy. As he explained his job and the thinking behind their Honda and Nike campaigns, I was sold. Life's question changed from "What do I want to do?" to "How can I do that?"

I quickly learned there is no cookie-cutter planner and no defined check list to get into planning. It is more about accumulating life experiences and developing a strong point of view than knowing everything about advertising (though a passion for advertising is important).

Every planner I have met (to this day) is unique, has different strengths, has different perspectives, and has different methods of getting to the answer. It's all because they have different backgrounds and traveled down different paths that somehow led them to account planning. How could I stand out?

I became my own brand campaign. From that point forward I was a planner, figuring out how to sell myself. Advertising became a passion. I took a class in logic, took some design classes, got an internship at Publicis, started painting, joined SMU's National Student Advertising Competition team, and went back to London as a research assistant. The final step was finding a way to organize my experiences and bring them together as a compelling brand: Rye Clifton.

Miami Ad School's Boot Camp for Account Planners offered a way to tie everything back together. Three months of organized chaos: planners flying in on the weekends, case studies, creative teams, pitch presentations, and living on South Beach.

By the end, I had a website, www.ryeclifton.com, and a portfolio that looked dramatically different than anyone else's. My theory was simple: In order to sell myself, the most dangerous thing I could do was blend in. It worked, and I started work at The Richards Group about two weeks after leaving Miami.

However, even with universities and portfolio schools offering planning programs, there are still other ways to get your foot in the door. Both Integer's Kramer and Deutsch's Stephanie Walton used undergraduate degrees in advertising to launch their planning careers.

Fallon's Heller majored in economics, and SS+K's Snitow studied anthropology. He combined that major with an advertising internship and involvement with his school's Ad Club to gain the understanding that helped him get his start in planning at Foote, Cone & Belding. In short, even today there are still lots of ways to get started.

The Get It Factor

Planners come from a variety of educational backgrounds: business, advertising, psychology, anthropology, film, journalism, even art (to name just a few). What do all planners have in common? Curiosity, cultural savvy, and a great brain for understanding how people think.

Sure, certain majors or jobs might make breaking in a little easier. But if planning seems like the career for you, you still don't need to have formal training. However, you will need to highlight the right skills and maybe add a few more to your repertoire. Here are a few ways to do that.

Internships: "Yes, Yes, and Yes"

Internships are a great way to see if planning and advertising are right for you. Both Kramer and Heller landed planning positions after interning as planners. But what if you're graduating? No problem. These days many agencies are willing to offer internships to recent graduates. Some even require that you have already graduated. And remember, the better the agency, the more clout it will carry on your résumé.

Most agencies with at least a few dozen employees offer some kind of internship. Look for those that will provide an opportunity to do hands-on project work. Unless it is someone from your personal network who is committed to your education, if the agency doesn't have a plan for the internship (as in "oh, we'll find something for you to do"), skip it. You are apt to be making coffee and copies. Good internships have some structure that allows you to practice advertising, not just provide administrative support.

A number of agencies now offer internship programs in account planning. But if agencies in your area don't offer that sort of opportunity, don't worry. Just make sure the agency where you intern has account planners.

Then get involved as much as possible with the planners at the agency. Volunteer to do extra work. Attend the brown bag lunches they host. That'll give you insights into how planners think through problems and help you make contacts you can use later.

Collect Experiences

Disrupt your own space. Challenge yourself to do something new every day — even if it is just walking a new route across campus (on a really busy day). Take up fencing, try new foods, read something you normally wouldn't read, practice talking to strangers — beyond discussing the weather. Goodby's Thorpe recommends "reading as broadly as possible. You have to get a feel for the business. So read from as many views as possible — even Naomi Klein, James Twitchell, or *Adbusters*. You have to know the limits of the business and what is harmful or inappropriate."

Showcase Your Strategic Thinking in a Portfolio

If you're looking for a job as a copywriter or art director, you have to have a portfolio to give interviewers a feel for the kind of work you do. These days the same is true for planners: You need a portfolio or book that showcases your strategic thinking.

Maybe your book includes samples of research you conducted, your insights into specific groups of people, and an example of how you would illustrate the insight visually; maybe the portfolio has some strategies or briefs you've come up with for products or even a thoughtful analysis of the strategies behind some current advertising. There's no formula for what should be in your portfolio. The point is to show people how you think and that you can communicate clearly and in an interesting way.

For Deutsch's Greene, the value of graduate planning programs like those at VCU and the Miami Ad School is that they help you develop a portfolio. "What those programs do," she says, "is give you a book to take out on interviews. The hard thing in planning is getting your first job. After that, you are probably in demand. But you need to talk people through cases. Those programs provide the structure in which to create some case studies that you can talk about."

But what if you don't have the time or money for portfolio school? You can still create a book on your own and have a lot of fun doing it. The trick is to figure out what kind of ads to analyze, what sorts of consumers to study, and what sorts of insights to showcase.

You can take the same approach that agencies use. For example, there are magazines and websites for almost every interest. Pick up specialty magazines designed for a particular group of consumers like Oprah watchers, NASCAR fans, dog lovers, or gamers. Study the magazines, and see what sorts of insights you can get into a particular group of consumers and how you can use that insight to develop a strategy for a particular product.

In fact, Deutsch sends around magazines to its planners and asks them to study them in much the same way. Frequently, they find an idea that connects with a specific client or sparks a new thought.

You don't have to limit yourself to magazines. Watch a top-rated TV show or movie, or read a bestseller and try to figure out why so many people like it and what that says about the culture.

You can also go out and meet consumers on your own. Interview stay-at-home dads, senior citizens, or participants in a chili cook-off, for example. It's a great way to practice your interviewing skills, generate an insight, and meet some very interesting people. Then use your interviews to write a one paragraph consumer profile that makes the essence of the target come to life. Put the best profiles in your book.

Another approach is to pick some areas to explore that match up with your interests. Maybe you have a passion for sports cars, lacrosse, cooking, or *The Simpsons*. Use your own experiences to generate an insight into consumers who share your interests. And put some of those insights in your book.

Then when you present your book to an agency, you'll be able to talk about your particular interest. Doing that will show an agency that you can go deep and absorb the details. It will also show that you are passionate about something. That's just as important. After all, if you don't have something you personally care about, how can an agency ever expect you to care enough about a product to generate the kinds of insights their clients need?

Keep an Observation Journal

All of these portfolio-building exercises will make you more curious and more observant. You'll find yourself watching people in bars, restaurants, on buses, and at concerts as you ask yourself "I wonder why?" and "what if?" Keep an observation journal for your questions and your thoughts about why people behave in those ways. Put some of those journal entries in your book, too.

After all, planners are curious people who ask interesting questions. Your journal is another chance to demonstrate that ability.

What's more, planners keep these journals, too. In fact, TBWA\Chiat\Day produces *Shine*, an internal magazine where employees post observations on behavior, insights, and anything else that strikes them as interesting. Agency blogs are also loaded with interesting insights and commentary.

Using these sorts of exercises to put together a book will give you something to talk about on the interview. Sure, you can share your insights. But you can also talk about what you did to get them. That will demonstrate a passion for planning. And remember, agencies want to hire people who have a genuine love for the business.

Honestly, if none of this stuff sounds like more fun than work, you probably don't have the soul of a planner. Be yourself. If that doesn't work, maybe it wasn't meant to be.

The Interview

Planners need to be able to relate well to all kinds of people — from the boardroom to the bar. An interesting resumé may get you in the door, but the interview is especially critical — everyone interviewed for this chapter said in effect, "I'll know it when I see it."

If there isn't any energy or connection in the interview, it's over. "I'm amazed by the number of people who come in here for an interview, and they are very ploddy," notes Burnett's Saunders. "I'm thinking that 'I've given you 20 minutes to shine, and you've hardly got a pulse.' Some people must think it is all on the paper, so the interview is just a formality." But the interview is critical, and there needs to be some kind of chemistry.

One planner who works in LA says his test is whether he'd want to sit next to the candidate on a plane to New York. For others, it's whether they'd want to have a beer with the person, whether they can learn something new from the candidate, or if the candidate can make them think differently about a particular subject. Planners have to be able to lead discussions that stimulate people and generate ideas. The interview is one place to demonstrate you can do that.

When SS+K's Snitow interviews, he wants to learn as much about the person as he does about their experience. "I'm really interested in whether they are an interesting person. What do they do with their time? What do they do for fun? What kinds of things do they read? I'm trying to really understand what their life is like and what they think. So it may be about asking their point of view on issues, but it may or may not be about advertising."

As W+K's Taylor puts it, "The worst interviewees are those that don't have anything to say. I prefer to let the interviewee guide the discussion. That's a quality that a good planner has to have. They have to be able to think on their feet. To have a sense of humor. And, not take themselves too seriously — so there is a sense of humility as well."

5 Provocative Questions from Real Interviews

These are real interview questions. Agency names are not used so that they might preserve the remote chance of surprising you with the question.

1 • What do you think it would be like to work on a cruise ship?

2 • Why do you think *American Idol* is so popular?

3 • What would you do to get into the mind of a 54-year-old woman?

4 • Tell me what you think a day-in-the-life of a typical long haul truck driver might be like.

5 • Have you ever made a documentary film?

Be prepared for "why" questions and thinking questions. They might ask you, for example, to deconstruct a campaign. You have to have the confidence to articulate your own ideas and have a point of view. "I don't know" is not a good answer when someone asks your opinion. Everyone has a point of view. Don't be afraid of yours. If you come across as "who do you want me to be?" you'll never be able to persuade a client or a creative team to adopt a challenging idea.

Agencies also need planners with different styles and perspectives so they can learn from each other and challenge each other. As Saunders notes, "At the end of the day we are an idea business, and you don't want all of the same kinds of heads. You want different heads working on the problem so that you have different perspectives."

So if you have a great interview and don't get the job, don't let it discourage you. Maybe the agency already had planners with your perspective. But other agencies will be looking for the kind of experiences and point of view that you can bring to the table.

Investing in a Junior Planner: The Short and Long Term Returns
Adrian Ho, Director of Account Planning, Fallon, Minneapolis

I find that hiring inexperienced or junior planners can actually be more challenging than hiring senior planners.

It's possible to get a good grasp on how a senior planner thinks by simply asking them to take you through a few of their projects. Likewise, you can often tell a lot about a senior planner's style and commitment to both the discipline and the work by looking at where they've worked, how long they've stayed, and the overall choices they've made in their careers. Finally, it's easier to assess the kind of framework that a senior planner might apply to their thinking, simply because senior planners' lives and interests are more defined.

In hiring a senior planner, you are reaping the rewards (hopefully) of investments they have made in themselves and that the companies they've worked for have made in them. In hiring a junior planner, you are the investor; and that's really the crux of the problem.

As with any type of investment, there can be a short-term return and a long-term return. I believe that a fair contract for junior planners goes something like this: In return for fairly substantial parts of a senior planner's time, wisdom, and mentorship, you promise to supply energy, enthusiasm, and a willingness to take on any project big or small. In the process, you also promise to bring as much creativity and initiative to bear as you can, while soaking up knowledge as quickly as possible.

This contract qualifies as the way to measure short-term return. However, in investing it's the long-term investments that can really pay off. A planner who gets her start in the business through you could develop into a superstar.

If you're really lucky, she might develop into a leader in the discipline and a leader at another agency. She could go on to mentor and develop a new generation of superstars herself. In short, if you peg it right, she might be so much better than you that your reputation will grow because you were the genius who identified her potential before anyone else could.

Obviously, as you're starting to see, this is why it can be quite difficult to break into planning. The bar is extremely high, and the competition is abundant.

At this point, it might be reasonable to hope that you'll be rewarded for having read this far with a handy list of tips for sailing through the interview. Unfortunately, I'm going to disappoint you. There simply is no formula for being able to satisfy all of these criteria. For every individual there will be a different mix of attitudes, abilities, and interests that satisfy an interviewer of the astuteness of the investment.

In the unlikely event that two identically qualified candidates come along, I'd be prepared to bet that most department heads wouldn't hire both. Building a department of clones isn't in anyone's best interests.

A better place to start is to ask yourself the kind of returns you'd be prepared to deliver. In no particular order:
- Do you have the patience required to learn the craft of planning?
- Are you willing to do the very necessary but very mundane tasks that form the basis of good, rigorous planning?
- Are you passionate about culture and curious about people and what makes them tick?
- Are you passionate about communications, and curious about how communications work and how they can work as things evolve?
- Are you capable of looking at situations and seeing different solutions from other people?
- Do you have the confidence to make your presence felt, and are you confident enough for your contribution to be invisible?
- Are you someone people will want to listen to and work with, especially when they don't have to?
- Are you willing to work harder than everyone else when simply being smarter won't cut it?
- Are you willing to devote the time and energy required to become really good?

Unfortunately, for junior planners these are the sorts of questions that planning directors will be asking themselves as they speak with you and read your materials. Just as all planners are different, the questions planning directors use to get to these answers will also be different. The way that one candidate will convince me is also likely to be very different from the way another candidate will. Therefore, the only way to prepare for this is to ask these questions of yourself and to be able to answer them with honest conviction.

Finally, you'll probably only get a half-hour of someone's time to make your case. If you can distill your thinking down enough to make your case succinctly in this length of time, you'll have satisfied the last and final question on any interviewer's mind.

Giving Back: One Reward of Being a Planner

Most planners love pulling all of the pieces together to create a brilliant strategy and great creative work. KBP's Doody clearly loves the challenge: "It's really exciting when you come up with an idea — when you have all this information and you know the right idea but you can't quite articulate it." Of course, he adds, "There are always times when you feel that you don't know what you are doing. It's not working. But you have to trust that you will get there. Then you crack it, and there is such a rush. There is an energy you just can't replicate in other businesses."

Planners also value the ways in which they can use their skills to give back to the larger community. Most agencies do pro bono work where the agency works for free or at significantly reduced rates. It gives them a chance to do a different kind of work, to advocate for causes and give back. While it's rewarding, it isn't always easy.

Doody and his team found themselves literally hiding when they were working on the initial phases of the AdoptUsKids campaign. The agency was already working on two other big pro bono projects, and work with the paying clients was hopping. Within the agency, there was some discussion about saying "no" to the adoption project because they were just too busy.

But Doody and a couple of other people at the agency had already been to Washington, D.C. for the briefing and recognized the possibilities in the project. "So we [the team] hid from everyone in the agency. We figured they would forget about the project if no one was talking about it. Out of sight, out of mind. Any time the three or four of us were in the same area, we scattered. We would work in bars and restaurants...And, we worked hard on everything else, so no one had any complaints about other projects. We were passionate about it, and we never wavered. There was no going back." Their passion carried them through the initial reluctance by the agency, client reservations about the approach they recommended, and a grueling creative approval process.

Was it worth it? Doody doesn't have to stop and think about that one. "It's absolutely the most rewarding experience I've ever had in this business — both personally and professionally. Based on some of our recommendations and some brilliant thinking from AdoptUsKids, the Department of Health and Human Services committed their limited grant money to hiring over 100 people in newly-formed recruitment response teams. To have all of the efforts result in an increase in the number of people who stayed with the adoption process to the end was personally rewarding. I was able to use my skill set to make a bigger difference than I could ever make by donating money," says Doody. "I helped a kid somewhere get a better life."

  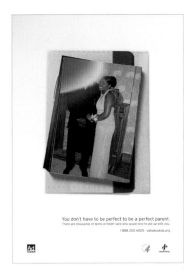

What's Ahead

The advertising industry is changing rapidly. More than ever, advertisers will need insights about how to position their brands. They'll also need to understand consumers and how consumers want to use all of the new media options now at their disposal.

While no one can predict what the future will look like, one thing is clear: Planners will be in demand. What's more, the need to balance art and science in marketing and communication planning won't disappear anytime soon. In the best agencies, planners are becoming more creative, and creatives are becoming more strategic. And it isn't limited to advertising agencies.

As boundaries blur between advertising, PR, entertainment marketing, media service agencies, and client marketing departments, there'll also be a need for more flexible, creative working relationships than ever. In short, if you like adventurous possibilities, it's an exciting time to be a planner.

As an account person, you're a general contractor. Meaning you're not the architect or the painter or the plumber. Those are specialists. But you're the person who makes this wonderful, beautiful house come together for somebody. It's a tough thing to do, requiring you to manage every single element of the project in a very professional way.

Jeff Steinhour
Managing Partner, Director of Content Management
Crispin Porter + Bogusky
Miami, Florida and Boulder, Colorado

Account Management

LET'S START WITH THE IDEA THAT GREAT WORK NEEDS someone pushing, probing, organizing, and orchestrating to make everything come together.

Ask account managers what their job is all about, and they'll talk to you about being a contractor, an orchestra conductor, or a coach. You could also call them generalists. Where other members of the agency team delve deeply into one particular area, account people take a broad perspective that enables them to guide the entire project. That's critical. After all, if painters, plumbers, and carpenters all showed up on a building site without anyone directing their efforts, you'd end up with a very odd house.

To manage a project's different parts and make sure those parts are working together effectively, an account person has to know something about every area of the agency from account planning and media to creative and production. "You've got to stick your nose in each of those huddles and have a working dialogue with all of those different disciplines," says Jeff Steinhour, Managing Partner, Director of Content Management, Crispin Porter + Bogusky (Crispin).

Being involved in every facet of the business is part of what account executives find rewarding about their jobs. Of course, players don't always listen to their coaches, and homeowners fight with their contractors. So account people also have to be skilled diplomats who can broker effective compromises and find creative solutions.

Account people have to be motivators who get people to say, 'we are going to find the holy grail for this client.' They have to be sellers of ideas and possibilities. They have to be business people.

Caley Cantrell, Senior Vice President, Group Management Supervisor
The Martin Agency, Richmond

In fact, account managers have many roles and wear many different hats, according to Caley Cantrell, Senior Vice President, Group Management Supervisor at The Martin Agency in Richmond, Virginia. "Account people have to be motivators who get people to say, 'We are going to find the holy grail for this client.' They have to be sellers of ideas and possibilities. They have to be business people. And sometimes they even have to be bartenders, meaning that they have to listen as clients and colleagues get things off their chests."

Account executives may be generalists who play many different roles within the agency, but when it comes to the client's business, they're experts. They study the company, it's history, products, and competition. That knowledge serves as their GPS system, helping them guide the advertising process, set strategic direction, and evaluate work to make sure it will deliver results. Then they combine that knowledge with a passionate commitment to their clients' success. Mike Sheldon, President of Deutsch in Los Angeles, believes wholeheartedly in that relationship. "The best account people are the ones who are most dedicated to the client's business. They consider their client's business as importantly as they consider the agency's business."

Making a Difference for Friday's
Mike Sheldon, President, Deutsch, Los Angeles

Our current work for TGI Friday's is a great example of strong account management skills and strategic decision-making. This is a client that has been in business for a long time. It's a brand that over the years had gotten a little dusty and a little stuck in the eighties. We had a client who said to us, "We're in no hurry for you guys to rush into some campaign and throw something on the air and then repair it over time. We want you to tell us exactly what you would do to turn this brand around."

So, we worked with the client as a team to determine what was wrong with TGI Friday's brand and how to repair it. The restaurant business is very difficult and very simple at the same time. Friday's had an image problem. People didn't think Friday's was a relevant brand for them anymore. Consumers felt that restaurants changed over the years, but Friday's hadn't.

Plus, with the dining industry becoming more competitive than ever, consumers had tons of new dining options to choose from. Friday's also had a little bit of a product problem, too. They needed to update their menu selection to make sure it was as appetizing and innovative as possible.

There is always a value component when consumers are making purchasing decisions about a product. Our goal was to show consumers that Friday's was as relevant today as it was in the past by updating the interiors of all Friday's locations and presenting amazing new menu options. Strategically, we focused on fun-to-watch, entertaining advertising that showcased a terrific product along with an explanation of how to get this product at a great value. Ultimately, we took the three problems and turned them into solutions. As a result, TGI Friday's business improved with increased traffic, sales, and brand awareness.

Account management is dissecting a problem and solving it. It's when you get out of the way of politics or any pre-conceived notions and just go. But you've got to have a great client. You've got to have a great partnership for a client to say, "We just want to fix this thing. Help us out." And that's what they did.

In short, account managers are determined to do whatever it takes to nurture and grow the client's brand. That's good for the client. It's also good for the agency because it can help the shop not only retain existing accounts but also produce the kind of work that brings new business in the door.

This chapter explains what account executives do for the brands they work on and how they use creativity, logic, and interpersonal skills to shepherd projects successfully to completion. It also shows the immense satisfaction that these folks take in the challenges they encounter along the way. And just to make sure we're on the same page, as used here, the terms account executive, account person, and account manager don't refer to particular positions. Instead, we use the terms interchangeably to refer to those who work at all levels of account service.

The Person at the Wheel or What Account Managers Do

The advertising you see on TV, in magazines, and online, for example, is the result of a journey that includes stops along the way not only to understand the business situation, the consumer, and the media but also to create and execute ideas. It can be quite a trip, and account managers are the ones driving the bus. They not only contribute ideas at every phase of the process but must also keep the bus on the road and see that everyone arrives at the right destination on time, on budget, and in one piece.

Wait a minute. A few seconds ago the account person was an architect or a contractor, planning and building this wonderful structure. Then a coach, a diplomat, a bartender all dedicated to better work, good communication, and a stronger brand. Now the account manager is a bus driver planning a safe trip, a fun time, even some sightseeing along the way.

Are you getting the idea that these are the folks that make things happen?

That's what we want you to remember. Now let's see exactly what that involves.

Developing the Strategy

When a major assignment first comes in, the account person assembles the agency team, reviews the project, and gets the team to agree to a rough schedule that will meet the client's objectives and timetable. "It's like a coach sitting in the locker room and saying, 'All right we're about to go out on the field, and here's what we've got to do,'" explains Steve Barry, an account supervisor at Wieden + Kennedy (W+K) in Portland, Oregon. Then the account executive and account planner get down to work to understand the business situation, the brand, and the competitive set.

Understanding the Client's Business

The account person takes the lead in getting a handle on the client's company. As Deutsch's Sheldon points out, the account manager must help the team "dissect the business problem and solve it." In fact, notes Crispin's Steinhour, account managers must ask themselves, "What is the business egg we're trying to crack? What is the business problem that people are paying us a whole bunch of money to solve? That's job one for account people."

The Get It Factor

Account people are business people who are able to identify the business problem and then work to solve it. They serve as the hub to provide a smooth ride for the account, the client, and the agency team.

One key to that job is knowing as much as possible about the client's business. Nobody will ever understand a company and its products the way the client does. But account people are determined to help the agency know as much as possible. Getting that understanding involves several steps, according to Jennifer Mitchell, Vice-President and Account Services Director at The Marketing Store, an integrated marketing services agency that has nine offices around the world.

The first step, Mitchell says, is to "learn what makes the client tick." That begins with listening to the client, adds David Dreyer, Account Director at TBWA\Chiat\Day in Los Angeles. "I really have to listen to what my client's objectives are, what keeps them up at night, and what they're worrying about not only from a communications perspective but from a business perspective." The account person must also take a hard look at the product, the packaging, the distribution model, where the company gets its revenue, and how the business is managed.

But the effort to come to grips with the client's business doesn't stop there. The next step for Mitchell is "brand understanding," which involves pouring over all of the client documents the agency can get.

Understanding the Competition

Once account managers begin to grasp their client's business, they work to understand the competition. "Obviously," Dreyer points out, "you have to stay on top of industry trends and competitive products, know what other companies are doing from both a communications and a business standpoint, and be aware of the retail environment so that you come to the table with a thorough understanding of the situation."

All of these steps involve research. Naturally, the account people will read everything they can find including past ads, annual reports, and articles in trade magazines. But that's just for starters. First-hand experience can be even more helpful. So account managers talk to employees and often arrange for the entire agency team to tour the company to see what it does and how it does it.

Depending on the client, the team might tour distribution facilities and visit with retailers, while the account executives might also travel with the sales force and attend sales meetings and industry conventions. Those on fast food accounts have even been known to flip burgers at a local franchise to get a better sense of the problems facing individual franchisees. And because agencies always work on extremely tight deadlines, information must be collected very quickly.

That sort of information gathering helps the team identify the business problem the creative must solve. There's no better example of how it all works than the process Crispin went through when they were awarded the Burger King account. Crispin's Steinhour explains: "When we won the account, we said, 'Give us a little time to get to know your business.' We looked at the entire category, the experience customers had in the restaurants themselves, and we did a very deep dive all the way back to 1965 when Burger King started and looked at everything they had ever done."

That research, he says, helped the agency identify "this interesting thing, which was that people loved The Whopper, but they did not especially like Burger King because the personality had been systematically stripped out of the restaurants.... So as a result the Whopper had literally become the brand instead of the restaurants."

That insight about the customers' less-than-positive attitudes towards the restaurant experience ultimately led to a wide range of creative suggestions. The agency recommended redesigning the restaurants and employee uniforms and looked at ways to make the cups, tray liners, and packaging more inviting.

Strong account management helped lead the turnaround of the Burger King brand as Crispin took the reins.

Then when Crispin turned their attention to advertising, they knew from their research that — in the consumer's mind — the Whopper rather than Burger King had become the brand. So, introducing the King made both strategic and creative sense. Of course, bringing back the character of the Burger King, which was a kid's doll in the 1970s, was also a smart move. It definitely gave the brand an iconic presence in popular culture and helped to start a cultural conversation around it.

Developing the Creative Brief

But identifying the business problem is only one part of the strategic process. The account executive and account planner must also work together to find a consumer insight that will connect with the key business problem that the brand is facing.

"It's a very tight partnership," observes Danielle Fuller-Keany, Senior Partner, Group Account Director at Ogilvy & Mather (O&M) in New York. "The account person is bringing what they understand from the client side of things, and the planner is bringing what they understand from the customer's side of things." By working together they craft a creative brief, which reflects "what the client wants and needs and what the customers understand and want."

The creative brief is the strategic document that will guide the development of the creative work. Account managers often have to push the client hard to keep the brief narrowly focused. Notes W+K's Barry, "Briefs are getting longer and longer because clients want more and more in there. But a brief should be brief, so you can give creatives something really clear to focus on."

There's one other aspect of the account executive's job that's evident during strategy development. Where other members of the agency team each focus on a particular part of the job, account managers take a broader perspective that includes both the work and the process. That's because they realize that the better and more inclusive the process, the better the work. So when they start to develop the brief, they make sure that creative and media people are involved from the beginning. Media planners, for example, can use their syndicated research and experience to help define the target. Creatives can help discover possibilities and refine the brief's focus.

"Creatives," says Eric Schnabel, Vice President, Account Director at Chicago's Leo Burnett, "are very good reductionists. They like to see things in very exact terms." So their input can give the brief a sharp focus. Getting their feedback early on can also help account people determine if the document is heading in the right direction and if it will be able to provide the creatives the insights they need to generate ideas. According to The Martin Agency's Cantrell, "If the brief is the kindling to help start a great creative fire, you want to know sooner rather than later if you've got wet kindling."

Of course, the account person must also make sure that the client feels a part of the process and is aware of everything that is going on. That means responding immediately to client phone calls and e-mails and doing mountains of paperwork like developing project lists, conference reports, and competitive alert bulletins. That sort of administrative work isn't the most rewarding part of the job. But it's necessary to keep the client and agency on the same page and the project moving forward.

> **We need account service to make sure that all the different departments are working together in support of each other.**
>
> *Mike Townsend, Director of Methamphetamine Demand Reduction,*
> *Partnership for a Drug-Free America, New York City*

Without account people functioning as attentive and efficient project managers, there'd be "chaos," warns Mike Townsend who spent 27 years in account service before moving to the client side as Director of Methamphetamine Demand Reduction for New York City's Partnership for a Drug-Free America (The Partnership). "We need account service to make sure that all the different departments are working together in support of each other" from the development of the brief right on through its execution.

After the creative brief has been developed and approved by the project team and the client, the agency can begin to develop specific creative and media ideas around it.

Developing the Work

Once the team starts developing ideas, it's vital for the account person to manage the process. Because the variety of media options has expanded, it's more important than ever for media planners and creatives to work closely together. Account executives make sure that happens by facilitating meetings between the two groups – something they would have seen no reason to do in the past. So you might say, the account manager is a matchmaker who brings the parties together and then steps out of the way as the creative sparks fly.

The Martin Agency's Cantrell believes that creating such partnerships "can help ideas get richer and more plausible." A creative team, she explains, "can say 'that's a great idea, but we'll never be able to pull that off.' And a media person can say 'well, yeah, we absolutely can pull that off, or we can't pull off something exactly like that, but we could do this.'"

Of course, account people aren't just facilitating such partnerships. They're also contributing ideas by exploring ways various media can amplify the message. To Burnett's Schnabel, "that's a key responsibility of today's account executives." In fact, he feels that account managers can set themselves "apart from the pack by understanding all the different ways you can bring creative to life and how you can take creative assets and push them across the spectrum of media channels. All of these false silos," he adds, "are falling away with the rise of things like YouTube. If you aren't thinking how you can push work into those areas, you're leaving money on the table."

But there's another reason account people stay closely involved with all of the departments during the campaign development process. That way, says Deutsch's Sheldon, they can "make sure that everybody in the agency keeps the client's business at the forefront of their thinking." According to W+K's Barry, it's about seeing the big picture: "Because you know more than anyone on your team about the client's business, it is your responsibility to keep things in check and know that you aren't doing anything that's off target, off strategy, or way over budget."

The Holidays at Starbucks
Steve Barry, Account Supervisor
Wieden + Kennedy, Portland, Oregon

Wieden + Kennedy was about to produce its second holiday campaign for Starbucks. We were given two clear objectives: 1) create a strong emotional connection between Starbucks and the holidays, and 2) drive awareness and trial of the holiday espresso beverages. Basically, the client wanted the holidays and Starbucks to be synonymous. And, of course, they wanted to sell a lot of beverages during this period.

The previous holiday campaign had been very successful. That was the elephant in the room. So the question was how do we create a campaign that can outdo what we'd done the year before?

We started by having Christmas in April. The whole team — account management, account planning, media, and creative — sat in a conference room and brainstormed together to figure out exactly what was particularly unique about the holidays and Starbucks.

With a lengthy brainstorm list of holiday traditions in hand, the account planner and account management team wondered if we could combine the unique moments of the holiday season with a few new traditions of our own. Every year, the Starbucks iconic white cup turns red. So why not make it the best new holiday tradition? What about an Eggnog Latte and a Peppermint Mocha? Can they be new traditions as well?

Eight months out, the account planner and account management team had locked in on a new strategy. It revolved around the idea of traditions. We knew there were those special moments and shared experiences that only happen

during the holidays. The creative team was briefed on the strategy and took the next couple of weeks to turn that thought into a tagline and direction: "It Only Happens Once a Year." The next step for everyone was making those moments come to life in a storybook way and mocking up the campaign for client presentations.

Using common holiday traditions that the whole team came up with, the creative team wrote ads that featured sketched illustrations with headlines. For example, "Men Decorate" celebrates that time every December when men, or dads, decorate the house in lights. In "Coworkers Dance," it's all about that truly classic moment at an office holiday party. Unique moments like these, along with the Starbucks holiday beverages, only come around once a year.

By June, the new campaign was officially approved. We then pulled in an art buyer and production team so that we could find the perfect illustrator and get the ads produced in time for the holiday season.

In "Long Lost Friends Become Found," the headline nods to the once a year tradition of sending out holiday cards. When the account management and media team saw this execution, we thought, why not turn the ad into an actual card that people could tear out of magazines and mail to friends and family? The media team called the magazines to secure the insert placement, and print production had the ad printed as an insert with perforated edges so magazine readers could tear it out. The main illustration of the ad became the front of a greeting card, with the inside saying "Happy Holidays."

The rest of the campaign featured a variety of components, including outdoor ads on billboards, wallscapes, and bus shelters. It also included animated short videos online and an interactive website. Wieden + Kennedy's efforts even earned the agency recognition as a finalist for the 2006 Kelly Awards for the Best Integrated Campaign.

Best of all, Starbucks saw a 10 percent increase in comparable store sales during the campaign period. And for the last three months of the year, their revenues increased 22 percent from $1.6 billion to $1.9 billion versus the same three months the year before. We managed to outdo ourselves; the campaign was a huge success. But no time to rest. When working on Starbucks, thinking about the holidays happens all year long.

The Martin Agency's Cantrell explains the account person's responsibility in this regard with an analogy: "You know how you can sometimes like the way a sweater looks, but then after you buy it and wear it for the first time, you realize that it really itches? You don't want to sell a client an itchy sweater — a campaign that at the end of the day the client isn't really comfortable with because it doesn't reflect how the company views itself or how its employees see themselves." To avoid that, Cantrell suggests, you establish "parameters, things that as the account person you know about the company's culture, that creatives need to consider as the advertising is being created."

Being a Good Creative Partner

How account people impact the creative work is perhaps one of the trickiest tasks they face. After all, the account manager doesn't have the authority to kill a concept; only the creative director can do that. Although most creative directors would be reluctant to present work that the account director is uneasy with, most account people would rather avoid such face offs, which can have long-term negative effects. Instead, they prefer to insert themselves into the discussions in a more casual way. But that's still not easy.

"If you're an account person," says W+K's Barry, "you'll do your damnedest to see the creative work well before it's due, so you can evaluate it, make sure that it's speaking to the brief, and can be produced within budget." But creatives are protective of their ideas. So they are often reluctant to show their work early on for fear that ideas will be thrown under the bus and killed.

Winning their confidence isn't easy. But the best agencies cultivate that relationship to everyone's advantage.

"If there is to be a strong partnership, not a tug-of-war" between account people and creatives, points out Deutsch's Sheldon, "account people have to respect the creatives, and the creatives also have to respect the account people." For TBWA\Chiat\Day's Dreyer, "It all comes down to trust. Everything you do from providing creative fodder to looking out for the creatives' best interests is a deposit in the trust bank."

That kind of effective partnership is the key to good work. As Chris Curry, Creative Director at O&M in New York, notes, "The best thing you can look for in an account manager is a creative partner — someone who gets why the creatives like their idea and who can also explain in plain English exactly what the client wants and needs and not just regurgitate the client-approved brief." To him, a great account manager is a career builder for both the creative team and the account team.

Being a good creative partner also requires the account manager to share the creative team's passionate commitment to the work. It's important, Dreyer believes, for creatives to know "that you not only want great work but can also recognize it because you understand the industry's best practices." That means something to everyone on the account.

O&M's Fuller-Keany, who sits on the account side, agrees. "It's really about digging down and getting underneath the first thing that's said and figuring out what the real problem is and then bringing that insight back to the creatives." After all, she adds, "the more informed you are, the more insight you have into the client's business and into what the problem is, the more creatives will feel you've helped the process."

The more informed you are, the more insight you have into the client's business and into what the problem is, the more creatives will feel you've helped the process.

Danielle Fuller-Keany, Senior Partner, Group Account Director, Ogilvy & Mather, New York

Barry, for example, recalls how one of the agency's creative people stopped by his office one day and "saw *Creativity* on my desk and asked, 'Why are you reading this?' And I said, 'You've got to read this stuff or else you don't know who's doing what and what's good.' And you could just tell by his question he was like, most account people don't even look at this magazine. But you could sense that he was thinking, 'You're different. You get it.' Just by my having that magazine on my desk."

Establishing a good relationship with the creative team can pay off in lots of ways. For one thing, Fuller-Keany points out, "If you're highly valued by the creatives, you can sit down with them during some of those early discussions when they're trying to get their heads around what the real problem is and brainstorm with them."

But she feels having a strong bond with the creative team yields even greater dividends later in the process. "Once a few ideas have started to form, the account person can come in and really help fine tune some of those ideas. So you might say, 'I understand where you're going with this, but maybe you want to put a slightly different angle on it that is more in line with what the problem is.'" Making those sorts of adjustments allows the agency to bring the best possible idea to the table. And that's in the best interests of both the client and the creative team.

While some account people work more closely with the creatives than others during campaign development, eventually creative, media, and account people meet to review the concepts. Together, they make sure that everything works against the strategy and that ideas have been pushed across the widest possible array of media channels.

Once the work is at last agreed upon and finalized, then it's ready to be presented to the client.

Presentation and Production

After weeks of work on the creative and media ideas, everything hinges on the presentation to the client. Without the client's approval, all of that work will have been in vain.

Account managers are critical to the meeting's success. If they have the client's trust, that can make all of the difference. As Burnett's Schnabel points out, "If you are going to do breakthrough advertising, sooner or later you are going to have to break category conventions. In order to do that, the client is going to have to take a leap of faith." And, he adds, "When you say to your client you're going to have to trust me on this, you're more likely to succeed if you've banked enough credibility through all of the effort you've put into their business over the years and all of the work you have done to learn what issues keep them awake at night."

No matter how strong their relationship with the client, account executives prepare carefully for the presentation because so much depends on it. In phone conversations with the client in the days before the meeting, the account manager warms the room by beginning to set expectations and lay the groundwork without ever revealing the idea that will be presented.

In the presentation itself, account managers review the strategic foundation for the work. As W+K's Barry notes, "If you don't set up the creative right, sometimes even if it's a great idea, it'll fall flat because the client may not remember what it is we're trying to accomplish." So in preparing for the presentation, Schnabel says, account people begin to think about "what insights about the consumer should be refreshed before this work comes up and what insights about the business challenge should be brought to the forefront. That way the work comes off of the target audience and the business situation as why would we do anything else. It seems perfect."

The Get It Factor

Work on presentation and pitching skills. Your ability to sell the good work your team creates is vital. Clients want to know you are confident and knowledgeable, that you're there to shepherd their brand, not merely to do their bidding. When you're smart, that shows.

The account person not only sets up the strategy but also manages the discussion. That's not as simple as it may sound, according to The Martin Agency's Cantrell. "You've got to be able to determine, OK, we're pushing too hard. The client just asked a question, and everybody is piling on trying to answer it. We've got to back off. You've got to be reading body language. The client just pushed back from the table, and nothing's going to get sold. And if the client starts rewriting copy in the meeting, you've got to shut that down." Paying that kind of attention takes a lot of energy, which is why Cantrell finds it "exhausting as well as exciting."

Even if the meeting goes well and the brand manager or chief marketing officer buys into the work, he or she will still have to sell the campaign up the corporate food chain where opposition might be encountered. That's especially true these days when a lot of work involves new media, which can be a new frontier for many senior-level executives.

Ask Crispin's Steinhour, and he will tell you that keeping great ideas sold is critical but not easy. It "takes getting into a foxhole next to the client and helping them make believers out of people. A chief marketing officer can have a boardroom full of people who pay his salary who are skeptical. So a lot of times you have to go arm-in-arm into these meetings with the client and really help people understand that this is a smart path to take. That becomes an enormous job particularly for senior account people."

Eventually the agency gets the client to approve a campaign. Once a project moves into production, the creative team is determined to make sure their idea achieves its full potential. So they'll fight hard to keep client changes to a minimum and see that they get the budget, talent, and time they need to realize their ideas. But the client may insist on copy changes, balk at the costs, want different talent than the agency recommends, object to certain aspects of the wardrobe, or find problems with the way talent delivers lines or even with how a television spot is edited.

At every step of the production, the account manager may need to carry on negotiations that would challenge the skills of a high-level diplomat. "A client definitely wants certain things," Barry observes. "But a creative may want different things. So you have to understand where each is coming from and do a lot of negotiating to reach a balance between the two." Naturally, he adds, the account person is not going to make everybody completely happy, but "you want to keep people sane and not make them completely crazy and upset." That's not easy to do. "You just have to pick your battles and explain that there are certain things we want to fight for, and there are others that we're just not willing to fall on our swords over." That sort of perspective is good for both the people and the work.

After weeks and often months of effort by individuals working alone and as a team to develop and execute the strategy, the project is at last completed. And the long hours and even the battles seem worth it as the client and the agency take pride in what they've been able to accomplish. Steinhour sums it up this way: "When we all stand on the sidewalk and look at this house we've built, we say 'wow.' Who's contribution was what? It doesn't matter. What you're looking at is a wonderful shared thing."

Learning to Drive: What Assistant Account Executives Assist With
Usually, you start out as an assistant account executive, a post that's also sometimes called account coordinator. Larger agencies may have both positions. In that case, the coordinator's job is the more junior and is focused on administrative support, while the assistant does some administrative tasks and a range of others as well. Since assistants do both kinds of work, we'll describe their role.

What exactly do assistants assist with? For one thing, they handle lots of paperwork to help keep everyone on the same page. Tracey Gardner was an assistant account executive at New York City's Grey Worldwide, where she worked on Procter and Gamble's Febreze account. Says Gardner, "The account group is in daily contact with the Febreze brand managers based in Cincinnati, Ohio." So each week there were dozens of e-mails and conference calls for her to summarize to keep the momentum going by reminding everyone exactly what was decided.

Gardner also had to be a skilled juggler and multi-tasker. In addition to writing call reports about client meetings, she had to keep track of each project's billing and stay on top of schedules and production costs for a range of projects like direct mail pieces, online ads, and point of purchase inserts. Plus, she not only worked with the client and account team but also got to be involved with Febreze's promotional agencies. That kind of team effort appealed to her. "It's great. Every week we have update calls with all of the partner agencies. So everybody really collaborates and works well together."

Assistant account executives also participate in strategic sessions. Naturally, they keep a record of what was decided. More importantly, they add their own ideas to the dialogue. Doing that is a way juniors develop the strategic muscle they'll need to be promoted to account executive. Notes Burnett's Schnabel, "One of the things I tell juniors is never check your ideas at the door. And the more you prove that you can add something to those discussions, the more of those discussion you get invited to."

It's a point of view Gardner echoes. "Don't be afraid to voice your opinion and speak up. Even though you are new, some of the best ideas come from the newest people." From day one, Gardner's boss encouraged her to participate in discussions and told her not to be afraid. Even if what she had to say wasn't exactly right, the team very much wanted to hear her viewpoint. "Don't for one second think that just because you are so junior that your point of view doesn't matter," Gardner advises.

That's not the only way assistant account executives are involved with strategic issues. They analyze research and write reports that spark ideas and serve as a foundation for developing the brand strategy. Assistants also attend some of the client presentations they help the agency prepare for. That gives them a chance to watch high-level account managers in action. From her many years of training junior account executives, The Marketing Store's Mitchell sees real value in their attending those client meetings. "Assistant account executives learn the vocabulary, vernacular, and parameters of the brand by attending meetings. They should become a sponge and soak up all of the information. It's like they are getting their own private tutorial."

> **My favorite part of my job is working with the creatives and developing creative work.**
>
> *Tracey Gardner, Account Executive, Grey Worldwide*

Assistant account executives also serve as facilitators between account planning, media, and creative to make sure everyone is working from the same playbook. "I like how you get to interact with so many different people and so many personalities," explains Gardner. In fact, she says, "My favorite part of my job is working with the creatives and developing creative work." Being part of the creative development process is "really exciting. Once you finally get a great commercial on the air, it tracks well, and you're getting great feedback and reviews, it's just a great feeling."

She is quick to point out that it's not all glamorous because the process of going from strategy to that final commercial is "lengthy," but it's worth it. In fact, Gardner urges juniors to pitch in wherever and whenever they can. Go the extra mile. She did just that and was promoted from Assistant Account Executive to Account Executive in one year.

WongDoody Junior Account Executive Brianna Babb works with Creative Director Monkey Watson and Traffic Manager Lara Johannsen to make sure the Kick It campaign is working.

Brianna Babb, Junior Account Executive at WongDoody in Seattle, feels the transition from school to an agency is big but can be mastered quickly. "I represent the agency to our client in the day-to-day operations of an account and that feels funny but right at the same time." Sometimes her job is to make sure the creative team has all the information they need to make decisions, and sometimes it's about the meetings constantly held to keep everyone up to speed. "I'm often here till six or seven each night," mainly so that she can become really familiar with every aspect of each account. "I look at our past work. I read the conference reports. I sit in my new chair and think, '*What else do I need to learn?*' to make it happen."

For new hires, that ability to throw themselves into the work is vital. In fact, says Babb, "Because I was ready to understand the processes here quickly, then to take initiative to organize and collect information that we may need to have to do our best work, I felt at home quickly." Like Gardner, she advises, "Don't be shy. Jump in and start offering your ideas and make them count. If you're smart, people will listen."

That's when you know you're ready for the next level.

Rungs on the Career Ladder

Account service "gives you excellent rungs on the ladder to climb" — a ladder that can lead all the way to top management, says Eric Mower, Founder and President of regional powerhouse, Eric Mower and Associates, headquartered in Syracuse, New York. Account people help bring in business, establish relationships with clients, and then maintain those relationships by growing the brand and the revenue it brings into the agency. So, as you might expect, their work is valued and rewarded.

The size of the agency obviously plays a role in how the account management department is structured. But most agencies will have some type of hierarchy that involves those in the more junior positions being responsible for executing tactics and getting work out the door, while those in more senior posts develop the strategy and set the vision. Naturally, advancement depends on ability, experience, and a proven track record.

After spending a year and sometimes more learning the basic processes and providing support, assistant account executives are ready to be promoted to account executive. Those holding that title are doers. They handle many of the details that go into developing broadcast and print campaigns. They're also responsible for much of the day-to-day client contact.

As they grow into the role, they begin to demonstrate their strategic smarts and their understanding of what makes for a strong creative brief. They also show that they can manage people through their mentoring of assistant account executives and less experienced account people. After two to three years in this position, an account executive can be promoted to account supervisor.

Understanding the Hierarchy

Account supervisors are the link between the doers (account executives and their assistants) and the broader, big picture thinkers (management supervisors). Where the account executives are the ones most involved in helping execute the tactics that grow out of the creative brief, account supervisors lead the development of that brief and then sell it through the agency and the client organization.

They also use their understanding of the client's business as a whole to provide insights, opinions, and recommendations. For example, that understanding enables them to determine which strategies and creative concepts are most appropriate for the brand. It also helps them generate ideas to grow the brands they manage and discover new revenue opportunities within the client organization. Their ability to do that along with their skill at managing those that report to them helps lay the foundation for their promotion to management supervisor after three to five years.

Depending on the size of the agency, there may be several layers of upper management including management supervisors, group management supervisors, and management director. Those who reach this level are closely involved with the client's senior management. They know the client's long-term needs and goals. So they are able to set the vision and see that the rest of the team understands and implements it. Management supervisors are also concerned with the financial side of the relationship. They make sure that the client's fees are sufficient to cover the agency's time and still allow for a profit. They also look for ways to enhance revenue by building the client's business or increasing the number of relevant services the agency provides that client.

Those in account management, like those in other departments, generally move from one agency to another to gain promotions and major raises. Such moves also provide opportunities to work on new pieces of business that offer fresh challenges. Some start at small agencies and then move on to larger firms, while others do just the opposite.

Some get the entrepreneurial bug. Eric Mower and Designworks' Michelle Belso worked for some years at larger agencies then left to start their own shops. A few begin their careers in the creative department, like Robin Koval, President of New York City's Kaplan Thaler Group, then decide it's the business-side of advertising that they have a real yearning for, and so they switch over to account management.

And, very rarely, there are the account managers like Bob Berenson, the former Vice Chairman and General Manager of Grey Global Group in New York City, who make their entire career at one agency. So there's no set pattern for career success in account management. You just need to decide how you'll plot your own account-management career path.

Something for Everyone: The Satisfactions of Account Service

Ask ten different account people what they enjoy most about their jobs, and you're likely to get ten different answers. That's not surprising. After all, account management involves every facet of the business from commerce to art and everything in between. And the satisfactions the career provides are as varied as the people attracted to it.

Some, like W+K's Barry, love the creativity. "I've always seen advertising as an art form and so have made it a point to work at the places doing the most entertaining, creative, breakthrough work." To him, coming to work every day is fun "because you help create things that can make people laugh or smile or even cry sometimes. You have the power to persuade people in that kind of entertainment way."

---

5 Great Tips for Working with Creatives

(All tips are quotes from senior creatives and account people.)

1 • Demand great work that benefits the client, the brand, and the agency. If you organize your time and efforts around that core idea, you'll be successful.

2 • It's not about "suits" and "creatives" anymore. That's history — bad history that ruined a lot of advertising over the years. Work together, and make good things happen.

3 • Eat lunch with your creative team. Go out for drinks. Take in an art gallery or just walk and talk. Even if you're busy, this shared time every-so-often helps immensely.

4 • Remember you're there to support strong work. Remember you're there to make that work be successful for the client. Those two guidelines should direct what you do.

5 • Know how to wrangle a meeting. Get to the point, be cheerful, follow an agenda. Have a strategy for making sure everyone knows what they need to do as they walk out of that meeting room.

For others, it's the strategic challenges that make their careers so satisfying. "I enjoy talking about ideas all day," points out Burnett's Schnabel. "I'm just a puzzle doer. I like figuring out what these brands should stand for and then making the connection between the brands and the people they target."

Account work is also tremendously varied. As Grey's Berenson observes, "The wonderful thing about the agency business is that you never know what is going to happen the next day." But it's not just that every day is different. Variety also comes from the range of businesses account executives work with.

When asked what is most rewarding about his career, Berenson quickly replies, "Unquestionably, the variety of business that you get exposed to. You are forced to learn as much about the business as your client. In fact, if you don't learn more you actually are not a good account person. Over the past 40 years I must have been exposed to 40 different kinds of businesses." It's that chance to "constantly be in a learning mode" that appeals to The Martin Agency's Cantrell. "I'm continually learning something new about an industry, a consumer, a media technique. If you're a person who's stimulated by increasing your knowledge base, then this is a terrific industry."

Account service, of course, requires lots of personal interaction. And for some that's what they love most about their jobs. Deutsch's Sheldon describes what so many feel about this industry: "The people in advertising are fun, smart, funny, and inspiring."

How many industries can offer such a dynamic and energetic path for building a successful career?

Changing to Keep Up with a Changing World

Account managers, like everyone working in advertising, are confronting fierce change. Not surprisingly, a primary cause is technology. Consider, for example, its impact on the media. Deutsch's Sheldon believes, "The traditional forms of advertising are not as relevant as they once were. So I'm finding new ways of getting the client's message out."

With more media options to choose from, there's more for both the media planners and account executives to understand and explain to the client. The upside of that, as Kaplan Thaler's Koval observes, is that, "The significant changes in media have made us focus on ideas rather than media vehicles."

The digital world has also accelerated the pace at which account managers are expected to do business. "The days of sitting in your office as an account executive and writing a ten-page, white paper covering an issue are over," acknowledges Koval. "Today, account executives are really valued not only for their ability to think clearly but also very quickly." Deutsch's Sheldon sees time management as key to today's executive. "You've got to be very quick on your feet. I think we generally have less time and fewer people to get the same job done — and business moved at a slower pace 20 years ago."

Clients are also changing. They continue to consolidate so that the majority are now owned by conglomerates and are publicly traded. This has drastically changed the relationship that account managers have with their clients. Grey's Berenson puts it this way: "The largest changes come from the pressure of Wall Street on client earnings. This has forced most clients to make decisions based on quarterly earnings as opposed to the brand. As a result, clients are... terrified of or concerned about not being able to increase their sales from month to month.... And that puts a different slant on agency relationships and what the job of the agency is."

Nor is Berenson alone in pointing to this bottom line focus. Koval also notes, "Our clients are under tremendous pressures, and they are very results oriented — very ROI (return-on-investment) oriented. There is a real need by today's account managers to show results."

What that means is that advertising, which has traditionally been viewed as a long-term investment in building a brand image, is shifting to types of advertising that can be measured in order to show client results. As Sheldon says, "We're doing a lot more direct marketing, a lot more database and data strategy. Many of our clients measure their business on a daily basis."

This concern with the bottom line has had an impact on agencies in another way. Clients have become more focused on the cost of the advertising. Mower describes it this way: "People in the client's purchasing departments are buying agency services as a commodity product. They're seeking the lowest possible costs and pitting agencies against other agencies."

Not only that, says Mower, but clients are also hiring consultants who promise "they can find economies which will further reduce agency costs." The problem is compounded by the changes in how agencies are compensated. Where agencies once received commissions on the media they bought for their clients, today they are mostly paid by the hour.

But here's the rub: Technology has made employees much more productive so they get the job done faster. Consequently, agency compensation is under additional pressure.

What all of this means for the account person is the need to keep a close eye on the hours devoted to each client to ensure that the agency does not spend more time on the business than is covered by the client's fee. If significantly more time is involved, senior account managers may have to renegotiate the client contract. No easy task in this age of budget-minded clients.

Keeping the agency profitable also means that account executives must help generate critical new revenue streams by leading successful new business pitches and by providing existing clients such excellent service that they award the agency additional work. In short, the changes in the industry are making the account manager's role both more challenging and more important than ever. So it's a great time to be considering a career in this area.

What Entry-Level Account People Must Bring to the Table

Here's the good news: Employment in advertising is expected to grow faster than the average for all occupations through 2012, according to the U.S. Department of Labor's Bureau of Labor Statistics.

But don't get too comfortable yet because landing an entry-level position in account service requires planning, a proactive attitude, and real effort.

Consider these odds, and you'll get the idea: "Every advertising posting on Monster.com gets 500 to 600 applications" says Karen McGee, who is the Career Development Director at Syracuse University's S. I. Newhouse School of Public Communications.

Kaplan Thaler Group's Koval reports that at her advertising agency the list of applicants gets winnowed down through an "initial screening process." From there she and her colleagues "consider only 15 resumes for one real entry-level account services spot. So, yes, it's tough," Koval notes.

What exactly are recruiters and account service directors looking for? Without a doubt, it's someone who can bring some real skills to the agency. As Grey's Berenson explains, "Agencies can't afford to train people any more. They have to start them right off because we need the people working on the accounts."

That means you'll need to be able to contribute from the get go. Majoring in the field is one way to do that. But it's certainly not the only way. After all, advertising also requires that you know a lot about business and communication as well as consumers.

So agencies often hire graduates who have an interest in advertising but degrees in a wide variety of subjects from English and art history to business, psychology, and anthropology. Some would even suggest getting a double major in order to make yourself even more marketable.

Knowing something about advertising helps. But by itself that isn't enough. When Deutsch's Sheldon interviews applicants for entry-level account positions he looks for one thing: "Drive." This translates to bringing "a really good brain and really strong legs," to the account services department. Brainpower is "being able to think strategically."

But someone who merely ponders without having the gumption to pitch in to get the job done holds little value for Sheldon: "If somebody is a really great thinker but never rolls up their sleeves to get involved, then that person doesn't work very well around here. You've got to run fast and have a good brain."

The Reward and Challenge of Working at a Boutique Agency: More Responsibility Fast

Julia Kang, Account Executive, AdAsia, New York City

My advertising career got its start when I landed a job at AdAsia Communications, one of the leading full service Asian-American advertising agencies.

Even with an internship at one of the best ad agencies in New York City on my résumé, there were things I hadn't learned until I came to AdAsia: being responsible for a whole project, for example, managing direct mail productions, working with online advertising, having good relationships with vendors. Getting real hands-on experience and slowly becoming responsible for full-fledged projects have helped me make the leap from assistant account executive to account executive.

What makes my day at work so great are the people I work with. Good relationships with the creative team and good relationships with vendors are essential in successfully managing my accounts. Being a good people person is definitely key for an account executive.

I realize that account management is not only about managing the account well, but it's also about knowing how to think ahead and analyze every situation. If you just meet the client's needs, your role is no different from a secretary's. So the account executive must study and be a good interpreter for the client and go above and beyond their expectations. You must be able to show that client service is not only delivering what the client needs but also adding value to their brand. These are all the things I learned as I worked, and I don't think I would have been able to learn them any other way.

At a bigger agency each person has a very clear role with carefully defined responsibilities. However, starting out at a boutique agency like AdAsia, where I'm expected to fulfill many roles, gave me a chance to experience different areas. This gave me a clear sense of what I truly want to do. What's more, I was assigned projects that an assistant account executive at a bigger agency would not yet be ready to do. The responsibility and expectation level made me step up rapidly. Of course, being given duties typically given to a more experienced person can also result in a lot of pressure and stress.

The downside of working at a small company is mostly the working hours. Not having enough people to work on the projects causes everyone to stay late.

Working late hours weekly does affect my personal life, which means I get to spend less quality time with friends and family. However, at this point in my career, I want to take in everything as a learning experience. I'm ready for the next challenge that comes, and everyday provides a new and rewarding challenge in my role at this agency.

So what does an effective account person look like? Here are some of the skills and qualities that account managers must bring to the table.

Effective Writer

It's a must. Account people are constantly writing strategic briefs, budget rationales, proposals, meeting summaries, and a range of other materials. They may even write articles that clients then put their names on. So it's critical that account people be able to write clearly, concisely, and persuasively.

Writing effectively and concisely also forces you to determine which facts are the most critical. "One thing that's definitely relevant to account people," suggests Burnett's Schnabel, "is the ability to recognize the biggest issue on the table." He believes that the best thing that ever happened to him "was being a journalism major and learning about Associated Press-style writing. You're forced to think about what's the biggest, most important thing, what's the lead in my story here, and then to go from the lead to the supporting facts that are perhaps less broadly important."

Persuasive Speaker

You don't need to be a silver-tongued orator. But you do need to command a room, look people in the eye, and speak clearly, sincerely, and convincingly. Account people have to facilitate discussions and lead meetings at the agency and in front of the client. Account managers also have to think on their feet so they can answer questions, including unexpected ones, that come up during a presentation. No wonder some account people say taking an improv class can come in handy.

Relationship Builder

Account managers have to be able to develop good relationships with clients and other agency staff. That means being able to communicate effectively one-on-one. Crispin's Steinhour feels, "Listening is probably the most critical skill that account people can have." While being a good listener may sound easy enough, it's not. In fact, Steinhour calls it an "art." That's because he believes, "Listening goes beyond just parroting what was said. It's hearing what the speaker's underlying concerns are, which may only be hinted at, and then turning those concerns into a potential opportunity."

Communicating well one-on-one is also critical to negotiating effectively.

Account people have to do a lot of that. Clients, for example, make demands about how much work they want, how fast they want it, and how much they're willing to pay for it. Sometimes those demands are impossible. But account managers can't just say no.

Instead, they have to figure out how to get the client and agency team to agree on a compromise. As W+K's Barry points out, "Clients have certain dates they want to meet and certain things they want to get done. You go and talk to your team, and they may say 'no way.' Somehow you have to come to some middle ground and negotiate with both sides to figure out how to accomplish what everybody wants to accomplish."

Of course, no matter how skilled a communicator you are, you're still going to come upon situations where clients or agency staff are angry — maybe for good reason. "A good sense of humor tends to defuse tension and difficult situations," says Grey's Berenson. In fact, a good account manager "is the rudder in the storm," stresses Deutsch's Sheldon. As he sees it, account management requires someone "who can remain calm in a crazy time because deadlines always change, clients' businesses change, and nothing is ever in stone."

In short, the human side of account service is absolutely critical. "You have to be pretty gregarious and comfortable dealing with people," says The Partnership's Townsend. Working well with clients, he notes, "basically means dealing with people in a way that lets you earn their respect." Crispin's Steinhour agrees that respect is key. "Being liked is not the drill. But having people respect you because you are truthful, have the client's best interest at heart, and are trying to affect their business — that is precisely what good client-agency relationships are all about."

Comfortable with Numbers

You don't have to be a numbers geek, but, as The Partnership's Townsend points out, "You certainly have to have a penchant for numbers." To be effective, you have to keep a watchful eye on advertising budgets and production costs. You must be comfortable with all kinds of numerical data from quantitative research reports and the media plan's reach and frequency numbers to data on sales and market share.

And you have to be able to use the numbers to reach strategic decisions. That's why Townsend believes it's essential for account people to be able to interpret the numerical data.

As Townsend describes it, top account managers almost have an intuitive feel for the numbers. "What do these numbers feel like? Can you sense if something is right or wrong about these numbers before you can actually notice that something is wrong with them? If something doesn't sound right, then you go investigate. And, yes, you find that something is wrong. To have that innate understanding is critical."

Creative

Advertising is an idea-driven business. For Crispin's Steinhour, "Solving business problems creatively is literally the underpinning of the entire advertising industry." No matter what area of the agency you work in, agrees The Partnership's Townsend, "having a creative mind is helpful." That doesn't mean that account people need to be able to roll up their sleeves and write a commercial, but it is essential "to understand what is being written (by the writer and art director) and be able to contribute to the discussion."

It's true: Being able to recognize outstanding work and then logically and passionately explain why it is right for the brand can make the difference in whether a client accepts a breakthrough idea or not. As O&M's Curry says, effective account managers not only understand "why creatives like their idea" but also "can figure out how to sell that idea to the client as if they'd be crazy not to buy it."

Heron Calisch-Dolen landed a job in account management at Goodby, Silverstein & Partners a week after graduation. Part of what set her apart from other applicants was her ability to communicate her love of advertising. "I knew I had the technical skills for this job because I had great teaching and learning opportunities in college," she explains.

"But it wasn't until my now senior account manager, Robert Riccardi, praised me on my passion for advertising and the project I was explaining that I really knew I had the job. For some reason passion is never used to describe the job of an account person; it is often used to describe the work of a creative. Passion is equally important for all disciplines of advertising, especially this area that requires so much multi-tasking and problem solving."

Creativity is essential in another way, too. At every stage of campaign development, whether it's devising an advertising plan or a media approach, account executives need to be capable of contributing ideas.

Industry consultant Ed Russell knows this is imperative: "Account managers provide the team with non-stop ideas like product improvements, new product opportunities, new use possibilities, new pricing strategies, new ways to look at problems, PR ideas, and new media ideas." That's called being creative.

Kaplan Thaler Group's Koval expects the account people she supervises to be "creative people just as much as the agency's writers." She emphasizes that those on the account side should be held to "creative standards like everyone else at the agency because, frankly, great ideas can come from anyone."

Organized, Detail-Oriented and Buttoned-Up

Account people need to be creative, but they also need to be highly organized. It's a relatively rare combination. It's also an essential one. Account executives, according to Designworks' Belso, "are the hub person. They are managing projects, and if they are not organized, they get buried."

Where other departments are focused on one part of the job, account people are responsible for every aspect of it. They must keep up with thousands of details from budgets and deadlines to proofreading the copy and making sure any changes the client insisted upon are made. If something falls through the cracks, it not only costs agencies money, it can also cost them clients. So being good with details is critical.

Good Leader

Deutsch's Sheldon believes that one of the biggest challenges confronting account executives today is staying in the leadership position with their clients. "You always want to be an indispensable partner to your clients, so that they feel like they don't want to make a marketing or advertising move without calling the agency person."

But it's equally important for account managers to be seen as leaders within the agency. After all, they have been described as the conductor of the orchestra, the architect with a master plan, the lead driver of a convoy of trucks. They bring all of the disciplines within the agency together and focus their efforts.

One way to lead and motivate agency teams, notes Crispin's Steinhour, "is to be so effective at getting the client to approve and produce ideas that the account has momentum, and people are excited to work on your business." They'll also "want to be a part of your team if you help them shine," Burnett's Schnabel points out. "If you give your smartest people a chance to contribute in a bigger way, it can pay off. It's really a kind of key role of the account person."

Keeping people motivated by helping them deal with bad news is equally important. Despite an agency's best efforts, clients will sometimes kill a campaign. Delivering the news to the creative people takes skill and sensitivity. After all, says Steinhour, "What these creatives do is very, very difficult. They kind of walk naked through the building every single day and show what they've got. You have to understand that bad news can just take the wind right out of their sails."

But when you have to deliver bad news, he adds, "You can't spin it. You have to tell the creative team what happened. But you also have to be a kind of shield. Agencies take the hit for everything: 'It's the agency's fault. The advertising sucks. It's those bums at the agency.' You have to protect your creative team from the reality of that so you don't demotivate people."

W+K's Barry agrees. "You try to let the creatives down as easy as possible. Each person is different and takes bad news in a different way. Some people will get really mad, and some will want to just give up. You have to adapt and help them get through it."

Learning to deliver bad news from the client is a "critical skill that nobody teaches you," explains Steinhour. But he emphasizes that agencies value account managers "who can stay positive amidst the shelling and keep people motivated. And they pay them very, very well because they see them as positive momentum engines. Agencies have got to have that."

Being able to lead and motivate people is perhaps the most valuable quality an account person can have and — this is the most important news — it can be the foundation for a highly successful career. In fact, Sheldon credits his success at Deutsch LA, where he is the president, to his "being able to motivate. A lot of other people are really talented with numbers or really passionate researchers or really creative. I just consider myself someone who has a way of getting people to do stuff based on them feeling like they want to do it. As an account person, the more motivating you can be, sincere, honest, direct, and passionate — all these things make a great leader."

When that kind of leadership ability is combined with other necessary skills, it can take you to the very top of the agency.

Preparing for and Conducting the Job Search

There's no better way to ready yourself for an advertising job than an internship. Ask Syracuse University's McGee, and she'll tell you that internships are critical because they provide a real sense of what the industry is like and give you a better understanding of each area of the agency. That can help you decide not only whether advertising is right for you but also whether account service is a good fit. Of course, the knowledge and experience you gain through an internship also looks good on a résumé.

McGee puts it bluntly: "Employers don't want to waste their time with people who are merely thinking about advertising because it sounds neat. They want to see on a résumé that you have done it, and an internship tells them that." Designworks' Belso sees that résumé line as very important. "I want somebody coming in that really has a desire to be in the business. If somebody hasn't done an internship, I don't see the desire."

Develop a Portfolio

Your courses and internships will give you the skills and knowledge to get the advertising job you want. They will also give you something else — projects you can show interviewers to demonstrate your skills. "I love people who bring things to show me," says Kaplan Thaler Group's Koval. "It's not traditional for account people to have a portfolio; creatives do. But I love when account people are proud enough of their work to bring it in, show it to me, and (talk about) how they got there."

TBWA\Chiat\Day's Dreyer agrees. "I often ask about a project that was your baby. We've all worked on those projects where you stayed up late at night and you had to bring an event or numbers of people together. That shows drive, and it shows leadership, and those are the qualities that we're looking for in anybody that we bring in."

But what sort of work should you bring to an interview? For one thing it should be a project where you took the lead or in Dreyer's words, "a project that was your baby." You could show a competitive analysis you've done, for example, or a consumer profile. You could even show creative work and the strategy that produced it. That's what Grey's Gardner did. "I worked on a campaign for the Partnership for a Drug Free America in school. I always brought this along with me, and everybody I interviewed with was impressed."

If you show creative work, you'll want to focus on the thinking behind it even if you helped create the ad. After all, you're not interviewing for a job as a copywriter. But showing pride in both your strategic thinking and the advertising that was developed from it demonstrates that you value every part of the process and that you can work well with other agency departments. Using an ad to showcase your strategic abilities is also a visually interesting way to convey the variety of skills and proficiencies you can bring to the position.

Decide What Kind of Agency Is Right for You

It's not a one-way street. Sure agencies are interviewing you, but you are also making decisions about the sort of agency where you'd like to work. And it's important to realize that there are real differences between agencies. Some are account-driven. As Grey's Berenson points out, "The account management at Grey has always been the strongest and most important department. We have always been more interested in results than creative awards."

At the other end of the spectrum are creative-driven shops, which look to develop work that is both highly effective and also creatively fresh. At those agencies, like many of the ones profiled in this chapter, the account managers enjoy working closely with the creative people and are particularly skilled at defending the ideas and demonstrating why they're right for the brand. Those account executives also take real pride in the finished work and in being able to develop clearly focused strategies that make such work possible. Of course, most agencies are somewhere in the middle of that spectrum.

In making a short list of the places where you'd like to begin your career, you'll want to think about which elements of the account manager's job are most important to you and determine which agencies match your interests. Reading about agencies in trade magazines, studying awards annuals to see who's doing the best creative work, and talking with professionals at your internships can help you do that.

The Richards Group's Stephanie Hunter landed a job in brand management after an internship at the Dallas shop. "Once I got the internship, I worked really hard and contributed any way I could. I paid attention to the culture of the agency and learned a lot from the people I worked with," she explains. She had followed the agency's work throughout her college career, and she knew that the fit was right.

The Culture and the People: That's What Makes the Difference
Stephanie Hunter, Brand Management
The Richards Group, Dallas, Texas

In my first months out of college, I worked for the brand management team on the Chick-fil-A account. At another agency my title would probably be assistant account executive. But The Richards Group culture is very different from that of other agencies and in comparison has a very flat hierarchy. I have the same title as the rest of the brand management team even though they have a lot more experience than I do. One of the benefits of the culture is that everyone has ideas to contribute.

My responsibilities include writing traffic instructions, sending out program ads for collegiate sports, customizing grand opening ads for particular locations, managing point of purchase (POP) kits, and billing for my projects. My day is never the same as the one before, which is one of my favorite things about my job.

One of the biggest challenges in my job is managing multiple projects simultaneously. For instance, one minute I may be writing an e-mail about POP, and the next I'm having a discussion about talent payments. It's important to appear calm because your team is looking to you for guidance. But it's difficult when you're being pulled in so many different directions.

The hectic pace is made much more enjoyable by the people I work with, both at the agency and at Chick-fil-A, a quick-service restaurant with over 1,200 locations. Ten years ago, The Richards Group created the "Eat Mor Chikin" cow campaign. I studied and admired the campaign while at college. So I came onto the account already having a lot of respect for the company. But I couldn't have imagined what a positive impact the people at Chick-fil-A would have on me.

My main piece of advice during the job hunt is to be determined to get the

job. One of my networking contacts once told me, "Don't settle for the first job that comes along. Wait for the right job at the right agency because it will set the tone for the rest of your career." With that in mind, I interned at The Richards Group after I graduated from college. My goal was to work there, and I saw the internship as an opportunity to get my foot in the door and make a good impression.

Once I got the internship, I worked really hard and contributed any way I could. I paid attention to the culture of the agency and learned from the people I worked with. When it was time for me to interview for a permanent position, I knew which accounts were looking to hire, and I had done some investigating about the people who were going to be interviewing me. I can't say that I found the interview easy, but I went into it confident that my work as an intern would reveal the sort of employee I would be.

Size Matters

You'll also want to consider whether you'd like to start out at one of the large agencies found in a major market or a smaller shop. The difference between the two, notes Grey's Berenson, "is largely focused on the number of people you have to help you. The smaller an agency, the more likely you are to do all different kinds of work and that has a reward in and of itself. But you don't have experts walking around to help you."

Size matters in another way, too. Larger agencies give you more strategic opportunities. "It basically comes down to the size of the client's budget," explains Deutsch's Sheldon.

"So the larger agencies are going to have the larger accounts. The larger accounts are going to have bigger budgets. Now when you have a larger budget that means you are involved in more and different media, which means you have more tools that you can play with."

Finally, as Kaplan Thaler Group's Koval says, large agencies have "more infrastructure," and that "allows you to formalize the nuts and bolts of what it is to work in this business."

Put another way, that infrastructure means that large agencies have more narrowly defined jobs and a clearly marked career path. Smaller shops are just the reverse, which Koval suggests, "means you get to do more earlier on, which can be great."

But she is quick to point out that it takes a certain type of entry-level person to thrive at a smaller agency. "I think if you are reasonably self-disciplined, self-motivated, and an innovative person, then a small agency is for you."

In fact, she believes that it can make a lot of sense to start out at a smaller shop, "because you can rise so much more quickly." Because there are fewer people to do the work, in smaller agencies juniors are given more responsibility and more opportunities to prove themselves. Fewer people also means greater visibility. So good work gets noticed sooner by those with the power to promote you.

In short, both large agencies and smaller ones can be good places to start. It just depends on which one is right for you.

Work Your Network

Unsure what kind of agency you want to work for? Not only can networking help you make that decision, it can also open doors that can lead to a job. In fact, you probably have a larger network than you think, especially when you count your school's alumni. Networking played a key role in answering Gardner's questions and helped her land her assistant account executive position at Grey Worldwide. Alumni were particularly useful.

"I definitely think it helps to get in contact with alumni. They are always willing to talk about their jobs and what they do." Many are also willing to pick up the phone and make the calls that can help get you interviews.

The Interview

Not every interview has to be for a job. You can also use them to find out more about the job itself or about what agencies of different kinds and sizes are like. That's exactly how Gardner decided on the size agency that was right for her. "I went on some informational interviews at smaller agencies and then went to a larger agency. I think those interviews were really helpful in determining what (size) agency to pursue."

But some experts warn that informational interviews have to be just that. The term has a negative connotation with some professionals. Be honest when you arrange for an informational interview. Don't walk in pitching yourself with a bait-and-switch move. When you go in for an informational interview, make sure you keep the discussion about the agency.

Do Your Agency Homework

When you get a job interview, make sure you do your homework and learn a lot about the agency before you meet with them. You're likely to get questions about the agency and their clients. The research you did will help you answer them. You'll also be prepared to answer an even more important question: Why do you want to work for that particular agency?

Kaplan Thaler Group's Koval, for example, is looking for people who "really want to be in this business, who really love it." But that's not enough. She also is looking to see if they "really want to work here. They must say or do something that tells me they are really interested in our agency." After all, if you don't demonstrate that you care about the agency, you can't expect them to care about you. So it's important to have a genuine passion for the firm you are interviewing with.

Be Informed About the Industry

"I look for a strong point of view on the industry," TBWA\Chiat\Day's Dreyer notes. "I don't want somebody who says 'I just love advertising, and I actually cut out ads and put them on my wall.' That means absolutely nothing to me."

What interviewers are looking for is a specific perspective on the business. They want to know what appeals to you. For example, is it the creativity, the psychology, the strategic challenge? There's no right answer. Those interviewing you just want to hear what you think.

Then they want you to be able to back up your thinking with specific examples. Dreyer sums it up this way: "You're a consumer and are affected by brands all the time. So be able to tell me why you believe certain brands are doing it right and have your thinking go beyond advertising. Be able to explain what makes it a great brand — communication, the product, the people, the distribution. Give me a point of view." Doing that can help turn an interview into a conversation. And that's one of the keys to a successful interview.

Be Persistent

Landing a job as a junior account executive takes planning and perseverance. To begin the job search, Deutsch's Sheldon advises that you first "find an agency you respect and then do an all-out campaign to get in. Send letters, and be persistent."

And don't be deterred by rejection. While Sheldon certainly doesn't suggest making a pest of yourself, he is surprised at "how many people try once to get in and then stop."

That's a mistake, he suggests, because "oftentimes, it's not that they're the wrong person, it's just that, at that particular moment, there's no opening." Syracuse's McGee agrees, pointing out that too often the students she works with have a "naïve belief that miraculously because they want a job, the agency will land new business and new accounts." Persistence is everything. And it can definitely pay off.

Giving Back

"Advertising isn't just about selling shampoo," says the Kaplan Thaler Group's Koval. As a matter of fact, account managers often use their skills and expertise to tackle tough social problems. Take Mike Sheldon, for example. In addition to serving as president of Deutsch, Los Angeles, Sheldon also manages to find time to chair the California chapter of the Partnership for a Drug Free America. His agency is currently shooting a video for the chapter as well as organizing a Las Vegas night and a golf tournament as fundraisers.

Why do he and his colleagues donate their time and talent in this way? Sheldon's answer is simple: "It's the way we give back."

Nor is Deutsch unusual in that regard. As Koval says, doing pro bono work is "a great experience" for herself and the others at her agency, and it also provides a valuable service to non-profits. There may be no better example of this than the campaign her agency developed for the American Girl Scouts. The agency took on this pro bono project by invitation from the Ad Council, a non-profit organization that seeks out advertising agencies to volunteer their talents to create public-service announcements that will benefit the American public.

The Ad Council came to the Kaplan Thaler Group with a problem to solve: Help increase interest in science among young girls. The American Girl Scouts felt that this was a particularly important issue to tackle since more than 60 percent of all jobs require technology skills. If girls tuned out math and science, they obviously hurt their chances for future jobs.

So the agency created a campaign for the American Girl Scouts that encouraged girls to develop an early and ongoing interest in math, science, and technology. The first phase of the campaign spoke directly to parents and caregivers, prompting them to make girls excited about these areas. The second phase of the campaign targeted young girls specifically with PSAs that ask them to go to an interactive website (www.girlsgotech.org) featuring games,

quizzes, facts, and other activities that are designed to generate a strong interest in math and science.

The project has real meaning for Koval: "We won a White House Project Epic Award for the American Girl Scout campaign, which was special because it recognizes programs that advance issues that are important to girls."

Some account people like Mike Townsend find pro bono work so meaningful that they look to take their advertising skills and put them to work full time for a non-profit organization. After 27 years in the agency business, Townsend joined the Partnership for a Drug Free America as chief marketing officer, later becoming the director of the Methamphetamine Demand Reduction program for New York City.

He used his creativity and strategic ability together with all of the administrative skills he had developed as an advertising executive to establish a network of state and city alliance programs. The Partnership uses those alliances to solicit agencies to donate work and to secure free national and local media placements. In fact, that network has become one of the Partnership's most powerful marketing tools.

Helping one of the good guys set up that sort of program and then seeing its impact, Townsend says, gives him a real feeling of accomplishment. It's a feeling shared by thousands of account managers at agencies all across the country who use their talent and resources to benefit their communities.

There You Have It

Account executives use their knowledge and expertise to help create strategies, develop good work, get results, and strengthen client relationships. All of that does one more thing: It keeps the agency flourishing and profitable. Account people find these responsibilities immensely satisfying. "How many people," Burnett's Schnabel asks, "have jobs where every day they get to try and create cool, fun ideas that surprise and delight people in a world without enough surprise and delight?"

As Crispin's Steinhour puts it, "If you love being in the business of manufacturing cool ideas, it's a wonderful business to be in."

One-way communication doesn't work anymore. We need to leverage interaction between brand and consumer.

Anne Benvenuto
Executive Vice President for Strategic Services
R\GA, New York

Media

ONLY A FEW YEARS AGO, this chapter would have covered an easy-to-digest review of television and print planning and buying. And it would have discussed a fairly linear set of approaches and math skills. After that, you'd turn the page so you could get on with the other stuff.

Not so for this function, this page, this moment. Too much has changed. Media is not only the fastest growing area of the business, but it's also more creative and more central to the entire advertising process than ever before. And to add to the career planning challenges, the media industry runs the gamut from traditional forms of media planning and buying to new approaches reengineering the agency world.

A major reason for that is something you're very much a part of — the explosion of media choices. You now have many more ways of connecting with friends and accessing information, which means brands also have more ways of connecting with you. Faced with so many options and clients determined to find the most effective ones for their message, media executives have a more vital strategic and creative role to play than in the past.

DDB's Chairman Emeritus Keith Reinhard notes, "We can no longer place as much of the communications burden on our traditional creative departments. It must be shared by media people whose skills are those of strategists. More and more, we begin the strategy development process by asking not what we'll say to prospects but where and when we're likely to find them in media terms."

Media executives understand fairly well how and why people use traditional media. They've had decades to figure that out. But now to make informed decisions about which media are right for the target, they have to understand a new set of options that grow and change everyday. They have to identify trends before they become trends. They must understand new technologies and how consumers are using them. Media folks now have to consider media choices as a lifestyle rather than just a point in the day. And that changes everything.

111

Media

> **Media is, hands down, the most dynamic area in advertising right now. When you think about how the universe of media has changed in just the past five years — TiVo, satellite radio, interactive websites, blogs, cell phone sophistication — it hits you that you're never going to be bored when you come to work. Every day is a challenge, and every day is interesting. How many people get to say that?**
>
> *Lisa Christy, Media Supervisor, Wieden + Kennedy, Portland*

This interesting media environment means media executives also have to be more creative than ever if they are to use all of these fresh media options in ways that will stand out and engage the consumer. Crispin Porter + Bogusky's Executive Creative Director Alex Bogusky says he asks media people "to invent new types of media, new media units, and new technologies." Jim Poh, Crispin's Director of Creative Content Distribution and Bogusky's partner in genius work, adds to that: "What's important in media now is to stay open to new ideas about what might be considered media." In fact, at his agency media could be and have been everything from playful websites like the one featuring the Subservient Chicken to the labels on beer bottles.

What's important in media now is to stay open to new ideas about what might be considered media.
Jim Poh, Director of Creative Content Distribution
Crispin Porter + Bogusky, Miami, Florida and Boulder, Colorado

Maybe it's turning the side of a skyscraper into a race course as Adidas did recently. Or perhaps it's printing a million laundry bags with the line, "Everybody has a little dirty laundry," as a promotion for the ABC television show *Desperate Housewives*. It could even be drinking from paper coffee containers, which makes us understand that the visual context often helps convey the message, as in the advertising on cups for Toronto Plastic Surgery from DDB, Toronto.

But no matter what form it takes, media executives are busy inventing media and finding new ways to use traditional media in order to get consumers to pay attention to their brands.

Mark Rice, Managing Director of MindShare in Los Angeles, puts it bluntly: "Entry-level media candidates today are forced to be more creative and have more than just the 'numbers crunching' skills of the past."

Just so we don't mislead you about all of this, there are still lots of numbers to crunch. After all, media is where the majority of client dollars are spent. In fact, in recent years clients invested at least $150 billion annually in advertising in the United States alone. The media executives who plan and make those buys must use the money wisely.

For example, they carefully analyze audience numbers, circulation figures, trend data, and competitive spending reports to put recommendations together and then place the advertising in the venues that will deliver the right audience for the best price.

Today, media executives are at the center of the action and are deeply involved with every step of the advertising process from strategy development through creative execution and evaluation. They work closely with account planners to brail the culture, spot trends, and develop insights into consumers and their media habits. Then they put those insights into practice as they team up with agency writers and art directors and find ways to use these new media opportunities to engage consumers.

In short, the media specialist — media planner, media buyer, or media researcher — is a significant player in the success of the agency, the relationship with the client, and the work being produced.

Rice sums it up well: "Media today is so much more expansive than just television or radio. Media planners need to be both creative and analytical. The media industry's growing influence in the overall campaign process continues to expand. The media professional today is strongly recruited, highly trained, and positioned to succeed like never before."

This chapter will give you a good handle on this dynamic media world and provide an inside look at the job opportunities and perspectives of the three critical media areas.

Media planning uses insight into the consumer to determine which media the advertising should employ to engage the target. Media research uses quantitative and qualitative data to uncover the insights the planners use. And media buying is the negotiation driven, highly profitable world of purchasing placement for a client in each medium.

These areas are complex, tied to every facet of the larger media worlds of publishing, television, and online technology, and evolve at lightning speed. We'll touch highpoints and offer you some places to go for further networking and career ideas. But our biggest piece of advice: Keep tracking growth of technologies and changes in the way consumers — like you — use media. This will be your key to understanding where trends are going next and where job opportunities will flourish.

Media Departments and Media Agencies: All Shapes and Sizes

Today there are more kinds of media companies with more kinds of jobs than ever before. Before you start seizing these new opportunities, here's a quick look at how they came into being.

A few years ago (but it feels like something out of the Neanderthal age) the media landscape was simpler. There was primarily television, print, some outdoor, and radio. Agencies made money the same way they had been making it for decades. They had their own departments for media planning and buying, and the commissions on agency media buys were their primary source of revenue.

In the 1990s, media departments began to be unbundled from full service advertising agencies to form stand-alone media companies. Take OMD, for example. It was formed from the media departments of Omnicom-owned agencies, DDB, BBDO, TBWA\Chiat\Day, and Rapp Collins. Today, there are 14 major media agencies, and they control the majority of client dollars.

Establishing these independent media agencies made real economic sense. For one thing, it eliminated duplication of services among sister agencies. More importantly, it created far more business opportunities. Where a media department could only service its own agency's clients, independent media agencies weren't limited in that way.

But the formation of these media agencies was also a response to client concerns. Media constitutes the single largest expense in a client's marketing budget. As the media landscape was becoming increasingly fragmented and complicated, clients began to ask themselves if it made sense to buy the creative and media services in one bundle from the same agency. Was that, they wondered, the best way to get the kind of specialization, accountability, and business acumen they needed on the media side?

Buying effectiveness played an even larger role in the clients' thinking. Most major corporations produce a variety of products and may use a different advertising agency for each product. In the traditional model, the same agency handles both the creative and the media for a particular brand.

The new model allows a corporation to spread out its creative work but consolidate all of its media dollars at one media agency. That gives that agency enormous clout when its buyers start to negotiate costs, which can result in significant savings for the client.

Nonetheless, many small and mid-sized agencies such as Crispin, Fallon, and Goodby, Silverstein & Partners have retained their media departments. And the heads of many enormous worldwide advertising agencies lament that they ever gave them up. Here's why. Right after the media agencies were established, media exploded. Suddenly, there were far more options than anyone could ever have imagined, which allowed consumers to connect with brands in ways nobody could have foreseen.

But to take full advantage of these new kinds of media in ways that engage consumers, media and creative executives must work together more closely than ever before. That's more difficult to do when creative and media are housed in separate agencies. In fact, some of the most memorable campaigns of the last few years grew out of the partnerships that exist when media and creative teams work together within the same agency.

The Get It Factor

In deciding whether to work in an advertising agency's media department or in a stand-alone media agency, you'll want to consider how closely you want to work with the creative team.

As Charlie Rutman, CEO of MPG North America told *Adweek*, "There is still a little bit of a tug-of-war...for control between creative and media." When you work in an advertising agency's media department as a member of a larger team, you naturally surrender some of the autonomy and control over the process those working for media agencies enjoy.

But media departments and media agencies aren't the only opportunities. There are also small firms such as Los Angeles' Ambient Media, which specializes in place-based media like dry cleaning wraps. Or Seattle's Never-stop, which facilitates events like the San Francisco Steal Me Initiative where IKEA gave away furniture on the street — a buzz generator developed in cooperation with Crispin. Mix in the two fastest growing areas in terms of media spending — Internet advertising and out-of-home — together with a dozen other sub-specialties, and you've got a huge bagful of media planning and buying possibilities. And they're yours for the taking.

That Career in Media Can Take Many Forms

Both a media department within a full-service advertising agency and a stand-alone media services agency have roughly the same organizational setup. Each has areas devoted to media planning, buying, and research.

The jobs and career tracks in each area are quite different. A planner's job is very strategic in nature and involves analyzing data and trends. Then the planner makes recommendations to clients about what kinds of media to use as well as when and how long it should run in order to effectively reach the desired target. A buyer's job is more tactical. Buyers place the advertising in particular media vehicles such as a specific TV show or magazine. To do that, of course, they must select the appropriate vehicles and negotiate the most favorable rate based on estimates of how many people in the target audience the message is expected to reach.

The Get It Factor

A media planner's job blends creative insight with strategy.
A media buyer's job is tactical: They find the best bang for the media buck.

A buyer's key skills center around analysis and negotiation. A planner's key skills involve thinking strategically and holistically, making sure marketing goals are recognized and achieved, and bridging the message/medium divide. Both planners and buyers have to be on top of cultural trends — *Who's texting, and who's involved with gaming? How do consumers read newspapers in an era of 24-hour news? Where are the best places for delivering new experiences...coffeeshops or malls? How does consumer-generated content play into a media plan?* Both must also know how to translate those trends into various kinds of media. The third media area — research — provides ongoing support by analyzing trends in detail and developing insights into the target and their media behavior that will be useful to the planning team.

Let's take a look at some of the possibilities in planning, buying, and research that lead to fast career tracks and personal success.

Media Planners

Media planners are problem solvers who figure out the best way to get the client's message out to the target. Doing that means understanding the consumer's lifestyle and media habits. It also means thinking creatively about media options including some non-traditional possibilities that may never have been used as media before. But planners don't just select the best media mix. They also decide when and how long the advertising needs to run all while staying within the client's budget. In short, they must use their creativity to find the best ways of reaching the target, and they must be responsible with money.

"The beautiful thing about media planning is that it requires left brain and right brain working in harmony. Good media planners are creative thinkers who know how to use numbers and research to help justify their choices. It's strategic thinking in its purest form," says Wieden + Kennedy's Christy.

The planning process is a continuous loop. It starts with strategic planning, moves on to tactical planning, implementation, and evaluation, and then it starts all over again. On average, each full cycle takes a year. As you might expect, the strategic phase begins with a client briefing that's presented to both the media and creative teams. Planners take the lead at this stage analyzing both the target audience and the competition. You might expect the audience analysis to be a very linear process. After all, it's analysis, right? But it also involves intuition, a strong knowledge of people and their habits, and ways of addressing lifestyle that lead to a relevant connection with the consumer.

First, planners do have to sit down with research reports provided by companies like MediaMark and Simmons, which track product purchase and media usage behaviors. However, planners do more than just report the numbers. They cross tab the data and think about why a person who does one thing also does another. They must consider the human story behind the numbers if they are to gain an insight into the consumer.

One way they do that, says Andrea Javor, a media planner at OMD in Chicago, is by "creating a fictional person and imagining a day in his life. We think about things like during the day, how does he interact with media." And even that has begun to change: New planning exercises often ask a wide range of folks to keep media diaries, which focus on media choices and lifestyle rather than lifestyle only.

As one agency media guru mentioned in a 2006 speech to aspiring media planners, time-shifting and alternative-delivery mechanisms often show that two people who appear to have the same lifestyle have radically different media

Unilever won the One Show Client of the Year Award in 2006 because of its noteworthy ability to take creative risks in a broad multimedia campaign. Media decisions played a major role in this brand's success.

THE NEW LONGER LASTING AXE EFFECT.

consumption habits. It makes us rearrange all of our notions of what is "typical." And it forces media planners to reevaluate how they get their information and how they use it.

That also means shifts in office relationships. A media planner might be able to get interesting information by sitting for coffee with a designer and an account planner all working on the same innovative account. And oftentimes at small and medium-sized agencies, the media planners exploring consumer habits are working more and more in the same thought arenas as account planners thinking about consumer insights.

Annie Sarabia started right out of school as an assistant media planner at Crispin in Miami and then moved as a media planner to MindShare Interaction in New York City. She considers the account planner her "best friend and partner" since their insights can help drive successful media planning projects.

When media planners present to agency decision-makers and clients, their presentations might include insights gathered from account planners, conversations with writers and designers, intuitive moments from the planner's own research, plus the nuts and bolts of costs and logistics.

Once planners have established the overall strategy, they begin to develop tactics. They consider questions like how much of the target they can expose to the advertising and how often. To figure that out, they use specific quantitative measures like reach, frequency, and rating points. This is where the math comes in.

Naturally, budget plays a part too, requiring planners to balance reach against frequency. So they usually develop a number of options with some offering broader reach and less frequency, while others provide more frequency and narrower reach. They also have to decide on the combination of media — maybe cable, magazines, and some things never before used as media — that's right for the client's objectives and budget.

One thing should be obvious by now. The planning process is both logical and creative. As Javor says, "I love that this job requires a balance of analytical and creative thinking; nowadays clients expect their media teams to be more and more creative; it makes this work interesting and exciting and fun."

Companies also throw another challenge into the mix by requiring planners to provide certain "must haves," which differ for every client. Axe's parent company Unilever requires a minimum level of reach each week. So, Javor explains, her team "wanted to make it seem like Axe was 'everywhere.'"

That's why they planned a broad mix of media including cable television,

In 2004, Powell NY was able to give Rheingold beer a new brand image based on media that showed the "Don't Sleep" campaign theme in raw form.

second tier network television programming as well as college campus postering and sponsorship of spring break party events." The client's approach along with the work of media specialists and the agency developing creative (Bartle Bogle Hegarty) caused the One Show to name Unilever the 2006 Client of the Year for their Axe and Lynx brands. The solutions crafted for the brands ranged across media from napkins to television game shows to computer desk accessories.

Powell NY faced a similar challenge for Rheingold beer. Rheingold wanted to own the night in New York in their "Don't Sleep" campaign. Using only traditional media would have led the agency to a combination of late night television programming (like Conan O'Brien) and maybe dance mix radio. Instead, they went beyond the traditional and found a way to paint Rheingold advertising on the store-front grates (the protective window and door coverings commonly found in New York City) and on plain brown paper bags. The two interesting media selections connected because both are about the carousing nightlife. So when the stores closed at night, consumers on the streets in these hip, downtown neighborhoods would see Rheingold beer advertising up and down the streets at high-profile bars.

The Powell media planners explain it: The gritty street art was a hit, and the medium, which only appeared after hours, underscored that the brand woke up when everyone else slept. The media became door coverings, and this new way of connecting to an audience was lauded for its creativity and style. The planning function was key to that message coming alive.

As the Rheingold example shows, it's often not just a numbers game. It's an ideas game. Sometimes it's coming up with a sponsorship idea or media that doesn't "look like" media, as in Starbucks' powerful taxi-topper and snow globe ideas developed by Creature in Seattle. This smart concept won a Gold for Innovative Use of Media in the 2006 One Show.

Creative Director Jim Haven says that producing the idea was almost as funny as the idea itself, with creatives, producers, and media folks jumping in. "You would have thought we were redesigning the space shuttle. There were CAD drawings and a battery of safety tests, including running through a car wash." Smart media placement sometimes needs lots of brains to make it happen. This one ended up including taxi tops, coupons driving traffic to stores, an online movie, and lots of publicity.

Once the media has been placed and run, planners evaluate the results to see if the plan delivered the audience numbers they expected. That evaluation lays the groundwork for the next year's plan, and the process begins all over again.

What Assistant Media Planners Do

You may have a strong grasp of business or even advertising. And you may have tackled a variety of internships. However, you're still going to need some job training before you can handle all of the responsibilities assigned to the media planner. The assistant media planning position provides precisely that training.

As an assistant planner, you'll be part of a larger team where you'll work on projects associated with just one or two clients. You'll learn the client's business and the media business by analyzing data and entering it into spreadsheets, helping develop media plans, and analyzing target audiences and competitive spending reports. In short, you'll be doing exactly what media planners do, except somebody's got your back.

Starbucks' Red Cup campaign won a Gold for Innovative Media Use in the 2006 One Show for Creature of Seattle. Its power was in its simple media idea and the surprising but believable use of everyday moments.

You'll also get the chance to show your strategic smarts and your understanding of the fast-changing media world by writing major Point of View (POV) documents. POVs always deal with new developments. For example, someone somewhere had to write a POV about the effectiveness of media placements in bar restrooms or about whether blogs are a good place for advertising.

At some agencies, assistant planners may also help out with the implementation and evaluation parts of the media planning process. When Crispin wanted to do non-traditional transit advertising for Virgin Airlines, Sarabia contacted subway and commuter train companies to persuade them to do it. And she had to turn it around for a lot of different cities all in one day.

This is a big part of what Sarabia finds notable about her job. It's the challenge of thinking about things differently, tackling something new, and then figuring out how to get something done that maybe has never been done before. Add to that the fast-paced timing of this business, and it's no wonder Sarabia finds her job exciting. (You can also read about Sarabia in the Digital Media Chapter, since her Crispin and MindShare experiences use her knowledge on a highly diverse selection of media.)

As an assistant media planner at Goodby, Silverstein & Partners in San Francisco, Friday Werner worked on consumer planning for brand advertising. "I created flow charts, produced traffic sheets, and did a lot of competitive pulls using MRI and IMS. I found out what competitive spending information was and that info went to the planners. I also wrote POVs and evaluated buys by cost."

After that she moved to AKQA, then on to Carat in San Francisco, making the journey from creative shop to digital specialty to global media corporation. Her time as an assistant let her understand the tools, then gave her the opportunity to use those tools well. "It takes time to understand the process, but it leads to the understanding of what a media mix in a plan should be."

Figuring that out takes all of your talents. "I love the strategic thinking and planning I did with the creative team and the account and production people at Goodby and AKQA," says Werner. "The concepting is done with everyone not media only. I use MRI and Nielsen data and supplement it with psychographic information. I then marry the creative concept with what we know about the audience we are trying to reach and how that fits with the feel of the different media. I also enjoy the tangible part of this type of job. I can see a roadblock on a web home page and know I planned for that use of the medium."

Kelsey Bernert was hired as an assistant media planner at W+K and began two days after graduation. Her first week included using comScore to compile a list of websites for Old Spice ads; a conference call with the New York team which had the eerie feeling of a foreign language as they talked about "plumbing" and "commercial ratings" and "weighted rankers;" a trip to the W+K "nap room" for an afternoon massage; and the hurry-up-and-do-it of sending out a couple of dozen RFPs (request for proposals) to sites which looked right for Old Spice. Bernert hit the ground running and loves her job, the crazy hours, and the great perks which are all part of it.

Another Assistant Media Planner Possibility: The Digital World

Of course, not all media planning assistants work at traditional media agencies. Joanna Luu began as an assistant media planner at Carat Fusion, a digital media agency in San Francisco, then moved to Avenue A | Razorfish down the street. While some of her work is exactly like what she would do at a more traditional shop, she also spends a lot of her time "trafficking" ads — relaying ads from the agency to the Internet publisher where they will appear. Before sending the file to the publisher, Luu adds a special tracking code, which she uses to get data reports on the consumer's interaction with the ad.

"Every time someone clicks on that ad," Luu says, "the system records the interaction. One of my biggest jobs is to record the data and enter it into a spreadsheet." She looks at the spreadsheet data in a lot of different ways. She then turns her most compelling findings into a report, which the planner analyzes regularly.

While the job is highly quantitative, deciding on the significance of the numbers is a creative act. What Luu likes most about the work is that it gives her insight into "how consumers interact with ads. We see trends, for example, about how long it takes to 'see' an ad and 'click through' to the website and then how many pages the consumer views on the site." Luu is a cultural watchdog of sorts, seeing and understanding trends before they become evident to most.

Depending on the kind of worker you are, how quickly you learn new things, and the kind of work you get the chance to do, you can expect to spend any-where from six months to two years working as an assistant media planner. Somewhere in this period of time you'll find the opportunities you need to show off your skills and earn that promotion.

The digital media area is explosive. So much so that we've dedicated a chapter to letting you see where to take those interests. Check out Digital Media following this, and read about Joanna Luu's journey from school to industry.

The Media Planning Career Track

The next step after assistant planner and planner is media supervisor. This post is actually the entry-level position to middle management at most agencies. As a media supervisor, you will have a small group of planners and assistant planners who report directly to you and whose media plans and recommendations you'll need to approve.

You'll still have to use all of the analytical skills you've learned, but now you'll be learning how to be a manager, too. You'll learn how to assign work to the people who report to you. You'll learn how to assess the skills and abilities of your staff. You'll also learn the importance of keeping your staff motivated and on task. After another two to four years in this position, you should be ready to move up.

After supervisor, the next level is generally associate media director. Managers in this position usually oversee planning activities for a small group of clients with several supervisor groups reporting to them. Associate media directors are responsible for the positioning and strategic direction of media plans, and they collaborate with other departments in the development of the communications approach for the client. In this position you will be working directly with the client on a regular basis and you'll also be directing the teams who develop media plan solutions.

Or maybe you make your own title when you're at a certain point in your career, as Rachel Timmermann did when she moved to Philadelphia's Red Tettemer from Crispin in 2007. "I made up my title," she explains on the Red Tettemer website. "I'm a creative media strategist. Brands don't have to be loud to break through the clutter. They have to have the right rhythm. They have to be at exactly the right place at exactly the right time. It's my job to figure out the place and the time."

And so, in a small agency vibe, she's making the most of connecting big ideas to interesting, relevant places. That's a media career in a creative world.

Media Buyers

Media buyers are the high-powered executives who turn media plans into reality by buying the appropriate space (print and out-of-home), time (broadcast and screen media), and experience (viral or place-based). On any given day they can find themselves spending millions of the clients' dollars.

Buyers are strategic thinkers who analyze a wide range of media vehicles in order to recommend the combination that will provide the best value for the client. So they also have to be good negotiators with all of the interpersonal and bargaining skills that requires. Like any wary shopper, once they make the buy they keep a close eye out to make sure they get what they ordered. That means seeing that the advertising appears when and where it's supposed to and, for broadcast buys, that the program delivers the expected audience numbers.

If you're a buyer, you work on lots of different projects at once. No two days are alike. You work with an extended group of people far beyond your office walls:

the media planning team, the agency traffic department (the people who ship the advertising materials to the media), the agency billing department, the client (sometimes), and broadcast and print sales representatives. So it's a job filled with a large network of people and a variety of responsibilities.

The rewards are just as varied. It's a relationship business, and one way the media seek to strengthen ties is by taking buyers out to exciting events. "We get great perks," says Rachel Diperna, a national television investor for OMD in New York. "We go to fun games and concerts and eat in great restaurants."

Then there's the excitement of the media industry itself. "It's really great working with all of these cool magazines. You're in the forefront of what's going on," observes Julia Trinko, a print investor for OMD in New York. "It's fresh, it's media, it's pop culturesque," adds Diperna.

Most importantly, there's the satisfaction that comes from putting together a buy that offers clients the very best value for their money. "It's challenging," one senior buyer noted, and "everybody wants to be challenged."

It's no wonder Diperna says, "I truly love going to work every morning, and I don't know too many people who can say that."

Buying is not only a rewarding career but also a critically important job. Naturally, being able to place an effective buy at significant savings is highly attractive to clients. In fact, it is an ability that most agencies tout when pitching new business.

Even those advertising agencies, which have kept media planning inside the agency, often have the buying done by an outside buying service. Here's why. A buying service purchases hundreds of millions of dollars of media. So they have the negotiating clout that delivers great savings for their clients.

Rick Kloiber, who was a national TV buyer at BBDO before becoming vice president for sports sales at Fox Sports, points out that national television is still both the most visible and the most expensive part of any plan. "National TV," he says, "and the buyers of national television wield the most influence in the media marketplace."

Nonetheless, for anyone wanting to pursue a career in this area, Kloiber suggests understanding audience measurement in various media, not just television. Negotiation skills are a must. And the best place to acquire them, he advises, is a top media agency.

The reality: Buyers come in all different company sizes and media specializations — digital, out-of-home, sports marketing, print, radio, national television, and local television. But no matter which particular type of media a buyer specializes in, the basic skills and approach stay constant.

Putting a Buy Together

Just as account planners write a creative brief to initiate the development of creative work, media planners help the buying group get started by briefing them on the target audience, the kind of media that should be purchased, and when and how much of each media should be scheduled.

"From there on out," says OMD's Diperna, buyers "take the lead. It's our responsibility to do enough research and keep up with the trade magazines to figure out where the money should be spent."

In fact, print buyers spend a great deal of time familiarizing themselves with the editorial content of individual magazines, while those working in television must get to know the various programs. "I've definitely become a TV junkie with this job," notes Diperna. Buyers also scan the trades, attend presentations by networks or publishers, and study agency research reports to gain a good sense of how individual magazines or networks are doing. After all, OMD's Trinko points out, "When we recommend a book we want to feel comfortable that we really know our product and what we're talking about."

After being briefed on a new job, print buyers first evaluate alternatives. Then they ask each publication they're considering to submit a proposal that lays out the rates, the position the advertiser will get in the magazine, and any value added merchandising offers such as events, email blasts, or contests.

125

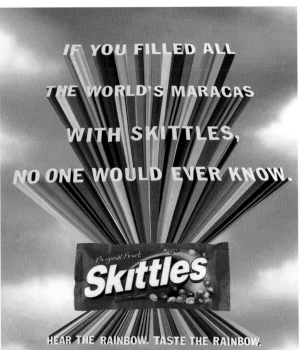

TBWA\Chiat\Day New York created a multimedia approach for Skittles in 2006, which won multiple 2007 Gold Pencils at the One Show. Buying television, OOH, and print for such a campaign means understanding the audience and its lifestyle

National television buyers invest much of their clients' budgets during the upfront market — a period in late spring and summer before the new television season begins when a large part of national television time is purchased for the upcoming year. Buyers can't purchase time on individual programs during upfront. Instead, they give the networks they're considering a budget, a tentative schedule, and programs they'd like to see in the final package. Then they ask each network to put together a program package that fits the specific advertiser's target and dollars.

Once proposals come back, the print and TV buyers evaluate them. To do that, they often create a spreadsheet in Excel where they consolidate cost and audience data and rank the alternatives. That's where math comes in. Buyers use a variety of formulas to determine important ranking criteria like cost per thousand and total impressions. Print buyers also look at the positioning and merchandising each magazine is offering, while their broadcast counterparts scrutinize the quality of the proposed programs, the appropriateness of the content, and the dayparts (prime, late night, sports, etc.) in which the networks are proposing to air the commercials. Then print and television buyers consider the intangibles like who's been a good partner in the past and who seems to want the business the most.

Carefully analyzing the proposals gives buyers the information and leverage they need to negotiate effectively. "It's not easy to sit across from someone and say, 'this is what we want,'" says Trinko. "It takes a lot of confidence, and you've got to really know what you're talking about."

Negotiating is Part of the Process

Sometimes the negotiation process is relatively simple. For example, says Diperna, "If I've been working with a network for a long time, I can call them up and say, 'take this out, add this in, and bump down the dollars to this.' And they will do it because they know how we work, and so they know what we expect to see."

Sometimes the negotiations are much more protracted and can go through ten or more different proposals before agreement is reached. "It takes cooperation and communication to build the kind of relationship necessary for successful negotiation," observes David Zamorski, a broadcast negotiator at GM Planworks in Chicago. Adds Diperna, "If I pick up the phone and start demanding things, they're not going to be as willing to help me out as they would be if we have a nice little conversation and I say, 'This is what I need. Now what do I need to give you to get this done.'"

Once the buy is negotiated, scheduled, and approved by the client, the order is placed. But for buyers the job doesn't stop there. They must also monitor the buy. Buyers or, more frequently, their assistants, check to make sure the print ad or TV spot ran when and where it was supposed to. Assistant media buyers play a key role here. In fact, it's a big part of how they learn the ins and outs of the buying business.

Media is a Social Network
Rick Kloiber, Vice President for Sports Sales, Fox Sports, New York

When I was hired at BBDO soon after graduating from college, I wasn't exactly sure what I had signed up for. My major in school was economics, and I had expected I would find work in investment or commercial banking or finance, but certainly not advertising.

But sure enough there I was. Truth be told, I wasn't even that big of a TV fan. To prepare for my final interviews at the agency, I read the new-season preview edition of *TV Guide* and tried to get a handle on what was new on the networks' schedules, and how, when it came up, I could sound informed about prime-time TV. If asked, my favorite show was *The Simpsons*, because it was. Of the new shows premiering that season, I thought that the *Fresh Prince* had the makings of a hit because rap music was starting to catch on with a wider audience, and the show was based on an MTV music video. Luckily, both questions were asked, and to this day I still think about the *Fresh Prince*. My banter about that show was borderline prophetic.

I couldn't have imagined a better place to work. The place was full of young people. The most senior people handling the day-to-day work seemed to be maybe 32, and all were eager to teach the young assistants about the business. The hours were long, and the pay was small, but the experience would prove priceless. Since our job was to learn how to buy national TV, a good bit of what we did was learn about the various network TV dayparts, including broadcast, cable, and syndication.

The sales people for these broadcast and cable TV networks were equally anxious to schmooze the newest members of the buying group. So when we weren't hanging around the office until 9 p.m., we found ourselves lunching at the best restaurants in Manhattan and enjoying trips to Madison Square Garden to see the Knicks and Rangers.

The hours are always going to be long, as agencies never seem to have enough staff. And the starting salaries are low. So after rent and student loans, there wasn't a whole lot of money left for entertainment.

Luckily, entertainment comes with the job in media. In addition to lunches with vendors, there are innumerable parties (everyone is always introducing something that requires a good party), events, award shows, concerts, sporting events, and other good ways to network and have fun. Again, the business is full of young people who are looking for good times, and, in fact, some of the more senior people in media never seem too far removed from their assistant days.

Socially, I'm not sure a better community exists than in media, at least in the largest centers of buying. Everyone knows one another, and contacts are well established and easily maintained as everyone moves around various aspects of the business, whether with agencies, media suppliers, or in the advertiser role.

What Assistant Media Buyers Do

If you like to juggle a lot of balls and keep your eye on every one, buying could be for you. Buyers and their assistants are detail-oriented multi-taskers.

They're also negotiators. But to be effective, negotiations need to be based on a good grasp of the audience a television show or publication delivers. Some of that knowledge comes from monitoring buys running in the market, and some comes from analyzing research reports. Even more comes from talking with the representatives for print and broadcast media and listening to their pitches.

As an assistant print buyer, you'll spend your time learning everything you can about the many thousands of magazines and newspapers that are most important to your key clients. You will discover the resources used to measure the unique audience of each publication and track changes in circulation — changes which can be critical when putting together a buy. Particularly for magazine buying, assistants use research resources like MRI to identify which magazine titles are used most regularly by the client's target audience.

Then the assistant buyer uses other resources like the Audit Bureau of Circulation (ABC) or the Publishers Information Bureau (PIB) to check statistics and evaluate the vitality of the publication. Assistants also use sources like SRDS to gather information about publisher rate cards for discounts and surcharges as needed. The assistant then passes this information on to the print buyer to help with negotiations.

Assistant buyers also usually have the responsibility for managing the buy after it is placed. In the world of print, this means checking magazines and review-ing tearsheets to be sure that the buy actually ran as it was supposed to.

It also means checking ads in magazines to ensure that the conditions of the buying contract were fully met. Conditions in print buying can include things like competitive separation (minimal number of pages between competitor advertisements) as well as special position placements like inside front cover. Such preferred positions generally cost more money, and so buyers need to be sure that the client gets what was paid for. This is all part of the important process of learning about the strengths and weaknesses as well as the unique capabilities of print publications.

Assistant broadcast buyers face a whole different set of challenges. You'll find yourself splitting time between the computer and the phone. And sometimes you're on both at once. You'll use the Donovan Data System to create and maintain digital job files for every buy your clients make in every city. That adds up to hundreds of files to keep up with. For each one, you'll need to input and then track the client schedules to make sure the spots run as planned. To try and help the stations get it right, you'll work the phones to guarantee that broadcasters know which buys are current and are scheduled to run that week.

Despite your best efforts, stations will fail to run some of the spots you've scheduled. So you have to continually review the details of your buy with the records showing which spots actually ran in order to find any discrepancies. When you discover an error, you have to get the station's media rep back on the phone and arrange for the station to "make good" the schedule by running the spot as ordered.

Securing an appropriate "make good" can require you to call on your negotiation skills. For example, if the spot failed to run during a one-of-a-kind program like the Academy Awards or even the season finale of a hugely popular show, it won't be enough to just run that spot another time. You'll have to negotiate with the station to make sure that the make good is a good deal for the client.

That's just one test of your negotiating skills. Here's another. Sometimes buyers need competitive information to help them negotiate a price or to reassure a client concerned about the cost of a particular buy. So you'll be asked to find out as much as you can about a competitor's buying activity. Getting that information won't be easy because stations know their advertisers don't want that kind of information passed along.

Gradually, your assignments will become more challenging and will prepare you for promotion to media buyer — a process that can take from six months to two years depending on how hard you work and how fast you learn.

The Media Buying Career Track

After two to three years as a media buyer, you'll find yourself in management as a media buying supervisor where you'll oversee a group of buyers and review all of their work before it is presented to the client. You might also continue to do some hands-on buying work and will be one of those who help present major buying recommendations to the client.

Then after five or so years as a supervisor, you'll become a group director.

On the broadcast side you'll be in charge of matters like creation and dissemination of all written points of view on relevant media buying issues such as programming changes at the television networks.

That's another exciting part of the buying job. When TV networks announce their new fall line-ups, the more senior people in the buying department often attend upfront presentations where they learn about the new programs and often get to meet the stars. It's just one part of figuring out what audiences will be watching so that you know what to buy.

Media buying supervisors on the print side will see and evaluate any new magazine titles that might prove useful for a client's advertising. The Magazine Publisher's Association tracked a total of 350 new magazine launches in one recent year. So this part of the job can keep you pretty busy.

As a group director, you'll also be responsible for negotiating and coordinating larger scale regional and national media buys. Plus, you'll be the primary buying contact for the media planning group and the media research group when they need critical information and input on issues like audience measurements and costs.

Overall, you will be a very important part of the agency's approach to the national media market including all aspects of strategic planning, implementation, and maintenance.

The next level up the ladder in a buying career is director. Print and broadcast buying each have their own director. Directors overseeing print buying are responsible for watching developments among publications old and new and for framing the overall relationship and subsequent negotiations between the agency and the print media. So they spend a lot of time with senior management at the many print publications.

The director of broadcast buying has many of those same duties with the added responsibility of having to predict the success or failure of the shows that the networks launch each year.

Directors for print and broadcast are also responsible for creating internal systems and processes that allow the department to function more effectively. For example, Mary Honan, Senior Vice President and Director of Local Buying for GSD&M in Austin, Texas, put into place proprietary systems to manage and track every single media buy more efficiently and effectively.

More Media Mean More Opportunities
Because there are media popping up everywhere we look, planners and buyers have a wider variety of opportunities than ever before. Here are a few of them.

Out-of-Home Buyers

Because we're spending more and more time outside the house, the emergence of OOH — out-of-home — media has become a big area for productive use of clients' media budgets. OOH includes everything from kiosks and video walls and floors to posters and panels on the street or in malls and airports. Plus, it covers media on and in buses or subways, outdoor boards, and even balloon marketing — large balloons with messages in key areas.

There are specialty agencies that use this medium to great advantage. A good OOH media firm will provide geographic and demographic data and will also draw up the planning proposals that grow a large range of OOH media. They'll negotiate with the bus company in Poughkeepsie as well as with a national commission of airport marketing. They'll produce and coordinate the trafficking of a set of outdoor boards to appear all over the United States or just in one city or one neighborhood. They will even use street teams to position balloons on street corners during high traffic periods. To make that happen, someone has to obtain permits, regulate size, and find the key times to execute.

The Get It Factor

Specialization in any one form of media can be a good career move. Planners and buyers who decide that interactive or OOH are areas of interest can find themselves looking at multiple job opportunities.

As one media supervisor at a creative agency put it: "OOH is so big right now because it provides the interesting 'other' type of media we all as consumers point at and remember." Agencies want to tie into that specialization. The growth in this area has been explosive in the last few years.

One OOH rep put it this way: "OOH is about inventing. Because of that we need smart, hip people who understand planning and buying and consumer contact." Apply now.

Direct Response Buyers

Darin Aho, Media Supervisor at Novus Print Media in Minneapolis, executes large scale print-buying in the print direct response arena. "Our staff works with the client to ensure the correct media will be used and the correct message conveyed in hopes that the best ROI is attained."

They work with a variety of media options: local market newspapers, national newspapers, national magazines, local magazines, Sunday supplements, shared mail programs, and direct mail. A national buying agency such as Novus spends millions of dollars across the country for a large client, looking for best buys and performance.

The upside of work in this area? It's all trackable and performance-related.

With every placement, the buyer can know what's happening with client investment. This happens because some kind of direct response mechanism is built into all of the ads: a website, a phone number, a specific call-to-action that can be readily tracked.

Direct response (DR) companies range from large to small and are found all over the country. Some agencies have departments geared for DR. At others DR will be included in traditional media departments, and one person with all the expertise and contacts will handle DR buying. Interesting news for your career decision: Over the next few years, the Direct Marketing Association estimates almost all television will include some form of direct response. Experts in this area will be important.

Research Analysts

The media researcher's job can be a lot like that of the account planner. They both use their understanding of the consumer to solve problems. As Debbie Solomon, Senior Partner and Group Research Director of MindShare in Los Angeles, explains, "My job is to help our media planning teams and our clients understand insights about the brand's consumer so that we can produce the most effective media plans."

The Get It Factor

Media researchers analyze quantitative and qualitative data to shape profiles of audiences and perceptions. Media usage and audience measurement are growth areas for this expertise. If you gain knowledge of trends and predictive strategies, you're building your portfolio for media research.

The media researcher's job has gotten a lot more exciting in the last few years. Once the work was primarily quantitative with researchers pouring over survey data provided by major media research companies like A.C. Nielsen. But today, notes Solomon, her job has gotten to be "a lot more about primary research and a lot more qualitative in nature." That's what it takes to understand how consumers think about new media channels like the Internet and cell phones and iPods and how media influences consumer buying decisions. That job is critically important if the agency is to take advantage of these changes to create more effective media plans. The research analyst is therefore the proverbial "go to guy" for all kinds of information.

In most agencies, research analysts support several different client-planning groups. Working on such a wide range of projects is part of what helps make the job interesting, and there's no better example of that than a recent day in Solomon's department.

The morning started with a meeting at Nielsen Media Research for Solomon and her team, including senior people and Assistant Research Analyst Danielle

Meglen. The meeting was focused around some of Nielsen's new initiatives in media audience measurement. For example, until recently, there has been no way to measure media usage by college students in their dormitories. Nielsen announced at this meeting that it was testing a way to do that. If successful, the test would allow agencies to determine with much more precision how effective they are in reaching the highly sought after college demographic.

Solomon and her team then headed off to a working lunch with another research supplier. Working lunches are common and cover a wide range of topics surrounding client research. Most large agencies run what they call omnibus research, a kind of continuous research program focused on a major client's business, a key target audience for several agency clients, or the way consumers use various kinds of new media. For such omnibus research, it's the research analyst who works with the supplier to design the questionnaire, then track and analyze the results over time.

After lunch, Solomon and her team tackled the regular challenges of the day, answering requests from media planning teams about everything from how fans feel about advertising at sporting events to how audiences use devices like TiVo to avoid television commercials. Solomon says, "We're researching communications channels now, not 'media.' We're using more qualitative research like focus groups as well as quantitative survey research to get a better understanding of how consumers feel about new communication channels in their everyday lives."

For example, Solomon points to a recent occasion when she sent her staff to interview fans at sporting events in an effort to measure the effectiveness of a client's advertising at the game.

She was planning to use a research company to conduct the research, but she sent her research assistants out on this job as a way to pretest the survey to make sure the agency would learn what it needed to learn. Such activities are also a valuable way, Solomon says, for her assistants to learn about media research and gain first hand experience about what sorts of survey questions work best. Plus, it gives them a chance to meet and talk with consumers: Real people with real opinions about media and advertising. Naturally, that kind of experience is invaluable.

What Assistant Research Analysts Do

Research departments run lean. So research assistants have to hit the ground running and carry their own weight right from the get go. That's the reason their assignments are more advanced from day one than those given to assistants in many other departments. Research assistants are responsible for data runs plus primary data analysis. They also find themselves in the trenches along side more senior analysts, handling requests from planning teams and meeting with a variety of research companies to design questionnaires and field survey research.

"A lot of my job is hard data runs," says Meglen, the Assistant Research Analyst in Solomon's group at MindShare. "But I also have people coming to me asking me, for example, 'Do you have anything on satellite radio?' And so I have to be prepared for that." That's one of the most exciting parts of the job, she says, "because you have to have your eyes on everything all of the time." So she spends a lot of time pouring over listserv newsletters from MediaPost.com, *Advertising Age, Adweek, Mediaweek,* and anything else she can find.

The assistant's job includes a variety of responsibilities. For example, on the day Meglen attended the meetings with Solomon, she returned to the office to handle a request from an international planning team looking for information on the U.S. Dairy market. She quickly looked up business reports and articles using computer research services like Mintel Online and Lexis/Nexis.

The planning team, she says, wanted "all the material in one place so they could do a deep dive to be informed on the subject. So Meglen put everything into one job folder with a brief bullet point summary and sent it off. At other times, those seeking data will want her to write up detailed findings in the form of PowerPoint slides that can be incorporated into a larger presentation.

After getting the report on the milk industry out the door and handling a few other requests, Meglen spent the rest of the afternoon on one of her ongoing assignments, the MindShare Clutter Report. The report tracks the number of commercial minutes or clutter delivered per hour of national television programming. It's created with data generated by a research company that watches TV programs and times commercials. Meglen sorts and tracks the data over time and then issues a Clutter Report twice a year. The reports help MindShare's media planning teams in offices around the world avoid the most cluttered media. That gives their commercials a better chance of standing out.

The assistant research analyst has an unusual amount of responsibility, and the promotion to research analyst does not greatly alter the nature of the assignments. Thanks to their variety and the challenges they present, most assistants find those assignments truly satisfying. Says Meglen, "I think everything about research is fantastic and interesting. I love learning how the whole process works; understanding why consumers buy what they buy and watch what they watch on TV. It's like I learn something new everyday."

The Research Analyst Career Track

After the assistant and analyst positions, the next step is supervisor. Although you have more administrative responsibility and must sign off on work done by those reporting to you, you still are deeply engaged in the work itself. It's much like what you did as an analyst. That's because this department's job is always about providing critical analytical support to the agency's various media planning teams.

As a research director, you have more direct contact with clients. You'll consult with them on all current media trends affecting their businesses. You'll also serve as the primary internal consultant to all of the media planning and buying teams within the agency. In that capacity, you will help with everything from detailed research and analysis on any number of specific media-related issues to wide-open advice and counsel critical to the development of agency new business presentations.

The number of these demands has led some large agencies like the Havas MPG network and OMD to create a new area within the media research department. This area does for media research what account planning does for message development. It provides deep insight about the target and their media habits. MPG calls this its "Catalyst" planning group.

Those working in this new area are not assigned to specific accounts. Instead, they assist with media planning for major assignments like new product launches or even annual planning for an especially large and important client. This new area plays a key role in an agency's growth, and those working in it have access to top posts within the client companies.

Coleen Kuehn, head of one of these specialist groups for New York's MPG, explains that the top people in this area are "a very special breed. They'll take larger leadership roles in the agency because media agencies more than ever need to form high-level partnerships with the client's chief marketing officer, chief financial officer, and chief procurement officer. And more often than not that person will be the senior media account planner."

Building a Career in Media

We've already looked at how people move up the ladder from entry level to supervisory positions. However, to gain more money and more responsibility, media people — like those in other advertising departments — frequently leave one agency in order to take a job with another. They move between full service agencies and stand-alone media service companies and from small agencies to large and back again. They even move between offices in the same agency network, although this is less common.

Still, Mark Rice says, "MindShare has a global HR process to assist in the movement of talent between MindShare offices." MindShare has a network of 91 offices worldwide so whether you need to move or just want to move, you might be able to work something out. From the agency's perspective, according to Patti Grace, who is the Human Resources Director at OMD in Chicago, it's a matter of managing to company goals and matching the best talent to the appropriate business need.

Lauren Harper, now a senior planner at Crispin, moved from assistant planner to planner to senior planner at a small agency in Ohio working primarily on Goodyear Tires, where she did planning and buying. Then she jumped to Miami's Crispin where she currently manages national GRP goals and planning on Burger King national.

"I remember being in school and about to look for a job," Harper explains. "I didn't really understand how all the pieces fit together. Simple things: When a client calls, who do they talk to? Or when an ad is created, how many people touch that ad? Who sets the budget?"

So you learn by asking and by internships. "Learn the difference between an associate media director and a media supervisor," Harper advises. "Find out what an RFP (request for proposal) is and how it fits into the business. Get the details right quickly, and it builds your career."

Kloiber of Fox Sports climbed the ladder at BBDO, beginning as an assistant TV buyer, then moving to national TV buyer, assistant TV supervisor, then vice president, associate media director. After that he made the jump to OMD where he was named vice president and group director of Pepsi and MGM/ United Artists. From there, he leaped to client side sales as vice president of sports sales at Fox. "I learned something valuable from every stage," he says, "and that's how you build your career."

Movement can also happen between the fields of planning, buying, and research. Sometimes people go from buying to planning. Sometimes we see planners go into research. And sometimes planners or buyers like Kloiber move out of an agency into the media, usually into media sales positions. Some agencies, like MPG, will start a person in one area and then watch to see which area best suits the individual. Other agencies, like MindShare, even offer a special entry-level hybrid position specifically designed to introduce junior people to media to help them ultimately make the right move.

Advice on Career Paths, Intuition, and the Intersection of Media and Life
Esther Franklin
Director of Consumer Contact Planning
Starcom MediaVest. Chicago

I got my undergraduate degree in marketing. And I first started working for a research supplier company. From there, I went to an advertising agency in the market research department. I left there and went to a publishing firm in the market research department. I wanted to see what the other side was like, so I went back to the agency side to account management.

About that time account planning was being introduced to the United States. I was very interested in that, and some of the agencies were starting to change over. Leo Burnett's market research department was making the transition to planning. I was there for ten years and left to start the department at Starcom.

Contact planning is our term here at Starcom. What we did was take the discipline of account planning and insert it into the media arena. That's very consumer centric: All about understanding motivation, influence, behavioral dynamics as people's lives intersect with the media.

Here's my advice for people starting careers right now: I think you should balance being scientific and diligent and rigorous in the gathering of information with intuition and your gut about what that information is saying or suggesting to you. Get comfortable with making hypotheses and assumptions based on the information you have available.

Make sure you're gathering information from a variety of sources, not just one. You can even get it from syndicated sources. There's a wealth of information from magazines and newspapers and people that are in specific industries. All are valuable for painting a picture about the consumer that can help you understand their media consumption and behaviors.

Here's my advice for the interview: The first assumption I make is that the person has some solid foundational training or they would not be sitting there, and they would not have the degree. Then it's about demonstrating a natural curiosity, an ability to put pieces together.

I want someone who is not afraid to take some risks. On the job there will be someone who is providing direction and some guidelines but not providing a specific roadmap. Demonstrate your ability to think.

Show me things you've done that help me see your process, whether it was in my business or not. Show me you're motivated.

What I look for when I am hiring someone is an understanding of consumer behavior and human beings. That can come from a variety of disciplines. It can come from psychology or any research disciplines.

If you're considering this area, I think you'll find that business and advertising are good places for you where you can get grounded and get some foundation.

What Does It Take To Get a Job in Media?

Exciting entry-level media jobs are everywhere. If you've decided that you want to set your sights on one of them, here's what you need to know about the knowledge, skills, and personal characteristics agencies are looking for.

What to Major In: Almost Anything

First of all, you'll need to complete your four-year undergraduate college degree. Literally everyone we talked to agreed on this point — an undergraduate degree is a prerequisite for entry to the media field. What they didn't agree on is what you should major in.

MindShare's Rice suggests a degree in advertising, marketing, communications, or media, but he says that other degrees can also work. Ed Hughes, who is the client communications director for OMD in Chicago, says any college degree can work.

But what Hughes is especially interested in is an aptitude for math. As a result, he would look at someone who majored in math or science as well as someone who majored in advertising or marketing.

Media planning is all about strategic thinking and problem solving. So the key is take the time to earn your degree and learn more about the world around you. In fact, Hughes, Rice, and Crispin's Poh all agreed on this point. Agencies can train you to work in media planning, but they can't train you to think. And thinking is what problem solving and decision making are all about.

On the research side, Solomon says they have hired people who majored in psychology, film, political science, and economics, among others. MPG's Kuehn is also open to a variety of studies and believes candidates might set themselves apart for her by talking about how they took a wide range of college classes including psychology and sociology as well as business classes in advertising, media, and economics.

Remember, media researchers are trying to understand important things about consumers and culture and how media influences them. That's why people like Solomon and Kuehn are looking for new hires with broad backgrounds in the social sciences in addition to an understanding of advertising.

On the buying side, Leslie Schwartz, Vice President, Regional Broadcast Director for Initiative in Chicago, agrees that any college degree is fine. GM Planworks' Zamorski majored in English literature. It may seem unusual, but he feels that his college degree has helped him be a better communicator, which is the heart of negotiating.

Even so, if buying is what you want to do, you might want to take classes in business and negotiation, and then be sure to point these out in your cover letter and resume. If you attend one of the colleges that offer a media sales class or a media buying class, take it.

Internships are Critical

Here's something else everyone agreed on: Internships are very important. According to OMD's Grace, "Internships are always valuable. However, the most valuable internship is sometimes when the student has tried something else in advertising or public relations and decided from experience that media seemed like the right area for them." Her point is that in trying something else you can learn what suits you best.

Initiative's Schwartz favors internships specifically in media and, even better, in media buying or media sales. According to Schwartz, "There's a lot to learn in this business." If you can get an internship where you can pick up even just the basic terminology, you will be one giant step ahead of the curve. Schwartz recalls interviewing one candidate and suddenly thinking, "Oh my god, you know what a make-good is!" The student had done an internship with one of the radio networks, and knowing just that one, specific term gave that student an immediate leg up on the job.

The Get It Factor

Math aptitude is still a basic cost of entry to the business. In fact, you should see math as a wonderfully creative tool that leads you to great information. Media folks see Excel as art. They love the complexity of a spreadsheet that tells them what they need to know. If you're not feeling it, don't apply.

Math: You'll Need It

No matter where you learn them, this work will require certain specific skills. You'll need strong quantitative and analytical skills. Look at the planner's job again. You have to be comfortable with math and spreadsheets in order to analyze the target audience and the competition. The same is true for research analysts working with research data and reports. Buyers have to be adept at balancing prices against audience estimates so they can negotiate buys that work within the client's budget.

Despite all of the new emphasis in media on creative problem solving, "You still need a good sense of the quantitative side," says Crispin's Poh. OMD's Hughes points out, "You don't need to be a math major, but you'll need an aptitude in math." Be prepared for this. Many agencies like OMD and Initiative will administer a math aptitude test for those candidates who reach the final round of interviews.

But don't worry, it's just basic math. "It's not like scary math class where there are no calculators," notes OMD's Trinko. "You have a calculator, you have Excel, you have peers to ask." In fact, ask Diperna of OMD, and she'll tell you, "The fact that math wasn't my strong suit in school hasn't prevented me from being able to do this job well."

If you want to be prepared, Initiative's Schwartz suggests that you focus on percentages. As she points out, "This is probably the one area that trips up most people."

Communicate Ideas Persuasively

You'll also need excellent verbal and written communications skills as well as strong interpersonal and presentation skills. Especially in media planning and media research, you'll write plenty of reports like whitepapers and POVs. Planners in particular also make lots of presentations.

Initially, you'll present to other members of your immediate team. You won't need slides or PowerPoint. You'll just be sitting around a conference room table presenting the key points of a report you wrote. Soon enough, you'll be making larger presentations to other departments in the agency and to clients. In either case, you have to be able to look people in the eye and explain with confidence why they should trust your perspective. After all, you'll be telling clients how they should spend millions of dollars.

In all areas of media you'll be working and communicating everyday with executives from other parts of the business. Planners have to interface with buyers, researchers, media representatives, creatives, and clients, among others. Buyers make their living by developing strong working relationships with media representatives. Researchers have the added requirement of sometimes working directly with consumers to learn more about how and why the target uses the media.

It's all about communicating effectively. That means inspiring confidence in people you don't even know. You can't do most of this work in media without the help of other people; you have to be able to make people want to help you. The bottom line is this: You have to have excellent communication and interpersonal skills to succeed in the media business.

Technology, Naturally

You'll also need to be comfortable with computers. Basic skills in analytical and communications software like Excel for spreadsheets, Word for word process-ing, and PowerPoint or Keynote for presentations are must haves. You'll also have to quickly master new programs that you will use daily.

Planners depend on proprietary software to create and evaluate media plan alternatives. Research analysts have to tap into their research suppliers' systems to conduct detailed data analysis. Buyers must constantly use the Donovan Data

System, which is the industry standard for buying communications between agencies and the media

Organized and Detail-Oriented

Planners and buyers have to stay on top of all kinds of information, and because of all the numbers they're working with, they have to be extremely careful to get it right. After all, says OMD's Trinko, "You have hundreds of emails coming into your inbox everyday. So you have to be really organized." And, she adds, "There are so many little things that go into everything. If you flip one number, it could cost you hundreds of thousands of dollars. So you have to be really careful."

Passion and Curiosity a Must

There are also certain personal characteristics that are unique to the people who succeed in advertising media. First, there's a sort of joy in all things advertising. At Crispin, Poh points out that he is "looking for fans of the advertising business."

Mindshare's Solomon notes that she looks for people with "insatiable curiosity who want to find out what makes people tick in media terms; they want to know why and how consumers use the media and how the consumers' motivations might influence their reaction to a product communication delivered through the media."

For MPG's Kuehn, it's "that person who's always wondering, 'What's next?' You have to be interested in new developments and new technology, and you have to be able to imagine how consumers might use the next new media."

Of course, you'll need a strong work ethic. As in most businesses today, you need to be self-motivated and willing and able to work hard in order to get ahead. OMD's Hughes calls it "effervescence; it's an enthusiasm and willingness to work hard all the time."

Initiative's Schwartz says she's looking for people who "can juggle multiple tasks and handle incredibly detailed work all on their own." How does she spot them? She says she gets a "gut feel" about this from the interview.

So it is very important to remember when you interview that you're communicating in all sorts of ways — with your words, the emotion in your voice, and with your body language.

How to Prepare for the Interview

Media professionals definitely have advice about how you should prepare for your interview. Do your homework on the media field in general and the agency where you'll interview. Prepare yourself to answer certain kinds of questions. Plan ahead for how you will work in key points about your particular job skills. And be prepared to ask smart questions.

5 Ways to Get Ready for a Successful Media Career

Your goal is to be nimble and smart about connections. This advice is offered by media planners interested in the long haul. So consider this list things they'd like to hear about from someone breaking into the business.

1 • Study the magazine racks. See what moves and who's buying. Make lists of new magazines. Read and digest their content and advertising support. This is a great interview talking point.

2 • Understand how people get their information: cable, radio, video streaming, iPhone and cell connections, billboards, newspapers, magazines, direct mail. Be a consumer of information channels.

3 • Write a POV (Point of View) report on a particular vehicle. Dig deep. And you don't need a school assignment to do this. Let your initiative guide you.

4 • Make lists. Keep a Top Ten list of the best websites and channels for talking to a particular audience. Good example: If you want to connect with foodies interested in smart healthy cooking, where would you look? How does that evolve in three months? Make your lists a passion.

5 • Tap into Google search and metrics to track keywords and trends.

You'll also want to find out more about the business and the agencies by reading trade magazines like *Advertising Age* and *Media Week*. MindShare's Solomon suggests you "visit the agency website or look up the agency in the *Advertising Redbook*. Keep up with blogs, trends, and what type of agency is doing what. Each agency has a different mix of clients, and each has a unique personality. Know which agencies suit you best, and think about how you might use the interview to show how you can fit into this particular agency.

We have mentioned that most media agencies are looking for people with problem solving ability. They're going to want to see how you think your way through a problem, and there are certain kinds of questions they'll ask that will force you to think out loud as you work through to a solution.

These are the weird questions you've probably heard about like which vegetable is better, broccoli or cauliflower or how many barbers do they need in Kansas

City? If interviewers ask you this question, know that they are not looking for your quick opinion; they want to see how you would solve this kind of problem and how effectively you can articulate the steps you went through.

If you want to practice fielding this kind of question, get yourself one of the prep books for any graduate school aptitude test like the GMAT. The book will offer guidance in working through such questions.

Plan ahead for how you'll work in key points about your job skills. The interview is your chance to shine. If you're that fan of the advertising business that Poh is looking for at Crispin, find a way to reveal that about yourself. If you have the insatiable curiosity that Solomon values, find a way to show off your belief that life is a learning process and you can't wait for that next challenge.

Be prepared to ask smart questions that reveal something about yourself. Use the questions to show you've thought about this work, this agency, this job. How you word the question and field the answer will reveal your character.

One question can be very tricky in an interview. So you should be careful about this one. OMD's Hughes says, "Ask me about opportunities for advancement." But Initiative's Schwartz advises, "Don't ask about growth opportunities." Many interviewees feel the question is a good way to show that they have ambition.

When we're interviewing candidates at The Media Kitchen, we still look for evidence that the person can add up a column of numbers, but we are just as eager to learn about his or her pop culture obsessions. Given all the technological support we now provide channel planners to manage data, it's becoming more important that our planners can see trends forming through a quick study of *Us Weekly* or the top ten Google search words. Being a student of pop culture is just as important as having wiz bang math skills.

Barry Lowenthal, President, The Media Kitchen, New York
writing in TalentZoo.com, May 30, 2007

But some interviewers may see the question as overly ambitious or maybe even arrogant. Schwartz favors other ways to show your ambition. For example, you might find a way to talk about what you did to work your way up in your part-time job from waitress to shift manager. Or maybe you could talk about how you took classes over summers so that you could graduate early and get started on a job faster. Ambition is a good thing. But you just have to put it in the right perspective.

The takeaway is this (and you know we're not telling you anything new): Don't take the interview for granted. Be prepared, and you'll make a good impression.

How I Got a Job I Love in Media at
Crispin Porter + Bogusky, Miami
Annie Sarabia

When I graduated just a short while ago as an advertising major, I landed in Miami working in media planning at Crispin Porter + Bogusky! It wasn't that long ago that my friends used to tease me. They'd say things to me like "your major is a piece of cake." They wondered what I was thinking to declare a major in advertising. Well, to all of those who wondered, I say look at me now. I landed a great job, with a great company, working in the field I studied for. I love this job, and I believe that I will love this work for the rest of my life.

Typical day... talk to reps everyday. One day I had a client call and say they wanted to advertise in magazines in Canada. We already had a print campaign for them here in the United States, and some of the magazines had Canadian distribution. So we had to add some magazines to the mix. This meant that something else was added to my mix of responsibilities for the week. There's no way to plan for that. So it's important to be flexible.

I wasn't always so sure things would work out. Growing up in a predominantly Hispanic community, I arrived at college without a single connection and no built-in network. I started as an advertising major because I knew that was where I wanted to go with my career.

But it was my Intro to Advertising professor who really brought things into focus for me. My experiences in that intro class led me to study abroad in international advertising. That was intense. I learned about almost every major advertising agency in the world and about how each one operates. Then when I got back to campus I took the advertising media class, and I knew that I had found my niche.

I took every class I could in the media concentration. I had opportunities to learn about new technologies and new trends in advertising media. I got to develop strategies and media plans for real clients. Traditional media was always part of the process, but I also got to study some of the newest in interactive media technology. We were constantly challenged and encouraged to use our "propeller heads" to come up with innovative media ideas.

When it came time to start looking for a real job, I wasn't expecting anything more or less than any of my classmates. I certainly didn't have any inside track or built-in network to tap. I started my search online looking at some of the many advertising agencies we had learned about in classes. One day, my searching took me to a website for the CPB Group, www.cpbgroup.com. This looked like a pretty cool agency that worked on some really great clients.

So I looked further. I found they had a jobs link, and I clicked it. I was kind of bummed to see that the link was just an email link to the anonymous jobs@ cpbgroup.com. I went ahead and attached my résumé, thinking that I would probably never hear from anyone. But at least I could say I was sending out my résumé, right? Imagine my shock when I got a call two days later from Crispin Porter + Bogusky.

They flew me to Miami for an interview, and it was great. It wasn't anything like your basic kind of interview. I was there for a whole day, and it seemed like all we did was talk about the advertising business. And it wasn't boring talk and questions; it was more like relaxed conversation about the things we liked and didn't like about advertising. I felt really good about my day with Crispin, and I guess they liked me too. One week after my graduation, they called to offer me a job, and a couple of weeks later I was moving to Miami.

In 2007, Sarabia left her wonderful first job at Crispin for a media planner position in New York City at MindShare Interaction, a digital media concern. Her career is on the fast track.

A Lifelong Career

At the end of the day, media work is satisfying and fast-paced. OMD's Hughes enjoys "having the opportunity to work on lots of different kinds of businesses." After 24 years in the business, Crispin's Poh would agree that it has been a great ride "working with so many different and exciting clients." MindShare's Solomon loves the idea that her job, the job she's had for almost 20 years, is dramatically different today than it was just five years ago. For her, "the job is constantly changing and always really interesting."

We could hear it in their voices and see it in their eyes; every professional we talked to loves the media and the work they get to do every day. For them, the media world has been a source of professional growth and personal satisfaction. As you can tell, there are a lot of exciting jobs out there for people like you who might want to get started in this work.

Media is changing faster than any other part of the advertising business, providing more opportunities for growth and creative thinking than ever before. Professionals know that's true. Maybe that's why they were all so willing to share their stories with us.

Serious large marketers have effectively 'come out of the closet' over the last eighteen to twenty-four months and said, 'This is it. Interactive is the fulcrum on which all marketing efforts balance.'

Randall Rothenberg
*President, CEO Interactive Advertising Bureau
in an interview on iMediaConnection.com
May 11, 2007*

In the Media chapter, you took the broad journey through the media side of the advertising industry — planning, buying, researching — and found the media infrastructure evolving to meet the needs of more media choices, smarter consumers, and savvier brand management.

Now we take a closer look at part of the advertising media world with ever-growing implications and huge opportunities to match. If ever there were a growth industry for you to be keyed into, this is it. One Internet guru puts it this way: Think media, then add words like *on steroids, frantic, fever-pitched*, and *near chaos*. It's so new and driving so hard that little has been written or gathered from which incoming industry leaders can learn. It's full of data management, invention, creativity, gut instinct. Here's your chance to jump in.

Understand that almost all agencies are looking to carve a place in the creative interactive world by hiring digital designers and conceptual idea makers nimble enough to tap into digital. With that comes a need for media intellect involving engagement, planning, buying, and analyzing. This area is new territory — still — for developing a career path.

Traditional agencies are bringing in digital specialists in media, strategy, and creative. At the same time, a few agencies have carved their reputation only in the digital realm. Both of these types of agencies need smart media planners and buyers. Consider these reasons why digital media has become the focus of new career possibilities and a burgeoning new industry in its own right.

The Get It Factor

A digital or interactive agency offers digital brand strategies, Internet advertising and marketing, and creative services for client brands. Purely interactive agencies first popped on the scene in the 1990s before traditional agencies had embraced the Internet. Now, almost all agencies — traditional, interactive, small, large — have some digital component to service brands. Everyone knows that the digital landscape is part of a smart media effort.

First, the Internet shook up the advertising media industry in a dozen different ways. Traditional mass media concepts are being redefined to fit new media forms — including the definitions of reach, frequency, and cost-per-thousand. This means new opportunities to those who see the opening. It also creates sparks when traditional media encounters new media. And all of that translates into billions of dollars of investment in media technology and the accompanying support capabilities of the larger communications industry.

Second, this shake-up is spawning a new generation of *entry-level* media thinkers that are unlike any preceding generation of media professionals. These new media professionals — just like you — are uniquely equipped to handle the shake-up because they were the first generation ever to be totally immersed in digital media. Computers aren't magic; they're appliances. *What's the big deal? Why wouldn't it work every time?* E-mail was a middle-school phenomenon. They are on their third or fourth cell phone...one that's fully Internet, GPS, and QWERTY enabled. They've never been out of touch. IM was a seamless adoption. Blogs and social network websites are simply more and better than the other media they've experienced.

Digital media is about understanding how audiences are adopting, using, and interacting with an explosion of new media forms that were completely and totally unimaginable five years ago.

Tom Bedecarre, CEO of AKQA, the San Francisco-based interactive agency that is a global leader in the field, explains his take in a recent interview with technology entrepreneur and blogger Sramana Mitra: "What we see happening is a very interesting convergence of the agency and marketing service providers, and the technology providers and ad serving platforms," he says. "The ad networks and the new exchanges and the publishers all seem to be converging, taking looks at similar models but from different angles. I think what's happening is every one of those four areas is looking around and saying, 'What else do we need in order to be more connected with the trail of customers, advertisers, and data?' I think it's going to be a really exciting time."

New industries based on innovation and convergence of ideas plus a whole new way of doing business. Is there anyone more qualified to understand this vibrant new media landscape than you?

Hello, This Is Your Wake-up Call

Except for the heady days of the dot-com boom, when hiring decisions were driven by greed and common sense left on extended vacation, there has never been a better time to jump into interactive advertising or, more generally, digital media.

Call into the interactive media department of virtually any agency in the country. Talk to anyone at any level from an entry-level interactive media coordinator up through a media director. Ask if she or he thinks it's a good time to get into digital media.

"Yes!" says Annie Sarabia, who started as an assistant media planner for Crispin Porter + Bogusky in Miami and then moved to MindShare Interaction in New York City. "My first job at Crispin was part traditional and part interactive. I saw both sides of media. Now I'm fully on the interactive side as a media planner. Is it crazy to say that I love coming to work and doing what I do?" Interviews show this kind of career enthusiasm coming through from many first-year digital media specialists; the high-energy, technology-driven, change-happening-daily agenda is alluring.

In fact, Kelsey Bernert, Media Planner at Wieden + Kennedy (W+K) in Portland, Oregon sees her foray into the digital world as making advertising better. "Playing in the online space, there are endless opportunities to get creative with the brand. It expands beyond boxes and skyscraper banners. Editorial integration, user generated content, interactivity — when a user sees the brand's advertising as content and not banners, that's when advertising gets smarter." And that, she adds, is why she knows digital media is absolutely the way to build a career.

Rounding out this trio, Tracy Soledad, Senior Media Planner at Houston's Fogarty Kline Monroe (Fogarty), makes the possibilities clear. "Opportunities are everywhere — on the client side and on the agency side, within permission marketing and specialty shops focused on SEM (Search Engine Marketing). The digital field is wide open."

Mercedes Guynn leads a digital media team discussion on content targeting versus behavioral targeting in GSD&M's Network TV conference room.

To make it perfectly clear, just consider this simple media fact: The Internet's age can be measured by counting up only a few years; it's probably younger than you are. Get it? If you're interested in the part of advertising that's filled with opportunities and that's being led by professionals not much older than you, consider a career in digital media.

What's Going On?

Why is everyone so excited? First, advertisers are returning to the Internet. "After the dot-com bubble burst in late 2000 and the tragic events of 9/11, the economy went tight and clients pulled back from the Internet," explains Terry Young, Group Account/Interactive Director for Rapp Collins Worldwide. "It's now a growth area. The agency is having different conversations with our clients based on some great results."

So let's be smart. Before we explain job descriptions and annual salaries and qualifications, let's take that short journey through the *how did we get here?* world of digital so that you can state the obvious: *I'm ready; show me where to go and what to do.*

Internet advertising, or more properly, digital media, is obviously the growth area in advertising today. While it represented only 2.3 percent of the total advertising spending in the United States in 2003, according to *AdAge's Fact Pack*, its 15.4 percent annual growth rate was over four times advertising's overall rate of growth. It easily eclipsed every other medium in the report, including both broadcast television and daily newspapers. A late 2007 *eMarketer* report predicts that by 2011 online advertising will reach $1.3 billion. What's more, *eMarketer*, a well-known provider of industry statistics, also estimates that online advertising will grow at an annual average of 6.4 percent over the next four years, an exceptional business growth rate by any standard. And, to your advantage, that growth rate looks sure to continue.

In short, the outlook for the future is bright. And the predictions for the success of online advertising lead to one important conclusion: Career paths in this area are the way to go.

The Get It Factor

Digital planning and creative career openings are in a huge growth curve. Many traditional agencies are mainstreaming their interactive units, often growing those areas to the same size and scope as traditional media and creative. Sometimes they work as stand-alone departments within the agency; many times — think Goodby, Silverstein & Partners, for example — digital is simply integrated into the agency flow.

In a July 6, 2006 special report on *The Economist's* website, Internet advertising in America is pegged at "about 6 percent of total advertising expenditures last year." And in 2007, it wasn't just revenue that grew. There was an explosion of consumer-generated content, social networking, not to mention the Google, Craigslist, and Yahoo worlds of brand experience.

Looking to 2010, things get brighter. A lot brighter, according to Morgan Stanley's Mary Meeker, one of Wired.com's ten influential "inside players" in the Internet revolution.

October 13, 2006

Industry View
Attractive

Internet & Consumer Software
US Internet Advertising Outlook, 2006-2010E

We remain upbeat about the five-year outlook, and project a 20% five-year base-case CAGR for U.S. Internet advertising revenue growth, with above-average growth rates of about 25% for search and rich media. Internet advertising spending per household could move from $177 in 2005E to $362 in 2010E (comparable to 2005E radio advertising spending per household, but still far from $980 for newspapers). Internet's share of US ad revenue could rise from 7% in 2005E to 13% by 2010E.

She expects a five-year 20 percent compound average growth rate. That's explosive growth. And the prediction comes from one of the Internet's most knowledgeable and most highly respected financial pundits.

So? What does all of this mean to someone who is breaking in and beginning to explore their career options?

Advertisers are demanding that their agencies address this phenomenal audience shift. The smartest agencies are realizing that the digital component of their task is real and powerful. Because of this, agencies are trying to quickly backfill their skill sets after the Internet's initial stumble. The outlook for digital expertise is bright indeed, whether your skills are in media, management, research and planning, or creative.

It is future-oriented, convergent, and all about inventing the culture of this young century.

It's an opportunity you can't ignore.

What's Different?

Two issues underpin digital media's growth, and these two things clearly differentiate digital from traditional media. The two are: "measurement" and "accountability." These two words have rarely been linked to advertising in a positive way. In fact, John Wanamaker's famous quote from the 1870s rang true to advertisers for over 120 years.

> *Half the money I spend on advertising is wasted; the trouble is,*
> *I don't know which half.*

So why are "measurement" and "accountability" so important? Put very simply, digital media knows what part of advertising works. It even delivers the news about which part doesn't work.

This is beyond being a big deal. It's revolutionary. None of the traditional forms of media can claim to know this most important piece of evidence. Not network television. Not cable television. Not radio. Not newspaper. Not magazine. Not out-of-home. Not PR.

Because an interactive agency's media team now has the ability to directly measure online behaviors, they know exactly which banner ad generated the most number of clicks. Or which news article's "call-to-action" motivated the most people to request a white paper. Or which athlete the audience likes most.

We're constantly refining and exploring the measurement of digital buzz for clients whose careers and businesses hinge on this. The concept is simple; the execution is incredibly complex. Digital conversations unfold in text across thousands of conversations. Those conversations are in shreds and bites spread across blogs, forums, online communities, and website content.

Jenifer Putalavage, Research Director, Nielsen BuzzMetrics, NY

"Only three things are important: accountability, accountability, and accountability," says Cassie Garza, Media Planner for Slingshot in Dallas. "The data are there. We buy impressions then we measure. It allows us to calculate CTR (click-through-rate), CPC (cost-per-click), and CPL (cost-per-lead). Our clients understand the value of that kind of information."

With this degree of precision, digital advertising expenditures can be matched to objectives. More to the point, digital advertising can be held accountable for results. Clients can calculate their return on investment (ROI) for digital advertising expenditures, and this drives budget allocations.

The connection to newcomers is big: Today's digital media measurement and analytic software tools are maturing. Not only are they more refined and more powerful than ever before, they're also dramatically easier to use. The emphasis is moving away from technological know-how and shifting toward strategic, creative thinking. That's what you bring to the digital marketplace.

What's New?

Digital media is not filled with geeks and nerds. Instead, it's filled with people who understand that the strategic fundamentals of media planning and buying haven't changed but the landscape has. Interactive media planners and buyers compete on a dramatically different playing field than their counterparts in traditional media.

That landscape includes a change in research's role. "We're constantly investigating new media," points out Katy Sloan, Research Analyst for Ogilvy & Mather (O&M) in New York. "Consumers don't draw lines between online and offline. But we have to see the whole picture."

Jaime Onorofski, IP Manager at Chicago's Starlink Worldwide, adds that very few in the industry know yet how to fully address some of these new media opportunities. For example, she explains, "The current problems in the social networking space are real and so are the risks. Our job is to make smart decisions based on a holistic view."

What's more, creative thinking in the interactive world involves a much closer relationship between each member of the team than you normally find in a traditional agency. In this realm, digital media researchers, account managers, media planners, and creatives frequently sit down together in what are routinely dubbed "360" meetings.

These meetings are essential because interactive work produces immediate results, which can then be used by creative teams to develop new executions known as optimizations. Says Sloan, "We know the performance of the media. We know the performance of the creative. In a matter of days we can start to modify and begin our optimizations."

I pinch.

"We think about things in ways that go far beyond what's expected," says Haley Brothers, Interactive Marketing Planner at RPA in Santa Monica. "For Honda, we came up with a unique slant on our 'Element and Friends' campaign. The campaign's spots featured various animals talking with a Honda Element. So we purchased words corresponding to the featured animals. It turns out that 'crab', 'possum', and 'platypus' cost 10 cents, while traditional automotive search keywords run $1.00 or more. The results were literally award-winning. With that twist we turned a traffic driver campaign into a very efficient branding effort for our client."

Dynamic Search Engine Seeks Grad Ready for a Leap

Haley Brothers
Interactive Marketing Planner
RPA
Santa Monica, California

When I graduated from college in 2002, I moved near my family in California and began to look for my first full-time job. I wanted a career in interactive, but given the numerous layoffs from the dot-com bust I was out of luck.

I accepted a great position doing traditional media planning for an automotive account, but after a couple of years I became bored. I wanted the opportunity to do something that was less established. The nature of the job just wasn't a good fit for my personality.

I decided to pursue an interactive position again, but it seemed like nobody was willing to hire someone who didn't already have a job in interactive. Eventually, I decided I might find renewed interest in traditional media planning if I went to work at an agency that was quickly becoming known for their different approach to both creative and media. However, working in their satellite office I was disconnected from the best opportunities. I loved the agency, but I wasn't interested in moving to Miami.

One day I came across a listing for a search engine marketing job and interviewed just to check it out. My interviewer spoke almost the entire time and after his five-month search for a planner somehow decided I was the right fit. The only qualifications I had on paper were a few interactive classes I took in college and three years of traditional media planning experience. He was willing to teach me the essentials and trusted that I would catch on quickly. Later I learned that the agency was mostly looking for someone who seemed smart, showed an interest in the field, and had a personality that would fit with the agency's culture.

My gut told me I had to take the job. Despite a pay cut and the loss of my company phone, I just couldn't say no. When I took the leap I had no idea what I was getting into, only that I was thrilled by how dynamic it sounded.

In fact, it was so dynamic that I wished I had fully understood just how fast the industry was growing and changing. After less than a year at my agency, four search accounts quickly became 20.

Despite the busy schedule, I absolutely love that I get to be creative and find new ways to solve problems. I feel lucky to be a part of an award-winning search team that is always looking for the next big idea. However, there is also a downside. Technology errors are inevitable; you absolutely must keep up with trade e-mails; and it is extremely difficult to explain to your parents what you do for a living (especially if they still use dial up and/or AOL).

Haley has since left her small firm for RPA. She is on the fast track.

Digital Media's Job: Probably Not What You're Expecting

Before going any further, toss the idea that you'll be planning and running cheesy banner ad campaigns with pink flamingos surrounding a grid of 50 U.S. state abbreviations that change color with the cursor's movement.

Instead, you'll be:
- planning and running a wide range of "display" ads — from banner ads to microsites
- implementing permission-based e-mail campaigns tied to cell phone text-messaging
- bidding on premium placement and managing search key-word campaigns
- negotiating with content sites for product review placement and editorial mentions.

Wait a minute! If a blinking-pink-flamingo banner ad delivers better results than the cool flash animation featuring Dr. Dreamy favored by the creative team, you'll run the flamingos.

That is, you'll run the flamingos until their effectiveness starts to diminish. Then, because you *directly measure* the impact of digital advertising, you'll begin to optimize. As soon as you detect a downward trend in your daily ad results summary, you'll get together with your creative team to introduce new creative messaging or new ad units. You'll change to something that generates the desired reaction from your audience. That's called optimizing.

"Online effectiveness studies kick in immediately," says Cheryl Huckabay, Interactive Media Supervisor at Dallas' Click Here, Inc. "Analytics running all the time allow us to hit our optimization cycles."

Starlink's Onorofski explains: "The worst day (in an interactive campaign) is the day it begins. Then things begin to happen.... Boom! Are things going all right? How are users reacting? What do we do to improve results."

Great Story — But What Will I Do Everyday?

Digital media is a small but very fast-growing subset of total media. Virtually all agencies are in transition today, building or remolding interactive media departments to meet the rising demand for digital advertising.

As a subset of the media department, interactive media's organizational structure, job titles, position descriptions, reporting paths, and promotion tracks each closely mirror their traditional counterparts. Many agencies have media planners work on traditional and digital media in seamless fashion. Others — such as t:m interactive, Tribal DDB, and Tonic 360 in San Francisco — are engineered specifically to deal with digital media and digital branding clients.

Or consider how R/GA with offices in New York and London sees the digital media piece. The only Interactive Agency to be named to *Ad Age's* Agency A List in 2007, R/GA evolved from a pure design agency begun in the 1970s to an innovative digital branding firm ("the agency for the digital age"), housing its media functions under strategic vision in order to produce the most innovative work. R/GA media planners, working with account planners, take part in the entire creative process. Because of their design emphasis, a different organizational model is born.

R/GA New York created this online integrated project for Nike ID. It won a Gold Pencil in the 2007 Interactive One Show.

155

Yet in any of these organizational landscapes, someone must research and assess each new media, determine its true worth in context of a client's goals and objectives, inspect each new opportunity's composition and coverage, negotiate the best possible buy, implement the plan, measure results, tweak creative and placements, then integrate with all other traditional media. All in a never ending "research/plan/buy/measure/optimize" cycle.

What You'll Do

Digital media teams are tightly knit groups ranging in size from three to ten people — or whatever the needs of the agency and clients are — whose responsibilities cover the complete range of tasks necessary to any digital campaign. In contrast to larger, traditional media organizations, the core functions of planning and buying in the digital world are often combined.

This enables interactive media planners/buyers to touch a digital campaign from initiation to conclusion, which proves to be a very powerful motivator.

"In digital media, a media person really wears many different hats," says L. J. Kobe, Interactive Media Supervisor, at t:m interactive in Irving, Texas. "The departments are smaller and we typically work on multiple accounts. We are the media planners, the buyers, the implementers (trafficking), and we do the reporting/optimization."

Responsibilities overlap, and collaboration takes place in a very dynamic media landscape. "Creative works with Media more closely in interactive," says Huckabay of Click Here. Here's a more detailed look at exactly what digital media planners do:

Interactive Media Planner

What You Do	What It Means
CLIENT SERVICE	• Work alongside managers in all areas • Establish media goals and objectives
PLANNING	• Determine the overall campaign plan • Set appropriate goals based on audience characteristics • Review budget • Assess ongoing and prior campaign results • Track campaign history
RESEARCH	• Determine the initial pool of sites to consider • Create a weighted ranking matrix for sites and digital properties • Review new media developments
VENDOR MANAGEMENT	• Review "value-add" offers from sites and vendors • Assess technical capabilities • Explore enhanced creative opportunities • Determine targeting capabilities • Investigate other audience delivery opportunities • Evaluate site case studies and success stories
TEAMWORK	• Meet with Account Service, Creative, and Media • Hold interactive media team meetings • Set priorities for Assistant Media Planners • Assist the team in any capacity required

"No...really, Mercedes, what do you do everyday?"
Mercedes Guynn
Interactive Media Planner
GSD&M, Austin

Well, first know that I've been here for a couple of years, and I've never had a slow day. There's never been a day when I sat around and filed things. We also don't leave at 6:00 p.m.

When I was an assistant, my day started with ad metrics. Every day begins with an assessment of all the placements running in each campaign so that we can begin optimizing the plans and answer these questions: Are we on pace to deliver? Is every campaign on track to deliver the results we projected in our plan? What can we do to make this plan provide better results for our client?

That might be followed by having to create a report to evaluate a set of proposed sites by looking at a range of factors including site composition and coverage, targeting capabilities (SIC codes, .com | .gov | .edu, behavioral, and job titles, etc.), and then assessing both the technical delivery constraints (Flash, bandwidth limits, etc.) as well as potential on-line and off-line "value-add" offers.

The day also includes campaign planning (which never stops), meetings with various account teams, meeting with various sales representatives, top line planning and analyses, and dealing with everyday client requests. Escalated billing issues have to be resolved quickly, plan-versus-actual reports compiled, and minutes carved out to skim a few key newsletters and news sites.

In between all of that, I touch base with the assistant media planners, and we jump in to help others who are in a pinch. We all keep our hands on everything by hitting our ad campaign sites as well as the hot, new sites generating some industry buzz.

That's about it, unless we hit a technical hitch and everything kicks into high gear. Then things get very interesting."

The Daily Entry-Level Circus
Talking among themselves, media planners tend to shorthand things down to: "We plan, buy, traffic, and report," says Mercedes Guynn, an interactive media planner at GSD&M in Austin, Texas. Assistants-turned-planners like Guynn do all of those tasks.

Some of that work is detailed. While it can be a great way of learning the business, quite frankly, it's also not much fun. "Starting out, you will be doing grunt work, the stuff no one else wants to do but has done in the past," says t:m Interactive's Kobe. Unceremoniously piling on top, Carrie Murchison, Manager of External Affairs for eBay in Washington, DC, adds, "You start at the bottom of the ladder. So don't go in with a chip on your shoulder. The cream rises faster when you have work experience under your belt." In other words, start low, work hard, climb quickly.

So you're starting at the bottom and doing some jobs that may have you asking, "I went to college for this?" But there's also the excitement that comes from learning a new field — one nobody knows a lot about. There's also the rush of figuring something out for yourself. "You're not supposed to know a lot," says Fogarty's Soledad. "You're not supposed to know everything on day number one. You don't have to have a big background in digital media, but you must learn every day."

Look for an agency that's doing incredible digital planning, the ones thinking outside of the box and going beyond banners and making content that's meaningful. You have to be watching all the time to see who the industry leaders are on any day.

Kelsey Bernert, Media Planner, Wieden + Kennedy, Portland

Staying current on industry news is the only way to "figure out what is real and lasting, and what is a fad," adds Guynn. O&M's Sloan advises, "Create your own intensive course — dive in and do it."

And W+K's Bernert says you have to be a student of the craft. "A student should make sure she looks at examples of digital work the agency produces. Is it something that would irritate you if you were surfing and came across it? Or is it something that would engage you?" She adds that you should know who the industry leaders are in the field. "Look for an agency that's doing incredible digital planning, the ones thinking outside of the box and going beyond banners and making content that's meaningful."

This is the fast moving current flowing just below the surface of everything digital. "You can't depend on the company to train you; you must train yourself. You must have an interest in digital things outside the office. Digital has to be part of your personal life. Learn by doing. It adds to your decision-making in that area," Sloan concludes.

The Get It Factor
The best way to learn in this fast-paced industry is to train yourself. Be sure to explore all things digital. It shouldn't just be a job. It should be a passion.

So you're assisting, you're learning, and you're also doing some grunt work.

Let's see what that all looks like on a daily basis.

The tasks of the entry-level assistant interactive media planner would look something like this:

Assistant Interactive Media Planner

What You Do	What It Means
REPORT AD SERVING VENDORS	• Read daily advertising results reports from third-party • Assess daily every ad's performance against campaign objectives • Ask, "Are we on pace to deliver our goal?"
SUPPORT TEAM	• Ensure that team members have everything they need • Identify new needs
RESEARCH	• Review new sites and new media opportunities • Meet with vendors to assess capabilities and differentiating factors • Stay current on client-related industry news
DATA COLLECTION & MANAGEMENT	• Confirm that each ad's tracking mechanism is correct and in place • Implement and confirm all ongoing ad optimization changes
BILLING	• Verify insertion orders (placement) against delivered results • Confirm that client invoices are accurate and promptly processed • Resolve minor billing disputes with client or vendor
OBJECTIVES	• Work with the team and client to set campaign goals • Assess "above/below goal" status, as in did we meet the objectives for this quarter? For this campaign and flight?
ANALYZE	• Build insights from campaign results • Assess the user's total experience, including "post-click" actions • Identify opportunities for integration with traditional media • Identify client-side technical and business process opportunities

The Pace: Stressful But Worth It

Digital media's pace is set by the frequent new technology introductions, relatively small budgets, and a media team's ability to rapidly optimize interactive advertising's effectiveness with fast test cycles.

The 12-month planning periods and lengthy, expensive production processes required in broadcast and print are functions of those industries' intense capital structure and heavy regulation. None of that exists on the Internet.

"Know that you'll work a lot. There are some long days. If you don't know this going in, you'll be disappointed. We never leave at 6:00 p.m.," says GSD&M's Guynn. "It's lots of hard work but very rewarding."

"There are days when my brain wants to split," groans Katie Berger, Supervisor/Central Intel, at GM Planworks in Chicago. "It is fast-paced — at least twice that of the traditional side," adds RPA's Brothers. In fact, she points out, "There are times you have to make things up. But you'll never break new ground if you don't take risks."

"Almost every assistant planner wants to quit during the first four months," admits Guynn. "It takes a long time to know the job. Things do get better after the six-month mark. Some get discouraged and quit because they think they're not getting it and not doing any good. Have it in your mind to stay at least a year. It's a mistake if you leave too early."

"Digital advertising is ever-changing," concludes Ashlee Nekuza, Interactive Media Planner for Tracy Locke in Dallas. "You'll always be in at 7:00 a.m. and leave at 9:00 p.m. Things do go to hell." But despite all of that, says Nekuza, this is your "chance to make an imprint. It's worth it."

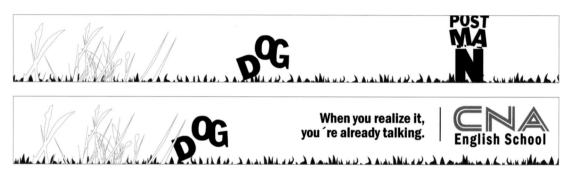

OgilvyInteractive/Sao Paulo created a series of banner ads for the CNA English School that won a 2005 Gold Pencil in One Show Interactive.

Wait! Where's the Fun?
The professionals who research, plan, place, track, and assess new digital media learn new lessons every day. They're learning how audiences engage the leading edge of today's advertising revolution. In this roiling, ever-changing environment, what kind of people can you expect to work with?

Digital media professionals have a sense of adventure but understand risk. They are keenly attuned to clients' objectives. They enter uncharted waters with a confident air and an oxymoronic "disciplined flexibility." They mix curiosity with courage. They are making marks in the industry.

They also laugh a lot.

They tend to be the assistant media planners with the gall and guile to walk into the office of an agency principal, introduce themselves, and then not be surprised when he or she is interested in what they have to say.

Here's the Fun

"Digital is a major shift in how people work, live, entertain, distribute information, and share information," says Cameron Maddux, Media Supervisor of the San Jose Group in Chicago. "I get paid to see how people are shifting."

Tricia Collum, who is the Director of Operations for The Integer Group in Dallas, extends the thought. "Pardon my French, but it's the newest, funnest thing to work on. Things move faster, are more interesting. We learn new things; we do new things."

Not only that, says Brian Wensel, Media Search Coordinator for Philadelphia's Razorfish, "It's so new I'm getting in on the ground floor; there aren't 10,000 experts." That means expertise is growing quickly, making leaps from traditional media systems to digital media buying and selling.

Rick Foote, Deputy Director of Online Communications for Public Strategies, Inc. (PSI), sums it up this way: "It's problem solving on two levels: Creative and logical. I'm a puzzle type. Where do the pieces go? How do we make the puzzle work?" He adds, "We focus less on technology; it's changing too fast. Focus on the user. We take what's been done and do it better. Our challenge is to make something better than the guy who invented it. Make it easy, go beyond the '[computer] monitor experience' and do new things."

---

5 Key Strategies for Jumping into Digital Media

1 • Make friends with comScore, AdRelevance, PointRoll, Donovan Data Systems, ORPs.

2 • Hone negotiation skills. You'll work with vendors, media reps, and agency folks with an agenda. Know how to work your way to the answers you want.

3 • Understand planner/buyer synergies. Even though they're two different paths, the more you know, the better off you'll be. And in some smaller organizations, you'll be wearing both hats. In the digital world, your career often combines the two job descriptions because things are happening so fast.

4 • Think metrics. How do you measure and report?

5 • Be proactive. Read up, invent, stay ahead of the curve. This industry demands it.

Readying Yourself for a Digital Media Career

As you've probably realized by now, digital media professionals are passionate about their field. It's that passion that drives them to learn new things and to use that knowledge to solve problems in new ways. So one of the best ways to prepare yourself is to be guided by your passion.

"If there's a piece of the industry that you know the least about, but are personally interested in, do that. Become an expert," offers O&M's Sloan. In fact, a random fact you may pick up by going deep can really pay off when it finally comes time for you to interview.

"You only need to know just a little bit, even if you can't see how it fits at the time," points out Razorfish's Wensel. He clearly recalls how during a job interview "the person I was talking to made reference to Nedstat, the name of a piece of freeware I had used to measure traffic to my personal portfolio site in college. I mentioned that connection, and the interview went to a new level. That's all it took."

Of course, you'll need to combine your passion with a few skills — some general and some more specialized.

The Get It Factor

Learn Excel. It's ten times more important in Digital Media than on the traditional side.

A Few General Skills

Traditional media basics include strong analytical skills coupled with strategic thinking, superior writing, and presentation skills. Digital media is that and more. So general courses in creativity, management, and strategy are important. Any business-oriented and strategically loaded class in consumer behavior will also help. Best assignments? Anything that makes you jump in and think hard about the why and how of consumer engagement in a new world.

More Specialized Skills and Understanding

The nearly universal digital media basic requirements span five areas, with one area repeated because it's so important. Note that technology drags in at fifth place. This is because ad-serving software is increasingly sophisticated and focused on ease-of-use. In other words, technology will continually be easier to use. Your brain and experience will be your most important qualifications.

- Pursue internships. Interactive and "a minimum of two," according to Integer's Collum.
- Deal with numbers. "Excel! Excel! Excel!," says Razorfish's Wensel. "Take online courses and practice."
- Repeat. "Learn Excel. It's ten times more important than on the traditional

side," notes RPA's Brothers. "It allows you to handle more data and build new perspectives. Formulas and pivot tables are critical. Practice and, as incredible as it sounds, create sample reports."

- Know third-party ad-serving software. Internships can help you get familiar with it. Also take seminars on Internet specialities and applications.
- Understand technology. Know basic HTML, ad-serving mechanics, social networking, and people.

Bernert of W+K tells a success story about a project she did in her first six months at the agency. The success, she says, hinged on knowing the target audience and communicating with them in a new and fun way.

"W+K created the microsite ExperienceOldSpice.com to communicate Old Spice's new experience positioning and allow deeper engagement with the Old Spice brand. The website included a 50 question quiz intended to measure a guy's 'experience.' Positive chatter about the quiz was found online and drove additional traffic. This example shows that when users can engage with the 'advertising,' and in this case when it's entertaining content it is successful."

Do the Research on Where Big Ideas Are Happening

Where's the best place to start a career in digital media — a large national agency or smaller local firm?

The answer mimics the general rules of thumb true for all of advertising. You'll wear more hats and do just about anything and everything advertising has to offer in a smaller agency. On the other side of the equation, a large national firm has the client base and overhead structure to support a stable full of talent. So you'll be surrounded by young, like-minded professionals. Joanna Luu began her career as an assistant media planner at Carat Fusion, then made the leap to media planner at Avenue A| Razorfish in San Francisco.

There are a few digital media twists, but the answer most often skews toward national firms. "If there are no resources, you can't implement good ideas," says ebay's Murchison.

"Opportunity is everywhere," says Rapp Collins' Young, but the keys are agency size and billings."In the national arena all pitches are big. Reputation counts."

Large, sophisticated clients can't talk to everyone, and there are opportunities that smaller agencies don't get. Bigger revenue means the agency can attract the best talent at the top, and this translates to better thinking at all levels."

Integer's Collom agrees. "Go bigger. You'll appreciate the structures in place, and there are more people to learn from. Also, the chance of finding a mentor is higher. You'll have access to more resources and training. Research is available. You'll have time to gather confidence as you're groomed for a higher role."

"If you're starting out, interview at all of the large agencies. Ask them the pros and cons of working there as well as working in that type of environment. Remember, in an interview you are interviewing them as much as they are interviewing you — it needs to be a mutually beneficial situation," says t:m interactive's Kobe. "You interview with the people you will work with," notes Guynn, a thought worth keeping in mind as you walk into an interview.

The Transition from School to Media Career
Joanna Luu
Interactive Media Planner
Avenue A/Razorfish

It's been a relatively short while since I started my job as assistant media planner at Carat Fusion. When I joined, that agency was still known as Carat Interactive. The name change alone reveals the dynamic nature of the advertising industry, one of the characteristics that attract so many to the field.

I graduated from a program that has a reputation for producing bright, passionate, creative thinkers. The media program at my university gave me a basic understanding of the business. I knew who the key players were, had two internships under my belt, and had been exposed to the top agencies in New York. When I graduated, I strongly believed that I was prepared to enter the hip and exciting world of advertising. Nevertheless, I have to say that there have been a number of surprises.

In a fast-paced business like this, mistakes happen, and all you can really do is try to learn from them. In my college classes, the professors warned us that advertising is a fast-paced business. We all thought, "Yeah, yeah, sure." With a solid education and internship experience, we were confident that we could handle it. Well, it's even faster than they say.

Supervisors who are supposed to be training you are so swamped themselves that it is up to you to make the best of situations. You'll find yourself making decisions you don't feel qualified to make, and you'll make mistakes. Struggling with this, I asked for some advice. The Account Director looked me in the eye and responded, "You are good because you care."

That was my *a-ha!* moment. College prepared me to think strategically, to ask smart questions as well as to ask dumb ones. It did not prepare me to take mistakes less personally. Is there a class that teaches that?

Many times I find myself wishing I had learned more about working in teams. The professors told us that teamwork is a fact of life in this business and made sure that we were well seasoned by the time we graduated. Similar to classroom team projects, everyone at work has specific responsibilities and a designated contribution to make to the team.

However, the dynamics of team interaction can be very different in a corporate setting, especially if you are interacting with the same team everyday for eight hours a day. Things can become very challenging when members of the same team have different creative views and/or a different work ethic.

But even with my two internships, I can tell that I am still learning new things every day. I would have to say that the biggest thing I've learned on the job is that you have to keep learning on the job. This seems to be especially true in the ever-fragmenting world of media. My experience is teaching me that no matter how hard you study in college, you can't learn to think outside the box until you have lived in it.

If the Job You Want Doesn't Exist, Create It

In this environment, sometimes it's best to offer your vision of the industry and your career as a starting point. So much is being invented so quickly, great brains are needed to fulfill what agencies and the marketplace will produce. "Ask for the job you want, not the job they have to offer," suggests eBay's Murchison. "Don't ask what's available. Tell them what you want. Make them create the position for you. Create your own destiny. The innovative, exciting times are still ahead of us."

After all, new job titles are being created everyday. Take Katie Berger, a Supervisor/Central Intel for Chicago's GM Planworks. That's not a title you'll run across most places, but it's the perfect one for her job. "At Central Intelligence," she says, "we act as information and knowledge gatherers and sharers. Our job is to identify, access, and keep tabs on emerging technology opportunities."

The possibility of creating your own destiny exists in this field. Just be ready with the right skills, the right information, and a great measure of adventure and hard work to back up what you promise.

The Fast Track

Because of the real need for digital media planners, this area is the fast track in media. Starting salaries can be 10 to 20 percent higher, especially if you have a resume that includes significant interactive internship experience and evidence of strong depth in at least one technical area.

Few things are standardized in this area, but the career ladder happens to be one part that is. Dropping the word "Interactive Media" for the sake of clarity, the progression is generally: coordinator, assistant, planner, supervisor, associate director, and director.

"Promotions are faster because digital media is growing so fast. Agencies are expanding by creating new groups within groups. Digital media planners set their own pace. People will see that you're ready to be promoted, but if you're just going through the steps, it won't happen," says Click Here's Huckabay.

The Get It Factor

Starting salaries in Digital Media are higher than in traditional media and most other areas of the agency. Your digital expertise is a valuable commodity. If you can stay nimble with the everchanging flow of technology and information, you can build a formidable career.

Personal initiative and being proactive are the way to get ahead says Fogarty's Soledad: "You must keep up to date. Add something new each day. Take on a project that you don't know much about. Request the user manual for your ad serving software and read it. Do things that make you nervous. Teach yourself."

Razorfish's Wensel agrees. "You have to be able to pop out ideas. Learn what's going on. Be a half step ahead of your peers then go one step further. Sometimes it is hard to be passionate about daily tasks, but the future is worth it." In short, as Integer's Collom says, "It's easy to shine. But you have to have a 'go-getter' personality."

How to Get an Entry-Level Digital Media Job in One Sentence

This entire chapter was constructed to tease you, intrigue you, and lure you into considering digital media as a potential career path. Look closely at those we talked to, and you'll notice a distinct slant toward young professionals who are early into their careers. Listen to them carefully. They are living what could very well be your near-term future. And it's a bright one.

They are also well on their way to making marks in the digital media industry. They are working very long hours alongside other equally bright, interesting young professionals. They are working for supervisors and associates who understand the value of having a disciplined approach to creative thinking.

Digital media is not about technology. Digital media is about content, audiences, and using technology to directly measure audiences' communication and buying behaviors.

The Beginning

To get an entry-level job in digital media you only need to understand — *thoroughly understand... soaked-to-the-bone understand... able-to-explain-to-your-parents understand* — a single sentence.

That sentence is what allows you to know what part of your advertising works and what part of your advertising doesn't work.

That sentence is: "Using a third-party ad server, insert a uniquely named, one-pixel by one-pixel, transparent GIF image into your web page."

To figure out what the various words in this sentence mean, visit the following three sites:
www.webopedia.com
www.webmonkey.com
computer.howstuffworks.com/internet-channel.htm

Figuring out the technical mechanics will take about two hours of reading.

Figuring out the implications of those mechanics will take longer but can anchor a career.

Do those two things to hold the keys to a new way of thinking about all digital media — the direct measurement of communication and sales behavior. Everything you need to know about the Internet is on the Internet. Start reading. Find the "Beginners" section. Do the research. Get started.

"What are you waiting on," asks Tracy Locke's Nekuza.

What are you waiting on?

I'm handed a piece of paper that has some scribbling and some pictures on it. That script is like a big puzzle. To make it a reality and to make it great, I have to put it all together.

Scott Mitchell
Vice President, Director of Creative Broadcast Production
DraftFCB, Chicago

Production

BROADCAST PRODUCERS TURN SCRIPTS INTO RADIO SPOTS, TV commercials, and webcasts, while art producers transform layouts into print and digital advertising. But ask them what they do, and producers are likely to tell you that they put puzzles together. They assemble in just the right order all of the right pieces and people: directors or photographers, actors, locations, and post-production people. Putting that puzzle together is both challenging and creative. And a lot depends on it.

It's not for nothing that writers and art directors often refer to an idea as their baby. A print ad or TV spot that's scribbled on a piece of paper is as helpless as an infant. If it's to realize its potential and fulfill the dreams of both agency and client, it requires the care and nurturing of a great producer.

Listen to the stories producers tell about how they make that happen, and you'll find the kind of adventures and miraculous last minute escapes that would do Jack Sparrow proud. In short, the producer's job demands the same kind of creativity, intuition, and problem solving that art directors and writers need to imagine the idea in the first place.

Production is also critically important to both the agency and the client. After all, agencies win awards, build reputations, then gain and retain clients because of the power of their creative work. Clients are equally dependent on strong advertising to build both sales and brand image. The power of that advertising depends not only on the strength of the idea but also on the quality of the execution.

This chapter describes what it takes for a producer to protect and nurture ideas along with the rewards and challenges involved in that process. Broadcast producers generally work in television and radio, and art producers work primarily with print. And now there's a fast growing legion of producers dedicated to the digital realm. The basics of all of these jobs are similar enough that we will describe them as if they were one. Of course, where there are significant differences, we'll tell you about those as well. And we need to make one other thing clear: Art producers are sometimes referred to as art buyers. In this chapter we call them art producers unless the person we're quoting uses the other title.

"Bringing Up Baby" or How a Producer Turns an Idea into Reality

The producer's goal is to serve the creative and make it sing. But sing for whom? The creative team and the account people who represent the client's interests all have the same goal. But they may have different priorities, a situation which can often lead to conflict. "There's a reason why there's an account side and a creative side," notes Jeff Yee, a broadcast producer at Los Angeles' TBWA\Chiat\Day. "You think they're on the same team, but they are oftentimes opposing forces with separate priorities like marketing strategy versus creative execution."

Sure, writers and art directors care about the product being advertised, but they often care even more about their idea. It's their baby, if you will, and they want to make sure that nobody mistreats it. On the other hand, clients are especially concerned with how their product looks in the advertising and want its benefits to come through clearly. They also want to make sure that the money invested in the idea is spent wisely so that the production comes in on budget and on time. If the final product is to be an effective piece of advertising that everybody loves, the producer must balance those two points of view. Doing so is satisfying. It's also not easy.

But let's not get ahead of ourselves. Generally, the process begins happily enough. After weeks of labor, the agency and client have finally produced an idea, which they all consider to be their brainchild. And who isn't happy when a baby is born? Everyone — client and agency alike — envisions a bright future for the apple of their collective eye.

Trial by Fire: It's a Great Way to Learn
Nate Brown, Associate Producer, DDB, Chicago

What I enjoy most about my job is the chance to manage a commercial production from start to finish. I am involved at every stage from bidding out the job to the final "finishing" just before the commercial is shipped for broadcast. For someone like me, who has an interest in just about every part of the production process, that opportunity is very rewarding. It allows me to meet and observe the work of talented artists and craftsmen in all areas of the industry. It also allows a continuous change in scenery.

Some days I might spend my morning supervising an edit at a post-production house, and later that day I could be running around Chicago shooting a spec spot for a new business pitch. The change in scenery also includes many trips to Los Angeles, New York, and other popular production destinations where I supervise casting sessions, productions, or even post-production work.

Recently, I traveled to Los Angeles four times to supervise visual effects on a commercial at a major Hollywood visual effects facility. It was a lot of work, but it was also a great experience.

I studied economics in college, and this taught me a very intuitive way of looking at the world. Producing is very much the same. I believe a successful producer is much like an economist: They both have their own unique ways of interpreting information and strategizing a game plan.

I guess you could refer to it as "producer goggles."

A good producer's approach to a project includes proactive thinking, strategic communication, diplomacy, and the ability to manage huge amounts of information and communicate it clearly. These skills cannot be taught in a textbook. This is experiential knowledge you have to acquire in the trenches working as a professional in the industry. Nevertheless, my work in high school and college producing low-budget short films and spec commercials taught me plenty and prepared me to be an agency producer. It's also what ultimately caught the attention of the agency I now work for.

There are so many things I wish I had known before starting my job, like understanding the quasi-parental role you play with your art director and writer while on a production. You are there in part to make sure your creative team knows where to go, is on time, and is happy.

I've also learned a tremendous amount about managing personalities. Advertising is a mix of art and business, and there are people and personalities on both sides. Finding harmony between business and art can sometimes be challenging. So diplomacy is a big part of my job, and it takes practice. I think trial by fire is the best way to learn these things. It takes many years and many failures (and successes) to become a good agency producer. Do the legwork to get the opportunity to be thrown right into the trenches, and let the learning begin.

(To see some of Nate's work, check out his website: www.nathanpbrown.com)

First Steps: Selecting the Photographer or Director

Before selecting a photographer or TV director, the producer needs to fully understand the idea. It sounds simple enough, but it's not. Jessica Hoffman, Senior Integrated Art Producer in the Boulder, Colorado office of Crispin Porter + Bogusky (Crispin) explains: "Getting what the art director needs and helping people translate that into a visual can be a delicate process."

No matter how detailed the storyboard or layout, it's only a sign pointing to the vision inside the creative team's head. As DraftFCB's Mitchell points out, "To grasp what the creative team wants, what they have in their heads, and what they're hearing in their ears... and to understand what is so central to the idea that we cannot as an agency or as a creative team ever let go of it, the producer has to ask the writer and art director a lot of questions like what do they want this to look like, to sound like, to feel like." Only by thoroughly understanding the idea, will the producer be able to explain it to others and ensure that the final product meets everyone's expectations.

After getting a good understanding of the creative idea, the producer is ready to begin selecting a photographer or film director depending on whether the advertising is print or television. This is probably the single most critical decision that will be made. Everything hinges on the talent of the director or photographer because that person is largely responsible for shooting the images and directing the actors that will make the agency's idea a reality.

Finding a Photographer Who Could Make a Guy Fly
Sebastian Gray, Art Producer, Crispin Porter + Bogusky, Miami

Our number one criteria for the photographer we would hire for the Mini "Grab Handle" print ad was obviously the ability to give us the look the art director was after. Two photographers came to mind. They both did the super grainy, hyper-real, de-saturated thing pretty well. Stylistically, either guy could have worked. But there was a technical dimension to the shoot. The talent would need to fly in the air while holding onto the grab handle.

Our decision to go with Jim Fiscus was mainly due to his solution for making our talent fly. He wanted to suspend our talent in flying harnesses and use a wind machine to imply motion. The other photographer's approach was to cast gymnast types to fly through the frame via a launch trampoline. It sounded cool. But we felt the approach was a bit ambitious given our need to place our flying bodies at very specific angles while holding the grab handle just so. We went for the harness approach for the added control not to mention the broader pool of talent.

The ad didn't just call for a man. There was also the small matter of the dog biting the man's leg. We cast three Jack Russells, a breed known for its spunk. The idea was that we would get a dog pissed enough at a fake leg to really clamp down on it, allowing us to swing dog and pant leg into frame.

But our dogs didn't hate the leg enough to really sink their teeth into it so we could swing them through the air. At the last minute we had to find another dog. I called my brother who happens to live in Manhattan and also happens to own a Jack Russell. I asked him to bring his dog by for a try. Pickles, a non-pro, is a truly psychotic ten pounder. She clamped hard and saved the day. And then she swallowed the pant leg.

No two directors or photographers will approach the concept in the same way. So choosing the right person is essential, and there are thousands of people to choose from. Ask Jeff Selis, a broadcast producer at Wieden + Kennedy in Portland, Oregon, and he'll tell you, "Knowing who's out there and who is great at what they do is probably the most important thing a producer does." That's why producers spend a good deal of time meeting with artists' representatives and reviewing work. Then when a job arrives on their desk, they can immediately suggest the names of directors or photographers they want the creative team to consider.

What makes the selection process exciting, according to Selis, is, "You don't have to stay in the stack of reels of advertising directors. You have the whole creative world out there to draw from." For example, Selis remembers considering directors for a Miller High Life spot when one morning the art director came rushing into the office saying, "I just saw the most amazing movie, *Fast Cheap and Out of Control*, and we have to use this Errol Morris guy." Errol Morris is a documentary filmmaker who at that time had never made a commercial. Nonetheless, after talking with him Selis and the art director were convinced that he was right for the spot. The commercials went on to win awards, and Morris has now become a well-known commercial director.

But producers find talent in many other places besides Hollywood. Tattoo parlors, for example. Cindy Hicks, a senior art producer at The Martin Agency in Richmond, Virginia, tells how she found the perfect illustrator in a bar. "When we had Saab as a client," she recalls, "an art director wanted an illustration done by Big Daddy Roth of *Mad Magazine* fame. But he had passed on. Then I was out at a club one night, and I saw a couple of friends who had these fabulous tattoos that looked exactly like the style I was looking for. And the guy who did the work happened to be there that night. So I ended up hiring a tattoo artist to do the illustration."

In short, good producers have an eye on what's happening around them. That helps them get ideas and find solutions almost anywhere.

Bidding the Job

Once the producer, copywriter, art director, and creative director agree on a short list of directors or photographers to bid, the producer sets up a conference call with each one so that all of the key players can discuss the project. The call is partly designed to check out the vibe between the agency and the photographer or director. "Life is too short to work with assholes," as DraftFCB's Mitchell says. "And if you're not gelling on the phone, chances are you're not going to gel on the set."

In addition to a chemistry check, the initial phone calls are designed to see if the photographer or director is in synch with the creative vision and can bring something to the table that will make the idea even stronger.

During these calls the producer serves as an interpreter to make sure everybody is on the same page. Kate Talbott, an executive broadcast producer at Fallon in Minneapolis, puts it in perspective: "Part of the problem is that if there are four people in on the call, everybody could walk away with a different vision in their

Jeff Selis, broadcast producer for W+K, on location during a shoot with Tiger Woods for Nike golf.

head and all think this guy is going to be great because he's going to give us this. It's like no, he never said that. So the producer is sort of like the police and has to make sure everybody understands what was talked about."

Crispin's Hoffman explains, "It's just a matter of listening and making sure that when the writer or art director acknowledges what's been said that they're interpreting it properly. It sounds like a very small thing, but it's really the critical component." These calls also help photographers and directors get the details they'll need to submit cost estimates or bids to the agency. Not getting those details right can prove costly to the production company.

As with any other relationship, money can spell trouble. There never seems to be enough of it no matter how large the client's budget. Shawn Smith, Director of Art Buying at Fallon's Minneapolis office, points out that producers always "have to balance creative needs and desires with the realities of budget and timing." Doing that means "being resourceful — creatively and budgetarily," W+K's Selis notes.

Producers need to be able to review bid sheets and determine where costs can be cut. "If someone tells you they want $10,000 for an ad," says Smith, "you can't just take that and say, 'OK, they want $10,000.' You have to negotiate and try to get it down. And then you draw on your experience to know what's reasonable and if they're asking too much."

Finding Options that Satisfy Everyone

It's not just a matter of getting the production company to reduce the costs of certain items. Agency producers frequently have to work closely with the production company to see if there are less expensive or faster ways to shoot the spot or print ad.

For example, if a spot calls for multiple locations, one option might be to shoot the action in front of a green screen and then add the different backgrounds later during post-production.

It's all about finding a way to pull off what the creative team wants within the budget and time frame the client has provided. Doing that takes a lot of creative thinking and problem solving on the part of the producer.

174

Production

According to Char Eisner, Group Supervisor for Art Production at Leo Burnett in Chicago, "At the end of the process if the producer has handled it effectively, the creative team feels they have the people they need to execute their idea, the client feels like they are getting the bargain of the century, and the talent, be it a photographer, illustrator, or whatever, feels like he is being fairly compensated for his time and talent. And that," she says, "is indeed an art." In short, it takes vision to understand how to fulfill the idea in an effective way.

Pre-production and the Shoot

Producers are always busy, but their job really heats up once the agency moves into pre-production. That's when the details get nailed down. Every one of them is critical because it's the details that bring the idea to life. There are discussions about the kind of lighting, film, and lenses needed to convey the feeling the creative team wants. The photographer's or director's production company also sends out scouts to photograph locations, props, and wardrobe that might fit the creative team's vision. The agency team huddles around the computer debating the options the production company has e-mailed them. Casting sessions are held, and the agency scrutinizes the talent even more closely.

Once the agency and the photographer or director agree on talent, location, and wardrobe selections, those are shown to the client for approval. If the client rejects any of the options, then the search continues until everyone is satisfied.

While buttoning down the details, the producer is doing something even more important — planning for disaster. As Crispin's Hoffman knows, "There are so many things that can happen, you have to be prepared to deal with any devastating problem that pops up during the shoot." It's just a matter of having "a back-up plan and a back-up plan for that," notes Amy Favat, Senior Vice President, Executive Broadcast Producer at Arnold in Boston. "That way," she says, "when a problem does occur, you can say, 'OK, this didn't work out, but that's OK because we have this plan going into effect right now.' I think what people look to a producer to do is take care of the problem, minimize the trauma, and have solutions."

Even if you're performing emergency surgery right there on the set, you can never let them see you sweat. Jackie Vidor, a broadcast producer at Secret Weapon, a creative boutique in Los Angeles, explains: "Solving problems means internalizing things that you'd normally go, 'oh, my god, how am I going to do this.' Believe me, they don't want to hear that. They just want to show you what the problem is and have you go in and solve it."

> **Knowing who's out there and who is great at what they do is probably the most important thing a producer does.**
>
> *Jeff Selis, Broadcast Producer, Wieden + Kennedy, Portland*

The Best Laid Plans

But with all the planning during pre-production, what could possibly go wrong at the shoot? Lots. Like conflicts between the director or photographer and the creative team. Even though everyone may see eye-to-eye during all of the pre-production meetings, there can still be tension on the set. As W+K's Selis says, "You start out with this idea on paper, and that's the last time it's really yours. So expecting any creative team to just hand off their idea to a director is kind of ridiculous. But at the same time, we're always looking for the person that's best for the job, and so at some point you've got to step out of the way. The most demanding and stressful part of the job is when I'm on that set. It's kind of my role to balance the delicate egos of the creative team and the director."

Even when the creative team is in perfect synch with the director or photographer there can still be problems. The Martin Agency's Hicks points out, "An art director may say, 'You know what would be great,' and then the photographer goes, 'that would be fabulous.' And all of a sudden they're going crazy over budget. So it's my job to be the sort of bad cop in that situation."

Producers want to leave room for what Selis calls "happy accidents," new ideas that arise from the collaboration between the photographer or director and the creative team. However, shooting variations, whether print or broadcast, takes time and money. Producers are responsible for keeping an eye on both while making sure the ad is shot the way the client approved it. So they have to walk a fine line between flexibility and control.

The producer may also need to rein in the client. DraftFCB's Mitchell remembers walking onto the set to discover the art director and the clients in a furious argument over what sort of sunglasses the model should wear. That might have been understandable had it been a commercial for sunglasses. But it wasn't. It was a soft drink spot, and the focus of the scene was on the soda.

So Mitchell suggested that the clients focus their attention on how the product was being displayed and allow the art director to choose the sunglasses. As Mitchell says, "The client got it and backed off." No wonder Broadcast Producer Matt Blitz tells his production assistants at Burnett, "If you've ever served in public office, now's the time to start using your diplomatic skills."

Shoots almost always present problems that challenge producers. But it's those challenges that the producers enjoy. As Hicks puts it, "There's nothing cookie cutter about this job. It's often about how inventive and creative you can be in making a shoot happen. And that's what I love about it."

Putting Mash Ups, Historical Footage and a Hollywood Cinematographer to Work for Audi

Regina Brizzolara, Director of Broadcast Production and Senior Vice President, McKinney, Durham, North Carolina

With the "Progressions" campaign, we wanted to highlight the progressive spirit of Audi and applaud a few of their many innovations by showcasing the brand as it relates to innovations in such areas as music, sports, dance, and medicine. Each innovation sequence in the campaign showed a chronological progression of images moving from long ago to the present and incorporated a series of four shots that celebrated the four rings of the Audi logo.

Because we needed to show historical footage, the spot was complicated and required extensive stock searches and licensing through multiple houses. During pre-production we were searching tirelessly for stock, getting permission from the companies featured (including Apple and RCA), and figuring out what we could license and what we would need to shoot to tell our story.

Much of what we shot over our three days of stage and location shooting in L.A. was "in period," so that it would fit in with the historical footage that we licensed. Director Lance Acord, the director of photography for *Lost in Translation* and the cinematographer for *Being John Malkovich*, shot the entire wheel sequence shown here in Los Angeles. Lance used many of his old, handheld cameras along with specific black-and-white film stock to achieve the look within the wheel sequence. The location scout and art department did an incredible job finding the old barn, the vintage wheelbarrow, the old-fashioned bike, and the period clothing.

The music track also required extensive negotiation as it was a mash up of two David Bowie songs — *Rebel, Rebel*, originally released in 1974 and *Never Get Old*, first released in 2005. Through David Bowie's management, we were put in touch with three of the top mash up artists in Europe. The two Bowie songs are distinct, and the first two rounds of mash up demos fell short.

While the third round of demo work was going on in Europe, the clock continued to tick. So those of us at McKinney independently contracted another music house that ultimately created the mash up that Bowie, Audi, and the agency approved. During the creation of the mash up, negotiations for the use of *Rebel, Rebel* were taking place with the multiple parties that hold the rights to the track. We had to quickly get all of the parties involved to agree to payment, to use, and to sign the contracts that would allow us to go to air. As part of the negotiations around the two songs, we were allowed to host a mash up contest of the two songs online. The winner won a brand-new Audi TT. It was a complicated project. And it was completed in just 28 days.

Post-production: After the Shoot and
Before the World Sees Anything

Once the shoot is finished, the project moves into post-production. For a print advertisement, the photographer sends the agency the photos. The art director and art producer then review them and make the selections that will be sent to the digital imaging house so the images can be retouched and color corrected. In many cases, the imaging house will have to take several images and digitally compose them to make the final shot.

Post-production for a TV spot is even more involved. Once the spot is shot, the film must be color corrected and edited. In some instances, the edit is relatively straightforward. If the story dictates the arrangement of most scenes, it's simply a matter of selecting the best take. In other more cinematic spots, there are a number of ways the various scenes can be arranged. The order and rhythm of the shots determine the emotional color and psychological impact of the commercial. The editor's decisions can be as critical to the success of the spot as those of the director who shot it. The agency and client are sure to debate each of those decisions until they arrive at a version that everybody can agree on.

The edited spot is then handed off to the music house to create the music track. Although the agency gives direction as to the sound and feel that it wants, there are sure to be discussions about every detail from placement of sounds to pacing and instrumentation. Because the deadlines have often been pushed at each of the previous stages, the music house generally has less time than it wants to complete its job.

W+K's Selis points out, "You go to the music house you've selected about two days before your deadline and say we really need you to do something like this. And they usually do it. But it's extremely stressful. And you've just got to sweat it out and try and stay cool and know that it's all going to work itself out." Once the music track is completed, and the final edit is finished and approved, the spot is shipped out to the stations to air.

Every job brings a whole new set of challenges and opportunities to learn about random and wildly different things.

Jessica Hoffman, Senior Integrated Art Producer, Crispin Porter + Bogusky, Boulder

178

Whether print, broadcast, or digital, the entire process can take anywhere from just a few weeks to three months or longer. And what about all of the problems along the way?

Once the job is completed, agency and clients generally forget all about their disagreements and take pride in the work they have produced together. All of the near disasters so traumatic at the time become stories to entertain friends with over a beer. And the friends laugh and are jealous that anyone could get paid for the kind of adventures producers call work.

The Life of a Production Assistant

One agency's job description refers wryly to the "long, thankless, bitter years" spent as a production assistant. The job does involve long hours, lots of paperwork, and menial tasks like shlepping reels and portfolios from one end of the agency to the other, tasks that may leave you thinking to yourself, "I went to college for this?"

But production assistants also say — or at least most of them do — that it's the best job they've ever had. For one thing, even some of the routine tasks are hardly routine. Rebecca O'Neill, an assistant art producer at Crispin, tells of being sent out in the middle of summer to find someone who, in just two weeks, could knit one of those dorky holiday sweaters decorated with ice skaters and men cutting down Christmas trees.

Annalise Meyer, an assistant broadcast producer at Portland's W+K, recounts how she received a call from a senior producer who had lost his driver's license while out of town on a shoot. He needed her to break into his house, find his passport, and overnight it to him so airport security would let him on a plane the next day.

More importantly, production assistants say they are learning something new almost every day and can see how the skills and knowledge they are acquiring will get them where they want to go.

The variety is a huge plus. An assistant might be securing legal rights to an image one minute and the next might be meeting with animal trainers and taking photos of exotic birds being considered for use in an ad. Within a relatively short period of time, a production assistant's work becomes even more challenging and creative. Assistant art producers begin to negotiate stock photography and supervise illustrations and tabletop photography shoots. Assistant broadcast producers start to supervise radio productions and assemble and edit in-house videos. The hours may be long, but they're also interesting. That makes it all worthwhile.

What Assistant Art Producers Assist With

"The producer's overall goal," observes Alicia Kuna, an art producer at W+K in Portland, "is to find the right photographer or illustrator for the ad. Sounds simple. But it isn't. It's a hell of a lot of work."

An assistant art producer plays a key part in that process by staying in touch with photography and illustration reps. When the agency needs to review portfolios to select the right person for the job, the assistant producer contacts dozens of reps, arranges for portfolios to be shipped to the agency, schedules meetings where the work is reviewed, and then is responsible for returning all of the books.

While handling the logistics is not one of the most exciting parts of the job, getting to see all of the great work is, says Crispin's O'Neill.

Of course, production assistants also help producers arrange many of the details for a photography shoot. And it's not just tracking down props like a holiday sweater. It's also arranging casting sessions where the producer auditions talent for the ad. If the ad calls for the models to work with a St. Bernard, for example, the assistant producer also has to have one of those at the audition to make sure the talent isn't afraid of dogs or allergic to them. If the shoot is out of town, the assistant may have to put on a travel agent's hat and book flights and hotel rooms.

Then there's both the search and the research part of the job. As Burnett's Eisner knows, "You can get some pretty whacky requests from creatives when they're looking for inspiration or for different ways to execute an idea." Production assistants need the research skills to be able to go online and find whatever visual is needed no matter how unusual. More importantly, when either the budget or time makes it impossible for the art director to shoot an original photograph, the agency will need to purchase an already existing image that's known as a stock photograph. These photographs can be purchased from stock photography companies such as Getty and Corbis whose images can be accessed online.

The Get It Factor

Art buyers and their production assistants might find the perfect photo from a number of different sources: an original photo from a photographer, a photo previously shot by the photographer, stock photography sources, or online photo archives.

It's the assistant's job to find the right stock image, a task calling for both creativity and business smarts. The creative part means being able to look at the layout and understand exactly what kind of image the art director is seeking. That involves not just knowing what the visual needs to be but also what sort of emotional quality it needs to have. Selecting the perfect image means going through stock image banks and locating a number of visuals that have the right feel so that the art director has a variety of photographs to choose from.

Once the selection has been made, the assistant begins to negotiate the price and obtain the rights to use the photograph. Andrea Ricker, an art producer at Arnold in Boston, suggests that process gives the assistant "the experience of doing research, looking at a lot of photographs, doing the negotiation, and seeing a project through from beginning to end." Those are precisely the skills that the assistant will need in order to be promoted to art producer.

"It's still hard," according to Fallon's Smith, "to make that leap to producer. It's a big step to get the experience and be trusted to handle things." So agencies arrange for assistants to take several small steps. After handling stock photography purchases, they are often given illustration jobs because those projects require very little monitoring once the artist is booked and the deal made. The next step may be tabletop photography assignments. Since no location or talent is involved, it's generally just a matter of working with the art director to make sure the product is lit correctly and properly shot in the photographer's studio.

Such projects allow assistants to develop confidence in their creative judgment as well as hone their ability to recommend and book talent, arrange shoots, oversee schedules, and handle contracts and legal clearances. As they get ready to take the next step and become an art producer, assistants move on to more complicated projects involving locations and talent.

What Broadcast Production Assistants Assist With

"The first thing I would tell new production assistants to do," says W+K's Selis, "is to make time to sit down and watch as many reels as they can in a week. That way they can get familiar with who does what and get an idea of what they like." The key phrase is "make time" because assistants are scurriers with little free time. Nonetheless, finding that time is critical. After all, knowing directorial talent is key to what producers do.

What's more, familiarity with commercial directors will allow production assistants not only to hunt down the reels of directors being considered for a job but also offer a suggestion or two of their own, so they feel less like go-fers and more like knowledgeable support. That's also the kind of initiative that impresses the agency's senior people.

After the producer and creative team put together a short list of directors they are considering bidding for a job, the assistant has to contact each one's rep to see if the director is available for the shoot dates. As the spot moves into production, the assistant sits in on meetings and takes notes about what is decided and also handles a variety of other details from helping obtain legal clearances to making sure that the client sends enough product to the shoot. Once the spot is completed, the networks require an "as produced" script, which lists each shot in the commercial and the dialogue, music, or sound effects that accompany that shot. That task falls to the assistant along with cataloguing all of the elements from the shoot before they are sent to storage.

While accomplishing all of this, the assistant also needs to practice putting together budgets. As Selis puts it, "Once I start a production I would expect a new assistant to watch me do a budget and then try to do a budget on their own." It's critical to make the time to do that, according to Burnett's Blitz, "because it's not uncommon for a supervisor to say 'just go ahead and do this project,' which would mean you'd have to put together a budget. If you hadn't already made the time to sit down and kind of learn how to do one yourself, suddenly you'd have to take a big crash course."

Producing In-house Videos and Radio

Assistant broadcast producers master their craft and prepare for larger jobs by being responsible for producing quick turnaround material such as radio and in-house videos. Agencies generally create in-house videos for clients to use at sales events, online, or at other employee meetings, which several hundred people may attend. So these projects are important and must be done well, though they might not require the high level investment of a senior producer.

While a few of these videos use original footage, most are built around footage from movies and other sources and use a voiceover narration plus existing music. Since nothing new has to be shot and no music has to be recorded, such pieces are easier to put together than a television commercial, yet involve many of the same skills. W+K's Meyer sums it up this way: "When I'm doing a video, I may have a list of 25 different kinds of scenes I need, and so I'll either call and get movies or research databases online. I have to know how to scan and mark the footage I need and how to find the music. I have to put together an estimate, hire an editor, coordinate with the creatives to show them the rough cut, and then work with account service to set up a meeting to show the video to the client. A lot of it is time lines, schedules, and budget estimates. That's a lot of what producers do. That's how we're practicing what we're going to be doing."

---

5 Great Reasons to Jump into Production

1 • You have to eat culture for a living. Museums, art galleries, films, places, and ideas are your toolset.

2 • Watching reels or reviewing photographs is part of the job. You see the great and not-so-great directors and talent everyday.

3 • You locate the impossible. Chicken suit for a website? Monkey wrangler — and monkeys — for a TV campaign? Photographer who jumps from planes...in Alaska? You can find them.

4 • When you make it to the bigtime: You watch the money (big bucks); you find the location (Johannesburg, Thailand, or Aspen?); you see the big picture.

5 • You work with outstanding photographers, film directors, casting agents,

videographers, performance artists, typographers, and people who make beautiful things every day.

Such projects aren't just logistical challenges, they're also creative opportunities. "It could have just been a boring sales video," says Chris Folkens, a production assistant at Burnett, about an in-house video project, "but we wanted to make it slick and exciting and think about how we could cut it together and structure it so that it would be very engaging. It's a challenge. It's what you do with that challenge that really makes the job fun."

What production assistants do with such challenges tells senior producers a lot about their talent and passion for the business. Those that consistently make the most of such opportunities will be given more complicated projects and promoted faster. For a closer look at what goes into an in-house video project, check out what DDB Associate Broadcast Producer Nate Brown has to say later in this chapter about producing the Battling the Ordinary video.

One of the more complicated projects production assistants handle early on is radio. To produce a radio spot, the assistant must audition talent, make travel arrangements if the recording session is being done out of town, find and hire a music house, make sure rights to the music are available and affordable, locate any needed sound effects, and work with the creative team to supervise the recording and editing sessions.

As Meyer points out, "A lot of it is time management, planning and being organized, and always thinking several steps ahead. You're always on your toes, and you're always juggling." But, notes Folkens, whether it's an in-house video or a radio spot, "At the core of it is knowing how to sit down and talk to editors, sound designers, and composers and really get something out of the final product that's going to sell and that's going to stand out. Helping make that happen is basically what this job is all about."

What a Junior Interactive Producer Might Tackle

Because the interactive production world is growing by leaps and bounds, you should realize how interactive job descriptions match those of other media and how they differ. Interactive producers work on scoping the digital project, concepting its idea and architecture, then building and delivering the site or online campaign on strategy and on deadline. Like their broadcast and print counterparts, they work with creatives, account people, programmers, and the usual mix of agency personalities to get content out of the initial stages and then produced quickly.

An assistant interactive producer comes into the job with a few key digital tools: basic programming knowledge, web design and architecture skills, and an

183

understanding of the software that makes it possible to make great ideas look good. The intellectual skills are the same as those required of any good producer: produce on budget and on time, work well in a team, and know what makes good work happen.

In fact, go online and look at the hundreds of calls for interactive producers at all levels. When you hone in on the assistant or junior producers, the job call will probably look something like this:

We need an assistant producer in our Interactive area yesterday. The right person will be super-organized, ready to learn, and good at working in teams. You already know some front-end web and email development tasks, you love Flash, and you have a lock on basic Java script and html coding. Motion design and knowledge of social networking sites a major plus. You'll work to make our Senior Producer's life easier by pushing digital campaigns through the pipeline and working with creatives to implement their ideas. You might even get to show off that video and animation talent you've been meaning to use.

Stress Has Never Been This Much Fun

Although the work is stressful, producers say there's a lot to love about their job. One reason for that, W+K's Kuna believes, is that production provides "an opportunity to be involved in both the creative side of things — helping art directors find the right photographer or illustrator — and the logistical side of things — organizing shoots and solving production issues."

Marni Beardsley, Director of Art Buying at Portland's W+K, echoes that thought: "Creatively I enjoy supporting talented photographers and illustrators and giving them the opportunity to elevate the work. But I also enjoy the production process and finding solutions to every situation." As Kuna says, "It's the best of both worlds, very right brain and left brain."

Certainly, both art and broadcast producers love the creativity of the job. Burnett's Blitz describes it in personal terms: "I always wanted to be in entertainment. I love the idea of creating things that make people's emotions do different things."

The creativity appeals to assistant producers, too. Burnett's Folkens puts it this way: "I love the fact that I get to be creative and have fun at my job so that it doesn't feel as much like work as it did when I worked at an Internet service provider. We are trying to tell a story just as much as a feature filmmaker is. And that's exciting."

Then there's the variety. Secret Weapon's Vidor likes the adventure of each day. "I enjoy not necessarily knowing what I'll be doing when I walk in the office. You walk in having no idea that today they're going to come to you with a board and that tomorrow you're going to be sitting in a meeting with Tom Cruise. Those things are fun, and they happen."

It's not just that every day is different. Every project is different, too. What Crispin's Hoffman loves is this: "Every job brings a whole new set of challenges and opportunities to learn about random and wildly different things." While that can be invigorating, it can also be challenging. And that's especially true for production assistants.

W+K's Meyer points out that the learning curve is steep. "When I get home at night I'm exhausted because it's like a new job everyday. The benefit is that I'm pushed and pushed and pushed. I get to learn things that are new and different and interesting everyday. But the drawback is that it's so draining because there is so much more to learn."

For many, an unexpected perk is the travel. Producers are frequently on the road. They not only spend lots of time in New York and Los Angeles but also in cities all around the globe from London and Prague to Auckland and Rio. Sure they're working, but travel also gives them the chance to have experiences they might not have otherwise.

Best of all, perhaps, is the satisfaction taken not just from a job well done but from the whole experience as well. Ask Burnett's Eisner, and she'll tell you, "When you're flipping through a magazine and see something you've done, you feel really good about it, either the deal you struck, the camaraderie you had with the creatives, or the relationship you had with the photographer. Not all projects are fun, and I'd be lying if I said they were. But there's enough joy in the biz to come back and do it all again."

Speed Kills or How New Technology Is Impacting Production
The speed that new technology makes possible may not kill, but it certainly can endanger the quality of the final product. Because digital technology allows everyone to move faster, the production team is expected to drive the project at warp speed. According to Samantha Jaffoni, a senior art producer at Publicis in New York, "The faster turnaround time for an ad often doesn't give enough time for creative development." In fact, says Arnold's Favat, "When the production process is super accelerated, sometimes you don't even have time to take a breath to reflect a little because you're just jamming through it. But is that the best way to work?" Whether it is or not, producers admit that accelerated schedules are now a fact of life.

185

Technology also opens new possibilities for all producers, no matter the media landscape they're in. As Crispin's Hoffman indicates, technology makes it more important than ever to consider how the campaign elements can all work together. For example, she explains, her agency was working on a campaign that would be built around an animated character. When the creative team was discussing how they would shoot the print ad, they realized they could photograph it in a way that would allow them to use the shots of the character in print, on the web, and as the basis for the animations on TV. That kind of thinking, Hoffman notes, allows the client to extend the money devoted to print and use it to cover a variety of media.

Moreover, shooting spots for the Internet and television at the same time offers the producer, writer, and art director interesting, new creative opportunities. For TBWA\Chiat\Day's Yee, "Shooting a spot for the Internet can be really exciting and challenging. Since you aren't just limited to 30 seconds, you can tell a bigger story."

There's no better example of that than the award-winning BMW films, a series of eight short films all starring Clive Owen with such A-list directors as John Frankenheimer, Ang Lee, John Woo, and Tony Scott. Developed by Fallon Minneapolis in 2001 and 2002 and released on both the Internet and DVD, the project was both a creative and a marketing success that generated more than 14 million viewings while building a powerful brand image for BMW.

Most creative teams would agree that having to work a bit faster and do even more planning in advance is a small price to pay for that sort of opportunity.

Helping Sorel Take to the Slopes
Eric Terchila, Copywriter and Jeremy Boland, Art Director, Borders Perrin Norrander, Portland, Oregon

Sorel's non-traditional campaign communicates how the boots are designed for winter survival, recreation, and fun. However, due to a limited budget, we had to find media placements in highly visible locations at little or no cost. What better place for the "In Case of Emergency" boxes than a ski resort? We launched in Snow Bird, Utah at the beginning of the ski season. The only media cost associated with the campaign was for our lift tickets.

The production costs, however, weren't so simple. We realized it would be quite difficult to produce three-dozen well-crafted boxes on our limited budget. We sought estimates from promotional companies but quickly discovered this project exceeded their capabilities. Finally, we came upon a company on the east coast that could design the boxes for one-fourth the price of the other suppliers we contacted.

About two weeks before the ship date, the owner called with some unfortunate and unexpected news — he didn't think he would be able to have the boxes ready in time to meet the agreed upon ship date. We calmly explained to him that an extension was not an option. He told us he would work around the clock if he had to, but missing our launch date was a real possibility.

We arrived in Utah on a Friday night, collectively holding our breaths. Our shipment arrived on two enormous shipping flats the following morning, a mere two hours before our client expected them to be positioned at various locations on the slopes.

Once our truckload of material arrived at Snow Bird, only one obstacle remained — permission to install them. We approached individual chairlift operators and told them if they allowed us to place our props near their stations, they could have the boots at the end of the day, provided nobody actually took them (which, in many cases, people did). With that personal incentive, they obliged. And the end result, albeit at the eleventh hour, was a true work of craftsmanship. Nothing says beauty like a 20 cubic inch violent orange box containing a pair of burly boots.

For the weekend, our bright orange boxes were displayed in plain view of each and every skier and snowboarder as they got on and off the chairlifts. Our placement couldn't have been more effective. The concept was well received — especially by those lucky size niners with enough audacity to break the glass.

Skills Producers Need to Bring to the Table

Let's say production is starting to sound interesting. What kinds of skills and knowledge will it take to turn your interest into a job? Having a few specialized skills can certainly be an advantage. What's just as important is having enthusiasm plus the kinds of abilities and interpersonal skills that can be developed in school, during internships, or even in some of those totally meaningless jobs you've probably held while in college. As Burnett's Eisner says, "Many skills can be learned, but I think personable people excel at the job."

Specialized Broadcast Production Skills

Nobody is going to expect a broadcast production assistant to pick up a camera and shoot a spot or sit down and edit one. Even producers aren't expected to do that. But it will be extremely helpful to at least be familiar with what the Avid and editing programs like Final Cut Pro can do. Knowing how to tell a story in film, having a grasp of the editorial process, and understanding what makes for an effectively edited sequence are even more important.

That sort of knowledge is necessary for putting together the kinds of in-house videos that most assistants handle early on. Of course, it's the sort of thing that could be picked up on the job. But there's so much else to learn, it's a real advantage if you already have a handle on the basics of film storytelling and are familiar with some of the equipment and computer programs used in the business. Any additional technical know-how will also come in handy. Burnett's Folkens makes the point well: "Because I had a working knowledge of sound editing from doing it on my own, I could communicate an idea in the editor's terminology. And that helped me be more effective on the job."

Nonetheless, many producers say they've hired assistants who didn't have a film background. "When you start out as an assistant," notes Arnold's Favat, "you're not shooting spots; you're not producing anything. You're doing a lot of start-up work. So while it's great if a kid has gone to film school, we don't want to exclude anyone by what their degree is in." For W+K's Selis, "it's not so much knowing how to do it as being able to learn how to do it quickly."

Battling the Ordinary:
Producing Internal Videos that Grab Attention
Nate Brown, Associate Broadcast Producer, DDB, Chicago

At the end of every year, the Chicago office of DDB showcases the talents of its employees through its Enemies of the Ordinary program. Enemies of the Ordinary is an art gallery of sorts that's set up in the halls of the agency to display artistic works employees do in their free time — everything from woodworking and dog training to painting and even Boy Scout leadership.

To document this program, I often produce an internal agency video, which is shown at the agency Christmas party. In mid-October, I'm assigned an art director and writer, and we start working on a concept that creatively ties all of these people together and emphasizes the very meaning of being an "Enemy of the Ordinary." This process is very much like producing a TV commercial, except our budget is less and the video's running time is longer, typically two to five minutes.

I especially enjoyed producing the video that was built around a boxing theme and emphasized how DDB employees "battle" the ordinary through their artistic endeavors outside of the agency. The goal was to produce the video at a boxing gym in downtown Chicago and put DDB employees and their art work inside the boxing ring.

Once the concept was approved, I set out to find a boxing ring where we could shoot. Eventually I found a beautiful athletic club in Chicago. Then we had to secure a location agreement and make sure our production insurance, which is required for every shoot, was in place.

Since our budget was limited, we had to find a format that would maximize our production value while still falling within our small budget. We decided to shoot on high definition video, which gave us a dramatic, cinematic look.

The art director on the project is an aspiring director. So he signed on to direct the action as well as art direct the piece. He worked closely with me in determining the look, schedule, and production plan for the video. I made sure the videographer was aware of the shot list and the potential challenges. We even went to the location beforehand to walk through the shots. We had a lot of people to film in only one day of production. So planning was critical.

The crew shot for 12 hours and filmed 10 people from the agency. The director asked for a stylized look that included heavy use of a fog machine to add drama to the video and some texture to the empty space surrounding the boxing ring. For each take, we had to keep using the fog machine, and that slowed things down. We also needed multiple shots and extensive coverage of each individual to give us options in the edit. Our director also wanted the piece to be shot music video style, and this thorough coverage helped us achieve that look.

189

We designed our shots to cover each person in a way that was representative of their "art" but still in keeping with the battling the ordinary theme. For example, for an improvisational comedian, we lowered a microphone into the center of the ring much like an announcer uses at a boxing match.

Unfortunately, another 10 people involved could not make it to the shoot. So we shot background plates around the ring where we could composite in blue screen footage of them.

When we finished shooting, we took the footage to our in-house editor at DDB. The only sound we used was a rock track with a great beat. We went through a number of revisions and eventually locked the picture. We were then able to interest a very good colorist at a local film transferring facility to color the film and give it a unique, stylized look.

The video showed at the House of Blues for the DDB Christmas party and was a great success!

Specialized Knowledge for Art Production

Just as it helps broadcast assistants to have an understanding of framing and editing, so too it's useful for an assistant art producer to know what makes for a good photograph in terms of composition and lighting. While there's no need to know how to use computer programs like Photoshop, it's good to be familiar with how those programs can be used to retouch images. Knowledge of certain technical aspects of the photographic process such as resolution, film stocks, and printing comes in handy as well.

Such knowledge is hugely helpful but not essential. Producers say they definitely hire candidates who don't have it. What is most critical is having a good eye and a natural sense of what makes for a good photograph. That sense can, of course, be refined by just spending a lot of time looking at photographs in museums and magazines. "While I dabbled in photography in college," W+K's Beardsley recalls, "I spent even more time keeping abreast of talented photographers. When I should have been studying, instead I could be found pouring over the latest fashion magazines and scrutinizing the layout, design, and photography of each story."

Studying those images, Marissa Eller, an art producer at New York's Bartle Bogle Hegarty advises, can help you "begin to ask questions that allow you to see the bigger picture. The set they chose wasn't an accident. The models and wardrobe they chose weren't accidents. The lighting wasn't an accident. Every detail was planned." Considering those issues when examining a photograph helps develop the kind of larger understanding an art producer needs. That understanding will definitely come through in a job interview.

Specialized Knowledge for Interactive and Digital Producers

Just like the other areas, it's all about knowing what works in the medium. You have to know the basics — Photoshop, Illustrator, Flash — and then layer on some specialties. Maybe you love short films and can use Final Cut Pro in your sleep. Maybe motion programs are part of how you understand the online experience. Maybe you've gotten into social networking sites, blogging, or gaming. All of this expertise helps young producers grow the ideas placed in front of them.

"I walked in to my first production job knowing some basic game programming," one young San Francisco producer said, "and because I was the guy who could answer those basic questions, I got all the assignments. We ended up creating a digital cluster of games for one client because I was ready to stay late and try some new things." In three years, he's moved from assistant to senior producer, leading a team of five people in his department.

And, of course, the digital world now touches all areas of production. So soon interactive producers may see the job much the way any other producer does.

What Every Producer Needs

Sure broadcast, art, and digital producers each need a few specialized skills. But they also need a more general skill set and a wide range of knowledge.

Knowledge of Advertising, Business and Cultural Flotsam

Even though producers are dealing with creative and aesthetic issues, they need an understanding of advertising and business. "When I went to college," Publicis' Jaffoni remembers, "I focused on both business and communication. And I felt like that helped me because as an art producer you're dealing with the money side of it as well as the creative side." Moreover, W+K's Kuna feels that "as you take on bigger projects you need an ability to communicate with clients and understand their brands and their needs. Having an understanding of business and advertising definitely helps with that."

Advertising is a business where it's essential to know about a lot more than business. That's the exciting thing. Interests in things like anime, comics, thrasher metal, graffiti, mid-century furniture, costuming, and a host of other subjects can prove to be surprisingly valuable. "There's a certain confidence people have in you," notes W+K's Selis, "if they feel like you know what's going on out there."

191

After all, a producer has to help advise the creative team about all kinds of choices from music to art, and that team needs to have confidence in the producer's judgment. Art directors and writers will often simply refer to movies, music, or architecture, for example, in order to explain what they are trying to communicate. Producers have to understand those references.

"The All You Can Eat Buffet Is Not a Challenge" and Other Life Lessons from TLC

Molly Shaaf, Broadcast Producer, The Martin Agency, Richmond Virginia

Recently, I produced the TV commercials for the brand re-launch of The Learning Channel. The creative team worked with our client to come up with a brilliant campaign idea to complement the new tag line "Live and Learn."

The creatives began thinking of TLC not only as a place of learning but also as a place to learn funny life lessons like "merlot and e-mail don't mix." Then the creative team thought wouldn't it be cool if you not only learned those life lessons but could also collect figurines that would help you remember them. That was the key that brought the campaign to life. But the campaign was possible only because the clients embraced the thought of using humor and were willing to not take themselves too seriously.

We shot and edited 11 TV commercials in just three months. When we began production, the first decision we made was to hire an animation and visual effects company to design porcelain-like figurines. Because we only had 12 weeks to finish the campaign, we decided to save time by creating the figurines digitally rather than making real models.

KNOW WHEN TO NOT DO-IT-YOURSELF.

MERLOT AND E-MAIL DON'T MIX.

When you create an integrated campaign, you have to consider how elements developed for one area will be used in other parts of the campaign. So using digital figurines also made it easier to pass the figurines along to the interactive, manufacturing, and public relations groups, for example.

Of course, right before we were to shoot, we decided it was important to have a few real figurines made so that an actor could pick one up and reference it. Fortunately, we found a model maker who would do a rush fabrication in just seven days.

Once the figurine design and production were underway, we began our director search. As a producer, one of my main jobs is to be up on the latest directors. The trick is to find the one director who grasps what your project is about, who is interested in your project (not just for the money), and who can add something to it. Many times, you work on a script for so long that you become almost too close to it.

So it's great when a director and editor come on board and can offer new perspectives that make your campaign that much stronger.

We found an excellent director in Matt Aselton of Epoch Films. He directs talent effortlessly and enables the actors to be so comfortable in their environment that the performances get better with each take.

Matt had a number of suggestions that enhanced the commercials. One of his best ideas was for our Shoulder Pads spot in which a woman throws on an awful '80s outfit with very wide shoulder pads and makes the mistake of wearing it proudly to the office. Matt came up with the idea of putting a metal detector in the entrance of the woman's office building. When she walked through the metal detector in her massive shoulder pads she had to turn her body in order to get through. It was such a subtle moment and such a great addition to the spot.

The director gave our editors, Jason MacDonald and Lawrence Young from Cosmo Street Editorial, terrific material to work with. Then they took the spots to the next level by adding their expertise in cutting and comedic timing.

The spots have been so successful that My Space has over 30,000 registered friends of Life Lessons. TLC has also had great success in manufacturing the figurines for sale to anyone who wants to hold a piece of fun knowledge like "before getting intimate, turn off the TV." You can even send your own Life Lesson to your friends on their websites. So it's a quintessential integrated campaign. It was not only a joy to work on but also the most fun I have ever had on a production.

Juggling Skills

Producers also need to be skilled multi-taskers. Just to produce one campaign, says Marc Carter, a senior art producer at The Martin Agency, may require 300 phone calls and involve 600 to 700 details. Most producers are working on several campaigns at the same time all in various stages of production. Not only are there a million things to do, but all of them also need to be done immediately. That makes being able to prioritize and decide what needs to happen first critical.

Those decisions also have to be made fast because deadlines are extremely tight. And, oh yeah, things change. So it's important to be able to reorder priorities quickly. "If you're the kind of person who has to start at one and end at ten," suggests The Martin Agency's Hicks, "you're going to be frustrated. It's about being able to jump around and still keep it orderly because things change very quickly." Crispin's Hoffman says being a producer requires a unique personality: "It's handy being a type A to help keep everyone around you organized and in the loop. But at the same time you need to be laid back and able to roll with the punches when things go awry as they inevitably will."

Willingness to Play Psychologist

If you took a few psychology courses in college, they're going to come in handy. "A producer is also a therapist," points out Secret Weapon's Vidor. "You're constantly put in a situation where you're kind of trying to smooth out problems or solve them with a lot of egos, with a lot of creative people who don't agree and are angry."

Good listening skills and intuition will help you quickly understand someone else's perspective. That ability also helps producers listen to differing points of view and then guide the discussion to the proper conclusion without alienating anyone. Doing that is not easy. That's why producers need to be comfortable dealing with conflict and drama because there can be lots of both.

Of course, it's also important to be nice or, as one producer says, "to not be an asshole." It's a people-driven business, and "if you piss people off for a living, you're not going to get very far," notes Burnett's Folkens. That's because producers have to solicit favors from vendors whether it's getting a director to lower a bid or work within a tight schedule. W+K's Selis knows how important working well with people can be: "Somebody is going to have to have a reason to do something for you. And if you've got an attitude or are too abrasive, they're not going to want to help you."

A No-Task-Too-Small Mentality

Because producers are frequently surrounded by people with giant egos, they also need to check their own egos at the door. That's especially important for production assistants. Publicis' Jaffoni is hardly alone in noting that many juniors don't want to do "grunt work." "Just because they're out of school, they don't think they're going to be doing things like schlepping books around or filing paperwork. I'm a senior art producer," she says, "and I still do it. I mean you're doing stuff, and you're like, 'I can't believe I'm doing it.' But you have to do it to get the job done right."

Of course, being willing to do the dirty work is also about a work ethic. And that's just as critical. As Secret Weapon's Vidor puts it, "If you are willing to start at the bottom and you understand that you have to start there and you're willing to work nights and weekends and you're the one that's always saying, 'Hey, I can do that,' those are the things that will get you noticed."

The bottom line is desire. That's what drives a person to do jobs others scorn and what makes them willing to stay late or to change everything at the last minute to make sure a job is done right. Every producer interviewed mentioned the need for that kind of heart. But nobody said it better than Crispin's Hoffman: "School helps. But passion is what drives the individual to find the solutions that make things happen." That's what matters above all else. So don't be cool. "Cool," says the noted architect Bruce Mau, "is conservative fear dressed in black." Be a passionate problem solver, and you'll also be a great producer.

The Get It Factor

You'll also need to decide what size agency you'd like to work for. Art producers have less choice in the matter because those positions are primarily found in mid and large-sized agencies. In smaller agencies, the art director often handles most of the duties of the art producer. But almost every size agency has a broadcast production department.

A Career in Production Starts Now

The best time to start preparing for a production career is while you're still in college, and there's no easier way to begin than with your classes. If it's art production you're interested in, art history classes help refine your eye by providing the opportunity to study the lighting and composition of great photographs and even paintings. Entry level photography classes can provide an introduction to film stocks and lenses.

For those interested in broadcast production, film history courses provide valuable insights into editing and composition, while film classes themselves offer an introduction to everything from developing a strong script and organizing a shoot to training in how to direct, light, shoot, and edit a scene.

Whether you're interested in art, broadcast, or interactive production, courses in advertising and business are also important. Producers need a larger understanding of advertising and branding if they are going to help make sure the finished work meets the clients' objectives and is appropriate for the brand.

Classes in interpersonal communication and leadership studies can be useful as well. According to Burnett's Folkens, "A lot of this is really about being able to rally people and not step on anyone's toes. My studying speech comm helped me be very well prepared to do that."

Find an Internship

Not surprisingly, an internship is also critical. As W+K's Meyer points out, "An internship is the best job interview you can have." Secret Weapon's Vidor sums it up this way: "Interns get to know the agency, and you get to know them. You get to know the work they can do, what they're capable of, and whether they're reliable and responsible."

So if you can get an internship with an agency in production, do so. But if you can't, then get one with a film director, photographer, or post-production house. Even better, do both. Understanding what goes into a shoot or how the raw film is turned into the final product will be invaluable if you become an agency producer. And who knows, you might decide you like the production side of the business enough to look for a job with a photographer or director. After all, there are lots more of them than there are ad agencies.

What Nobody Told Me and I Wish I'd known
Amy Jarvis, Senior Art Production Manager, Leo Burnett, Chicago

I think I am lucky because I'm happy in my job more often than not. If you think about how much time you actually spend at work, the scale better tip toward the good rather than the bad. In retrospect, it took me a while to get here. In fact, it took me seven years, and I'm still one step away from my true goal, art buyer/producer. The picture is getting clearer though, and there are definitely some things I wish I'd known about art producing when I started.

The majority of people you find in an agency have no advertising degree. For example, I have a degree in art history, my boss never went to college, and the VP of my department was a butler. We all found our way to art production through very different paths. From what I have seen and heard, it is all about contacts; just get your foot in the door. Get an internship, do as many informational interviews as you can, make as many contacts as you can and keep them. I wish someone had said, "Swallow your pride, don't be shy, and call anyone!"

If a career in advertising art production is what you want, beware: It takes a lot of work and patience to get there. Financially you are not going to be the next Gordon Gekko. And sometimes people (creative, account management, reps, etc.) are difficult and hurtful. But when you find that creative person you can partner with, when you meet that photographer who is truly a visionary, or when your jobs finally come in on budget 99 times out of 100, the job is worth it.

There is an old producer saying, "Cheap, Good, Fast. Pick two." It means you can have it cheap and good, but it will never be fast. You can have it fast and cheap, but it won't be much good. Finally, you can have it good and fast, but it does not come cheap. Production is about NEVER saying no (there is always a solution), getting in tune with someone else's creative vision (even when you are not a fan), and keeping your cool at all costs. No one wants to work with a judgmental, negative screamer. We must embrace the creative product and bring it to life.

The long and short of it is get out there and meet people. Get to know the industry, know what you want, know the job you are applying for. I recently interviewed a few candidates for a new position. The candidate that impressed me the most was a secretary who had called probably every person in the greater Chicago area she could get her hands on to research the company and the position. We got no less than seven phone calls speaking on her behalf. She came into the interview educated about the industry, confident in what she wanted, and not afraid to work. She got the job.

Start Networking

You'll also want to add networking to your to do list. As Meyer explains, "I learned that one of the key ways of getting jobs in this industry in general is networking. When somebody's got to hire a new employee and they've got 200 resumes on their desk and two employees say, 'wait, I've got somebody,' of course, it makes a huge difference." Not surprisingly, then, Burnett's Eisner believes, "You should take advantage of any friends you may have. It never hurts to have someone who knows you and knows your capabilities who will speak highly on your behalf."

Why start networking before you even need the network? Because it's not an efficient process. You can meet with family friends, join professional groups, conduct informational interviews, and keep the words "I'm looking to break into production when I graduate" on your lips no matter where you are. After months and months of effort, you may still have nothing to show for it.

Then one day, if you're lucky, the dime drops, and someone you talk to opens a door that leads to an opportunity.

Consider how DDB's Brown went about networking. While going to school in St. Louis, he met a junior member of the advertising department at Anheuser-Busch who offered to help and told Brown to call him every Friday. He did and got nowhere. Months passed, and Brown joined the St. Louis Advertising Club and began to get to know the professionals there. Then one day he met a man who knew August Busch III. That led to an interview with a senior marketing official at Budweiser who liked Brown's credentials and put him in touch with the head of production at DDB Chicago, the Budweiser agency. Thanks to all of his networking efforts and his credentials, when Brown graduated he had a job as an associate producer at DDB.

When the opportunity finally comes, you'll want to be ready. The classes and internships will have helped you polish your interpersonal and business skills, given you a grasp of the business, and maybe even some experience that an agency will find impressive. Hopefully, all of that experience has also given you one more thing: Work to show in an interview.

Create Work to Show

Certainly, having material to show isn't essential in order to be hired, but it can give you an edge if the material is strong. Says W+K's Kuna, when interviewing for an art production post it's good to "bring anything to an interview you feel will help you illustrate your skills. If you're a photographer, you should show some samples of your work." But what if you're not a photographer? The Martin Agency's Hicks advises, "Bring in ads that you feel have interesting photographs to show that at least you have an eye for photography."

It may be even more important to show work if you're interested in being a broadcast producer. While agencies say they hire broadcast production assistants who have little actual production experience beyond an internship, certainly if you have a reel of work that you can show, it can make getting in the door a whole lot easier.

As Brown suggests, "Get involved with production in college and even as early as high school. Gain experience by creating a body of work because that work says a lot about your credibility. That's ultimately what got me hired." Most of the spots on Brown's reel cost $500 or less to produce. In short, you don't have to be a millionaire to put together a reel. As he recalls, "The stuff I was doing was not comparable to high-end commercials. But my boss saw potential in what I'd done and knew I had experience producing at some level. He said that gave me an edge over the hundreds of other applicants."

In putting a reel together, Burnett's Folkens feels you should "just try to look at it from the perspective of the agency's head of production and think what are they going to want to see." Folkens assumed they'd want to see a bunch of styles and not just one.

So his reel contained music videos, spec commercials, and even a short film. In making the final DVD with his work on it, he made sure it was very professional, had a moving menu, and "showed that I had put a lot of hours into it and that it wasn't just plastered together in 30 minutes with a handwritten cover." As he points out, "It's a very image-oriented world out there, and you really have to think about how you're going to be perceived."

In the past, it wasn't easy for students to get broadcast production jobs right out of school. Reels were difficult and expensive to put together. So most candidates didn't have them, and that could make it difficult for them to convince agencies that they had the necessary skills for the job.

But today it's relatively easy to get the tools needed to assemble a reel, and that's opening the doors to more broadcast production jobs. "I think that there's going to be more and more young producers," suggests Brown, "because we grew up when digital video was really taking off, and it made all of these tools really accessible. So I think more and more people are going to have the opportunity to have a reel. That's the thing that's really exciting."

Decide on the Kind of Agency that's Right for You

Before starting your search for an agency production job, you need to make decisions about the kind of agency you want to work for and what size is best for you. Some producers are more interested in business issues such as budgets, negotiations, and contracts, while others enjoy the aesthetic and creative questions. You need to decide where your primary interests lie. If you prefer the business side, then you'll want to look for a job with a more account driven agency. If you are more excited by aesthetic issues, you'll want to look for a more creative shop whose work you admire.

Many industry professionals suggest that if you have a choice, starting at a small or mid-sized shop is best. For one thing, it's a good way to be exposed to more aspects of the business and be allowed to do a wider variety of tasks. The Martin Agency's Hicks believes that in smaller shops, "You wear more hats. The bigger the agency, the more you have to stay in your own little box."

What's more, observes Burnett's Eisner, "In a large agency the pace is frantic, and it can be a little daunting." In fact, "You have to buckle up, and keep your eyes and ears peeled and your hands and arms in the car at all times," points out Crispin's Hoffman. That can make a smaller agency a more comfortable place to start.

Happy Endings

Most searches have happy endings but not necessarily expected ones. So let's say you start your search, and the worst case happens. Despite all of your preparation, there's not a production job to be had in either a large or small agency. "Be patient, " says Secret Weapon's Vidor, "there are plenty of places to land." Both halves of that sentence are important. First off, be patient. Many of the senior executives interviewed said when they looked for their first job, a long time passed between the initial phone call and the moment when they got the job they had dreamed of. Just because a door slams, don't give up. That's not easy, and even telling yourself that it's happened to dozens of others doesn't make it any easier.

Crispin's Senior Integrated Art Producer Jessica Hoffman helps direct the visual component of the agency's creative work. As such, she must be ready to troubleshoot, find the best talent, fulfill the creative team's concept...all within the same hour.

What does make it easier is the second part of Vidor's advice: There are plenty of places to land and gain experience while you wait. As DraftFCB's Mitchell points out, "There are as many ways into this business as there are producers." Advises Fallon's Smith, "There isn't that one place where you can go and learn how to be a producer. People come into it from all sorts of areas like working on the production side with a photographer, being a rep, or coming in from other departments in the agency."

If you can't immediately find a job as an agency producer, you might want to look for a different job in the agency. As W+K's Meyer suggests, "Just getting your foot in the door is important even though it's not your ideal job." That way you are on the inside where you can learn more about the business, meet people, and demonstrate to them what you can do. Then when a production job does open up, you're sure to have champions inside the agency, and that will often lead to a job.

Another way in is by working for film directors or photographers, as artists' reps, or in post-production houses. "If you're working on set with a production crew," says Fallon's Talbott, "and if you have your eyes wide open and your ears open and you're hustling, you can take it all in." Crispin's Hoffman believes "that kind of production experience helps because you're going to know the tricks of the trade and all the other things you can do to pull off a job, especially one that's in trouble."

If you take a job in some aspect of production before applying to an agency, you're not side tracking yourself. You're simply following another path that ultimately leads where you want to go.

As Secret Weapon's Vidor puts it, "That first job may not be the place you want to land. But eventually, if you know what you're looking for and what you want to do, you'll get to the place you really want to be. And then you can start from there with all of the knowledge you gathered up along the way. And you'll feel good about the journey because you'll know that no time was wasted after all."

Building a Career

Once you take a job as an assistant producer, it usually takes between one and three years to become a Producer, depending on your experience and the quality of your work. Even though the wait may try your patience, you'll probably want to keep that job and not go looking for another production job until you're promoted to producer.

Once you are, you may want to start to look around. Moving to a new agency not only is the best way to get a major salary bump, but it also gives you a chance to work on new products with new people and to learn from those experiences. You can put what you learn to work as you move through the ranks from producer to senior producer to group head to head of production.

Making a Difference

Bill Bernbach, legendary founder of DDB, once observed that those who work at advertising agencies can use their influence either to "vulgarize society" or "to lift it onto a higher level." One way agencies lift up society is through pro bono work, which is done either for free or at cost, and advocacy advertising, which is usually done at a reduced fee. Producers play a key role in those efforts by finding ways to get the work produced inexpensively since the projects usually have little or no budget.

As The Martin Agency's Hicks points out, pulling off these low budget projects is "really about establishing mutual relationships with people because then you can ask them to do you a favor for a pro bono client." Adds Burnett's Eisner, "Finding a way to get the best possible person for the job and finding a way to work a deal with him where he feels honored to do this for no fee is very rewarding and gives me great personal satisfaction."

Pro bono clients are also rewarding in other ways as well. Hicks, for example, "loves working on the John F. Kennedy Museum Library because I'm exposed to things that normally I wouldn't see. Like photocopies of notes between John and Robert Kennedy. It's amazing to be able to read them and hold them in your hand."

The major reward that comes from working on advocacy and pro bono accounts is knowing that you are helping to make a difference. Take the Truth anti-tobacco campaign. It's credited with contributing significantly to the historic decline in youth smoking since the campaign's launch.

In an interview with *Shoot* magazine, one of the originators of the Truth campaign, Crispin's Dave Clemans, put it this way: "You don't get a chance to work for the common good of man every day in advertising. My girl friend teaches third grade, and we have this joke between us that she's helping America's youth while I demoralize them. This campaign helps keep the chips in my corner when that argument comes up."

A Pretty Cool Place to Be

Production is a very rewarding corner of the agency business. Producers get to solve interesting problems in highly creative ways, work with some of the most talented photographers, directors, editors, and musicians in the world, and travel to exciting locations, all while pulling down a very nice salary.

Even after being in the business for over two decades, DraftFCB's Mitchell still says, "I love every part of this job." Nothing says more about the satisfaction that comes your way as a producer.

Resources

Great Resources + Inspiration

---

5 Great Books to Read on Great Advertising
Luke Sullivan. *Hey Whipple Squeeze This. A Guide to Creating Great Ads*
Mario Pricken. *Creative Advertising: Ideas and Techniques from the World's Best Campaigns*
Warren Berger. *Advertising Today*
Joe Duffy. *Brand Apart*
Jim Atchison. *Cutting Edge Advertising I and II*

---

5 Great Books to Read on Account + Brand Management
Jon Steel. *Perfect Pitch: The Art of Selling Ideas and Winning New Business*
Douglas Holt. *How Brands Become Icons*
Robert Solomon. *The Art of Client Service*
Marty Neumeier. *Brand Gap*
Tim Williams. *Take A Stand for Your Brand*

---

5 Great Resources for Account Planning + Strategy
Jon Steel. *Truth, Lies & Advertising The Art of Account Planning*
Lisa Fortini-Campbell. *Hitting the Sweet Spot*
AAAA Account Planning Conference Annuals
Russell Davies. russelldavies.typepad.com/
The Account Planning Group. www.apg.org.uk/

---

5 Great Things to Read on the Media World
www.mediapost.com
www.imediaconnection.com
Helen Katz. *The Media Handbook*
Gavin Lucas + Michael Dorrian. *Guerrilla Advertising: Unconventional Brand Communication*
One Show Interactive Annuals

---

5 Great Things to Read to Make You Smarter
The Copy Workshop. *The Book of Gossage*
Seth Godin. www.sethgodin.com
Trendwatching.com
Arthur Asa Berger. *Ads, Fads, and Consumer Culture: Advertising's Impact on American Character and Society.* Third Edition
Edward Tufte on design. www.edwardtufte.com

5 Great Online Destinations to Inspire Creativity

www.visualthesaurus.com

The One Club Creative Showcase www.oneclub.org/co/showcase/

www.dannygregory.com

TED Conferences www.ted.com

www.howdesign.com

5 Great Things to Read for Career Planning (along with this book)

Sally Hogshead. *Radical Careering* + www.radicalcareering.com

Kevin Carroll. *Rules of the Red RubberBall*

Fast Company Magazine. + www.fastcompany.com

Brad Karsh. www.jobbound.com

Agency sites + blogs with inspiration such as www.bartleboglehegarty.com
wkstudio.typepad.com, www.cpbgroup.com,
www.goodbysilverstein.com, www.jwtintelligence.com

5 Great Opportunities to Show Student Work

The One Club in Portfolio Reviews + Annual Education Festival in May

Archive Competition

American Advertising Federation Addys through local ad clubs

Cannes Young Lions

CMYK Magazine

5 Great Trade Pubs/Sites to Get You Ready

one. a magazine

Adweek + adweek.com

Creativity + adcritic.com

www.theadfeed.com

Communication Arts + www.commarts.com

Your Résumé: Your Primary Weapon in the Battle for a Great Job

Brad Karsh

At some point after you graduate, there will be a company that will pay you tens of thousands of dollars a year to do something for them. Crazy, but true! My goal is to make sure you find one of those companies.

The tricky part is that there are often hundreds, and sometimes thousands, of people applying for the same jobs you are. That's not to say it's impossible to land one, but it does require some work.

It's NOT like applying to college, where even if you don't get in to your first choice there will always be a "safety school." In many instances, the job equivalent of a safety school is flipping burgers at the fast food restaurant.

The importance of this document is absolute. Read on and find out how to show yourself in the best possible way.

The Résumé

Ah, the résumé — a simple 8 x 11 sheet of paper is, for better or for worse, the key to your future. You've sunk an incredible amount of time, money, and effort into school, and you enter the battle for a job with just this one piece of paper as the primary weapon in your arsenal.

It better be as good as it can be!

The résumé is typically the first step in the job search process. Some people have résumés coming out of high school; others graduate without one at all. Your goal should be to land somewhere in between!

Quite simply, a résumé is an ad for you. Much like an ad you'd see in a magazine, you have one sheet of paper to tell your story. And just like an ad, you have to know your target and know exactly what you want to say to them.

The Target

Your target is the Recruiting Director or Hiring Manager for the job that you're applying for. Plain and simple. It's not your friends, or your parents, or your professors, or anyone else. As a result, everything on your résumé needs to be relevant, compelling, and easy to read for that particular Recruiting Director.

Here's the scary part. Recruiting Directors are flooded with résumés.

As a result, they're going to spend a whopping fifteen seconds max looking at your résumé. It's a frightening proposition. Four years of college, all of your internships, jobs, extra curricular activities, leadership, and more, and someone sizes you up in fifteen seconds!

So what are recruiting directors doing in their mysterious fifteen-second scan?

Let's clear up the mystery. They are looking for someone who:
- goes to a good school
- has excellent grades
- is involved in a variety of activities
- shows commitment and leadership in those activities
- has relevant internships or jobs

These points aren't in any particular order because every recruiter will look at these experiences differently. These are, however, the types of attributes that virtually any ad agency is looking for in a new employee.

However, don't freak out if you don't have a 4.0 from Harvard, weren't captain of the basketball team, and still do not have an internship at a major agency on your résumé.

And similarly, don't think that just because you were president of your ad club, you'll get a job anywhere you please.

What makes a great résumé is a combination of skills and attributes, elegantly told. You need to make sure the Recruiting Director knows your story and knows what you've done in the best possible way.

The Sections
There are three sections on every student résumé: Education, Experience, and Activities/Interests. Some résumés may include an Objective.

Objective
Should you have an objective? The answer is simple. Sometimes you need one, and sometimes you don't. For the most part, objectives can be wasted space. An objective like, "to obtain a position that utilizes my strong analytical, teamwork, and leadership skills" is quite frankly bogus. Of course, according to you, you are analytical, and a team player with good leadership skills. But let's be honest. Anyone can write that if they want.

If you are applying for a specific job, then no, you don't need an objective. Recruiting Directors assume your objective is to get that job.

The only time you need an objective is when you are applying to a large company that does not have a specific job opening. In that case, it's helpful for the Recruiting Director to know which department to forward your résumé to.

For situations like these, the objective should be simply, "to obtain a position in the advertising department at Pepsi." Short and sweet.

Education

This should always be the first section on your résumé until you've had your first "real" job. List your school, your degree, your major/minor and your graduation year. You'll want to include your GPA if it's above a 3.2, and you can include your major GPA as well, especially if it's better than your overall. Don't forget to include any study abroad programs.

You may also list any relevant academic scholarships or awards, including things like Dean's List. But don't simply list your scholarships. Make sure their meaning and importance is evident. For instance, many students will put down an entry like: *Skeeter McGee Honorary Scholarship.*

Unfortunately, the Recruiting Directors have no idea what this scholarship is. For all they know, it was given to you by your Uncle Skeeter to fund your enormous pizza habit. Or it was awarded to one student in the entire school based on superior academics, leadership, and involvement! Don't forget to let the reader know.

Here's how a typical Education entry looks:

> *Education*
> *University of Florida — Gainesville, May 2006*
> *Bachelor of Science in Advertising, Spanish Minor*
> *Major GPA: 3.6, Overall GPA: 3.4*
> *C. Arthur Hemminger Scholarship, granted to 20 students based on*
>   *academics*
> *Phi Eta Sigma Honor Society, awarded to freshman*
>   *with GPA of 3.5 or above*
> *Dean's List, Fall 03-present*

Experience

This is officially known as the "meat" of the résumé. The experience section is what will likely make or break your résumé.

What Goes in This Section

The obvious answer is all your relevant jobs and internships. The not-so-obvious answer is other great extra-curricular or volunteer activities you've done.

For instance, if the company you're applying for is looking for leadership skills, the fact that you held an officer position in your ad club is going to go a long way toward making you seem impressive. It's certainly more important to the reader than your job as a waiter at Sweet Willie's Rib Shack. Yet many folks bury this type of extra-curricular involvement in a section at the bottom of their résumé called "other experience" or something else. Don't be that person!

Think back to the beginning of this section. The Recruiting Director reading your résumé is going to spend about 15 seconds looking at it. So you will want to make sure that you always include the most important information at the top of the document.

How to Order Your Experience

Your résumé does not have to be in chronological order. Repeat...your résumé does not have to be in chronological order!

You should list the most important information first. The Recruiting Directors scanning your résumé start at the top and work their way down. If you haven't caught their attention at the beginning, they won't make it to the bottom.

If you worked as a lifeguard in the summer of 2005 but as an intern at FCB in the summer of 2004, put the FCB job first on your résumé. Always remember: Look at your jobs, internships, extra-curricular activities, and volunteer work, and then put them in the order that is most relevant to the reader.

Ordering isn't just top to bottom; it's also left to right. Often students will write:

Fall 2006, University of Virginia Ad Club (President)

The reviewer may not even make it to the word "President," which is, of course, the most important information. It should read:

President, University of Virginia Ad Club, Fall 2006

Dates are least important, and they should be listed last. Your titles or your companies should go first. It's a judgment call as to which you think the reader will find most impressive — just keep it consistent.

Using Your Experience to Set Yourself Apart

How you craft your bullet points under your experiences is the best way to distinguish yourself from everyone else.

Virtually all college students make the mistake of writing a job description as opposed to a list of their accomplishments. They simply describe what anyone in their position (internship, leadership, or extra curricular) did, as opposed to what they specifically accomplished. Let's look at an example:

Account Management Intern, Ogilvy & Mather, New York, NY, Summer 2006
• Assisted AE with new product launch

- *Prepared competitive analysis*
- *Attended brainstorming meetings and agency seminars*

The fact is, ANY account management intern in the history of the advertising industry, whether at Ogilvy or not, can write this exact same statement. All you've done is tell the reader what an account management intern does. And guess what? The reader probably already knows that!

If what is written in a résumé can be written by the person who did the job before, with, or after you, then you haven't done yourself justice. Résumés need to be infused with numbers, accomplishments, and specificity. It's the hardest thing to do, but it will dramatically improve your résumé. When listing your accomplishments, think about the following:

- How was the organization better as a result of YOUR involvement?
- What did YOU specifically accomplish?
- How did YOU do it differently than the person before, after, or in the next cubicle?
- How were YOU selected?

Use facts and figures whenever possible.

It doesn't matter if you were a White House intern or entered numbers into a database at your dad's office. Your ability to sound impressive in this section will dramatically improve your résumé.

Focus Your Experience Around Scope and Results

When you're thinking about what to put under the descriptions of your jobs, internships, extracurriculars, and volunteer work in the experience section, you want to focus on two key areas: scope and results.

Scope deals with the size of the project you worked on. To describe its scope, ask yourself questions like these:

- How many numbers did you enter into the database?
- How many press releases did you write?
- How many people received the newsletter you edited?
- How many accounts did you work on?
- How many ads did you pitch to the client?
- How many people attended the event you planned on campus?

To get a handle on the results of your efforts, consider questions like these:

- What did they use the database for?
- What publications picked up your press release?
- How many donations did you get from your newsletter?
- How successful was the campaign and account you worked on?
- Did your ads increase customer spending?
- Was it the largest campus event in your organization's history?

I cannot stress how important it is to fill your résumé with accomplishments instead of job descriptions. Most students think of their résumé from their perspective and not from that of a recruiting director. In your mind, you know what you did, how hard you worked, and what you accomplished. But that does you absolutely no good if the reader of the résumé doesn't know what you did and what you accomplished.

Recruiting Directors can be a cynical lot. They don't assume the best; they assume the worst. Do statements like, "responsible for all of the documents directed to project manager," "created progress spreadsheets," or "generated ticket sales" mean anything to you? Not really. You have no idea what this employee did. What happens is that a recruiting director ends up not really knowing the extent of your experience. They don't really know if you're qualified for the job. As a result, your résumé doesn't do nearly a good enough job in helping you get noticed.

Let's take a look at how to rewrite the Ogilvy job:

Account Management Intern, Ogilvy & Mather, New York, NY, Summer 2006
- *Assisted AE with most successful new product launch in history, exceeding projections by 15%*
- *Prepared 12-company competitive analysis presented to client's upper management resulting in $250,000 in incremental spending*
- *Overhauled company's advertising library with more than 2,000 commercials spanning 10 years*
- *Selected as one of 4 interns from a pool of 500 candidates*

Companies are looking for candidates who can hit the ground running. You want this section of your résumé to communicate "real world" skills that are easily transferable to a workplace environment. And that's not as hard to do as you may think.

Here's what this entry says about the candidate:
- Can handle a lot of work (reorganized huge tape library)
- Results oriented (competitive presentation resulted in more agency revenue)
- Works well in a team (helped with most successful launch in history)
- Great credentials (selected for highly competitive internship program)

That's not a bad list of skills to have for just about any company. An impressive list of accomplishments doesn't come just from having held great jobs either. In fact, some of those relatively meaningless jobs you've held during school can give you more résumé material than you probably think.

Oftentimes students will lament, "I just entered numbers into a database" and then write that on their résumé. But when you take the time to dig into it and question them about what they did, usually you discover that there's considerably more to it. Often you'll find something like:

Entered more than 1,000 numbers into company's first-ever new business database, helping to grow sales by more than 7%

The key to a strong résumé is an impressive list of accomplishments versus simple job descriptions.

Activities/Interests

Here's a chance to show how involved and interesting you are. This section should include brief listings of your:

- Extra-curriculars and club activities (unless you held a leadership position and listed it in your experience section)
- Intercollegiate, intramural, or club sports
- Volunteer activities and interests

It's a pretty straightforward section and goes something like this:

Activities/Interests
- *Habitat for Humanity, member, 2004 - Present*
- *University of Illinois Ad Club, member, 2004 - 2006*
- *Intramural Softball, captain/league champions, 2005*
- *Relay for Life, volunteer, 2004 - Present*
- *Interests include, biking, traveling, SCUBA diving,*
      and early American history

It's nice to have the last line help "round you out" so you don't seem so impersonal. It's also okay to have one of your last interests be something a bit "out there"...you never know, it could be a nice conversation starter!

Résumé Pitfalls

There are a few things that will hurt your chances of landing a job. Avoid these at all costs!

Typos and Grammatical Errors

With so many people applying for so many jobs, most Recruiting Directors simply throw away all the résumés with typos. It's estimated that 20 percent of résumés out there have typos in them. Don't let yours be one!

Proof it, but remember that spell check doesn't catch everything. Have at least two other people read it, and then read it yourself backwards — from the bottom to the top. Chances are you'll find at least one mistake.

First Person

Résumés should not include "I," "me," "we," or "our." They should be written in objective tense.

Long Sentences

All of your student life, you're trying to stretch when you write — "I need to write a ten page paper, and all I have is two pages of material." In the real world, it's just the opposite. Recruiting Directors don't like to read. So keep it short and compelling.

Use bullet points with your education, experience, and activities/interests entries. Use action verbs to begin each bullet — past tense for experiences in the past and present tense for jobs and activities you are currently involved with. And because you are using bullet points, there should not be any periods on your résumé.

High School

By the time you're a senior in college, you shouldn't have any high school activities or jobs on your résumé unless one is very specifically relevant to the job you're pursuing. Nobody cares anymore that you were Treasurer of the National Honor Society as a junior in high school!

Juniors can have a bit of high school on their résumé and then obviously more for sophomores and freshmen.

Multi-Page Résumés

Keep it to one page. No exceptions.

Crazy Fonts, Funny Colored Paper, Odd Layouts

These things don't help you to stand out; they just make the reader believe you have weak content on your résumé. It's fine to have nice, lightly colored linen paper, but leave the laminated purple résumé, printed sideways, at home.

There's a big difference between "good unique" and "bad unique" when it comes to résumés. Some people think the goal is to get their résumé to stand out any way possible. I've received résumés laminated to look like four-page menus; I've gotten cardboard cutouts of résumés in the shape of a star; and I've received polka dot résumés with streamers attached.

When you flip through a magazine, do you buy every product for every ad that stands out? Of course not. The same goes for a recruiter. What is going to make your résumé get selected is not a gimmick — that only says you have no substance in the résumé. What is going to make your résumé stand out is compelling content, elegantly told. Save the cutouts for art class!

Computer Skills

Unless the job asks for specific computer skills, there's no need to include them. The fact that you know Microsoft Word is not impressive.

These days, it's a given that any new hire is going to know Word, Power-Point, and Excel, or could learn them in a day. There's no need to list basic computer skills on your résumé, unless the job description asks for them. Of course advanced skills, those that are necessary for the job, should always be included.

Students sometimes say, "But I'll need to use Word everyday at the office. Won't they want to know that I know it?" Well, you'll also have to use the telephone everyday, and I sure hope you don't have "Ability to dial telephone" on your résumé.

By the same token, forget about telling recruiting directors that you know Internet Explorer. Is that supposed to impress them or let them know you'll be spending quite a bit of time at work checking out the latest deals on Ebay? Shockingly, about 10 percent of résumés still include the fact that the applicant knows how to use the Internet.

References Available Upon Request

Do you know anyone whose references are NOT available upon request? Don't waste valuable space putting that on your résumé. It's okay to include your references as an attachment.

Photographs and Detailed Personal Information

That's just plain weird.

Now that We've Covered the Details

The résumé is the basic building block of the job search — everything else is supported by your résumé. As you can see though, most students do not start with a strong foundation.

So remember, the key to a great résumé is to:
- Write your accomplishments and not just a job description
- Fill your résumé with facts, figures, and numbers
- Remember the perspective of the recruiting director reading it
- Format the document so it's easy to read
- Focus on the most important information first

Then, once you've crafted an amazing résumé, you're in great shape to dive into the job search.

Good luck!

The Interview

A few practical suggestions gleaned from the experts, collected here so your interviews go smoothly.

Before the Big Day

• Before you ever schedule an interview, practice interviewing with career counselors, job preparation companies, faculty mentors, friends, and family.

• Be proactive and seek out interviews. Openings are not always advertised. So don't be passive and wait to see what comes to you.

• Prepare for the interview by researching the company and, if possible, the person who will be interviewing you.

• Use the description of the position in the job listing to get a sense of the sorts of questions you may be asked. For example, if the job posting says that the company is looking for a detail-oriented person who is a self starter, think of examples where you showed initiative and were very organized and buttoned-up.

• Consider bringing a project or other materials you've worked on with you. Obviously, copywriters and art directors are required to have a portfolio. But account planners, media planners, and account executives can dramatize their relevant knowledge and skills in an interesting manner by showing relevant work. It can also help turn an interview into a conversation.

Make the Most of Your Interview Time

• If you're showing a portfolio, be ready to let the interviewer read without hearing your explanations. If they ask questions, answer with confidence. Don't make excuses for your work.

• Be prepared to talk about each item on your résumé including activities and even the college you attended. Know why you made the choices you did and how they impacted you.

• Be informed about the industry. Interviewers want you to have a point of view about the advertising industry and be able to discuss in a very specific way what appeals to you about it and even what brands you feel are doing it right and why. They don't want to hear you say that you just love advertising and cut out ads and put them on your wall. That tells them nothing.

• Be prepared for questions requiring you to think on your feet like why is *American Idol* so popular or how many boards are on a basketball court. Interviewers are not especially concerned with what you say but how you think through the problem and arrive at an answer.

• Be ready to discuss salary questions. Brad Karsh offers useful advice: Sometimes you can avoid giving a specific figure. For example, you might say something like you would consider salary in the light of the total benefits package, so it would be difficult to provide a figure without knowing what that package is. But if the interviewer pushes for a specific number, then you should be ready. Before the interview, research salary figures in the city where you'll be working for the type of job you're interviewing for. Then tell the interviewer what your research indicates the average salary is, and say you'd expect a salary in that range. You'll find average salaries listed online at sites like Monster.com.

The Job Offer is in the Details

• Bring extra copies of your résumé.

• Wear a suit or a sports coat, if you're a guy. Even if others in the agency are more casually dressed, it's better to be slightly overdressed than underdressed. Of course, if you're specifically told not to wear a suit, then don't. Exception: If you're in the creative area, dress casually but appropriate to the agency.

• Be responsive if asked to describe a weakness, and don't try to disguise a strength as a weakness. Again Karsh offers good advice: When asked about a weakness, focus on a real issue that could be a weakness in a business setting. Describe how you discovered it, why you feel correcting it is important, and what steps you're taking to do so.

• Be prepared for things not to go as you expect. And don't take it personally if the interview starts late or is interrupted or if you are interviewed by someone other than the person originally scheduled. The interview is taking place during business hours, and sometimes the press of business forces things to change.

• Be organized and engaged throughout. Sit forward in your chair, maintain eye contact, and take notes to indicate that you are listening and absorbing.

• Show you have a personality, are passionate and interesting in a way that is natural to you. This is your moment to shine. Make it count.

• Make all of your answers focused and relatively brief.

• Be honest, insightful, and interesting when answering questions.

• Have a couple of questions to ask at the end of the interview. The questions can be about such things as the company culture, the rewards and challenges of the job, or how the overall business environment has impacted the company. But these questions should never be about salary, benefits or vacations.

• At the end of the interview, ask when you'll hear back.

And Then There's That One Little Matter...

• Write a hand-written thank you note to whomever spends time with you. This is called sincere appreciation. It matters. And don't assume an email thanks will do; make this something that no one else might do.

• Whether you get this job or not, you're building a network. Think about the people you want to stay in contact with. Consider those you connected with during your interview. Send them progress reports about your job search. In five years, you'll have a group of friends in the business. And you'll be conducting interviews of your own.

Our Brain Trust

In writing this book, we sought out valuable insight, direction, and detail from many of the smartest advertising professionals in the business. Some offered hours of discussion and insight, others had interesting things to say as they heard about our project and wanted to help. And others we tracked down to add their perspectives to our pages. We thank them all for their wisdom.

Creative

Chris Adams, *Associate Creative Director, TBWA\Chiat\Day, Los Angeles*
Adrian Alexander, *Writer, Crispin Porter + Bogusky, Boulder, Colorado*
Dustin Ballard, *Writer, The Richards Group, Dallas*
Matt Barber, *Writer, Strawberry Frog, New York*
Warren Berger, *Author and Journalist, New York*
Shaun Bruce, *Art Director, Amalgamated, New York*
Scott Burns, *Filmmaker and Producer, Los Angeles*
David Baldwin, *Executive Creative Director, McKinney, Durham, North Carolina*
Rossana Bardales, *Group Creative Director, Mother, London*
Zach Canfield, *Creative Coordinator, Goodby, Silverstein & Partners, San Francisco*
Caroline Casey, *Strategist, 15 Letters, Chicago*
Bryan Chakel, *Art Director, Wexley School for Girls, Seattle*
Lisa Christy, *Media Planning Supervisor, Wieden + Kennedy, Portland, Oregon*
Ian Cohen, *Founder & Creative Director, Wexley School for Girls, Seattle*
Kelly Colchin, *Art Director, DDB, San Francisco*
Glenn Cole, *Founder & Creative Director, 72andSunny, Santa Monica, California*
Vince Cook, *Creative Director, Leo Burnett, Chicago*
Chris Curry, *Creative Director, Ogilvy & Mather, New York*
Russell Davies, *Founder & Strategist, Open Intelligence, London*
Danny Gregory, *Creative Director, McGarryBowen, New York*
Norm Grey, *Founder, Creative Circus, Atlanta*
Matt Heath, *Writer, 72andSunny, Santa Monica, California*
Mike Heid, *Writer, Peter A. Mayer Advertising, New Orleans*
Jelly Helm, *Executive Creative Director, Wieden + Kennedy, Portland, Oregon*
Kathy Hepinstall, *Freelance Writer and Creative Director, Venice Beach, California*
Lina Himorti, *Art Director, Wieden + Kennedy, Portland, Oregon*
Rachel Howald, *Co-Founder + Executive Creative Director, Howald & Kalam, New York*
Chris Hutchinson, *Writer, Wieden + Kennedy, Portland, Oregon*
Andrew Keller, *Executive Creative Director, Crispin Porter + Bogusky, Miami and Boulder, Colorado*
Mary Knight, *Executive Creative Director, DraftFCB, Seattle*
Dany Lennon, *President, The Creative Register, New York*
Mark Lewman, *Creative Director, Nemo Design, Portland, Oregon*
Kate Lummus, *Writer, Publicis, New York*
Matt MacDonald, *Writer and Creative Director, JWT, New York*

Rex McCubbin, *Writer, The Martin Agency, Richmond, Virginia*
Andrea Minze, *Writer, GSD&M, Austin, Texas*
Julio Olvera, *Art Director, McCann-Erickson, New York*
Jesus Ramirez, *Creative Director, Cartel Creativo, San Antonio, Texas*
Robert Rasmussen, *Executive Creative Director, R/GA New York*
Josh Rogers, *Chief Strategist and Writer, MargeotesFertittaPowell, New York*
Peter Rosch, *Freelance Director and Creative Director, New York*
David Roth, *Writer, Amalgamated, New York*
Beth Ryan, *Writer, Bartle Bogle Hegarty, Singapore + New York*
Brian Shembeda, *Creative Director, Arnold, Boston*
Luke Sullivan, *Executive Creative Director, GSD&M, Austin, Texas*
Dustin Taylor, *Art Director, DraftFCB, Seattle*
Kara Taylor, *Vice President and Creative Manager, Leo Burnett, Chicago*
Nancy Temkin, *Senior Recruiter, Greenberg Kirshenbaum, New York*
Kathy Umland, *Creative Manager, Carmichael Lynch, Minneapolis*
Janet Vestin, *Creative Director, Ogilvy & Mather, Toronto*
Richard Wilde, *Director of Advertising, School of Visual Arts, New York*
Hadji Williams, *Author and Marketing Consultant, Chicago*
Mary Williams, *Writer, MargeotesFertittaPowell, New York*
Betsy Yamazaki, *Vice President for Creative Services, Lowe Worldwide, New York*
Matt Zaifert, *Writer, BBDO, New York*

Account Planning

Tom Birk, *Director of Cultural and Cognitive Studies, Crispin Porter + Bogusky, Miami*
Jeffrey Blish, *Partner and Director of Planning, Deutsch, Los Angeles*
Rye Clifton, *Account Planner, The Richards Group, Dallas*
Adriann Cocker, *Planner, Deutsch, Los Angeles*
Earl Cox, *Director of Strategic Planning, The Martin Agency, Richmond, Virginia*
Russell Davies, *Founder, Open Intelligence, London*
Michael Doody, *Brand Strategy Director, Kirshenbaum Bond + Partners, New York*
Cheryl Greene, *Chief Strategy Officer, Deutsch, New York*
Karen Goulet, *Director of Ignition, OMD West, Los Angeles*
Andy Grayson, *Planner, Deutsch, New York*
Alyson Heller, *Assistant Account Planner, Fallon, Minneapolis*
Adrian Ho, *Director of Account Planning, Fallon, Minneapolis*
Kathleen Kindle, *Planner, TBWA\Chiat\Day, Los Angeles*
Darcey Kramer, *Assistant Planner, The Integer Group, Denver*
Julie Liss, *Planner, TBWA\Chiat\Day, Los Angeles*
Neil Saunders, *Senior Vice President, Planning Director, Leo Burnett, Chicago*
Alan Snitow, *Vice President, Group Planning Director, SS+K, New York*
Britton Taylor, *Strategic Planner, Wieden + Kennedy, Portland, Oregon*

John Thorpe, *Director of Strategy, Goodby Silverstein & Partners, San Francisco*

Jamie Webb, *Cognitive Anthropologist, Crispin Porter + Bogusky, Miami*

Account Management

Brianna Babb, *Junior Account Executive, WongDoody, Seattle*

Steve Barry, *Account Supervisor, Wieden + Kennedy, Portland, Oregon*

Michelle Belso, *Founder, DesignWorks, Syracuse, New York*

Bob Berenson, *former Vice Chairman, General Manager, Grey Global Group, New York*

Demian Brink, *Director of Development, The Martin Agency, Richmond, Virginia*

Heron Calisch-Dolen, *Account Coordinator, Goodby Silverstein & Partners, San Francisco*

Caley Cantrell, *Senior Vice President, Group Management Supervisor, The Martin Agency, Richmond, Virginia*

Chris Curry, *Creative Director, Ogilvy & Mather, New York*

David Dreyer, *Account Director, TBWA\Chiat\Day, Los Angeles*

Danielle Fuller-Keany, *Senior Partner, Group Account Director, Ogilvy & Mather, New York*

Tracey Gardner, *Account Executive, Grey Worldwide, New York*

Stephanie Hunter, *Brand Management, The Richards Group, Dallas*

Julia Kang, *Account Executive, AdAsia, New York*

Robin Koval, *President, Kaplan Thaler Group, New York*

Jennifer Mitchell, *Vice President, Account Services Director, The Marketing Store, Chicago*

Karen McGee, *Career Development Director, Syracuse University, S. I. Newhouse School of Public Communications, Syracuse, New York*

Eric Mower, *Founder, President, Eric Mower and Associates, Syracuse, New York*

Ed Russell, *Marketing Consultant, Chicago*

Eric Schnabel, *Vice President, Account Director, Leo Burnett, Chicago*

Mike Sheldon, *President, Deutsch, Los Angeles*

Jeff Steinhour, *Managing Partner, Director of Content Management, Crispin Porter + Bogusky, Miami and Boulder, Colorado*

Mike Townsend, *Director of Methamphetamine Demand Reduction, Partnership for a Drug Free America, New York*

Media

Anne Benvenuto, *Executive Vice President for Strategic Services, R/GA, New York*

Darin Aho, *Media Supervisor, Novus Print Media, Minneapolis*

Kelsey Bernert, *Junior Media Planner, Wieden + Kennedy, Portland, Oregon*

Lisa Christy, *Media Supervisor, Wieden + Kennedy, Portland, Oregon*

Rachel Diperna, *National Television Investor, OMD, New York*

Esther Franklin, *Director of Consumer Contact Planning, Starcom Worldwide, Chicago*

Melvin Goo, *Media Planner, Universal McCann, Hong Kong*

Patti Grace, *Human Resources Director, OMD, Chicago*

Andrea Javor, *Media Planner, OMD, Chicago*

Lauren Harper, *Senior Planner, Crispin Porter + Bogusky, Miami*

Jim Haven, *Creative Director, Creature, Seattle*

Ed Hughes, *Client Communications Director, OMD, Chicago*

Rick Kloiber, *Vice President for Sports Sales, Fox Sports, New York*

Coleen Kuehn, *Executive Vice President, Strategy Development, MPG, New York*

Joanne Luu, *Media Planner, Carat Fusion, San Francisco*

Dannielle Meglen, *Assistant Research Analyst, MindShare, Los Angeles*

Jim Poh, *Director of Creative Content Distribution, Crispin Porter + Bogusky, Miami*

Mark Rice, *Managing Director, MindShare, Los Angeles*

Derek Robson, *Managing Partner, Goodby, Silverstein & Partners, San Francisco*

Annie Sarabia, *Media Planner, Crispin Porter + Bogusky, Miami*

Leslie Schwartz, *Vice President, Regional Broadcast Director, Initiative, Chicago*

Debbie Solomon, *Senior Partner, Group Research Director, MindShare, Los Angeles*

Rachel Timmerman, *Creative Media Strategist, Red Tettemer, Philadelphia*

Julia Trinko, *Print Investor, OMD, New York*

Friday Werner, *Media Planner, Carat, San Francisco*

David Zamorski, *Broadcast Negotiator, GM Planworks, Chicago*

Digital Media

Tom Bedecarre, *CEO, AKQA, San Francisco*

Katie Berger, *Supervisor/Central Intel, GM Planworks, Chicago*

Haley Brothers, *Interactive Marketing Planner, RPA, Santa Monica, California*

Tricia Collum, *Director of Operations, Integer Group, Dallas*

Rick Foote, *Deputy Director, Online Communications, Public Strategies, Inc., Austin, Texas*

Mercedes Guynn, *Media Planner/Interactive, GSD&M, Austin, Texas*

Carrie Gurza, *Media Planner, Slingshot, Dallas*

Cheryl Huckabay, *Interactive Media Supervisor, Click Here, Inc., Dallas*

L. J. Kobe, *Interactive Media Supervisor, t:m interactive, Irving, Texas*

Joanna Luu, *Media Planner, Avenue A/Razorfish, San Francisco*

Cameron Maddux, *Media Supervisor, San Jose Group, Chicago*

Bart Marable, *Creative Director, Terra Incognito Productions, Austin, Texas*

Carrie Murchison, *Manager of External Affairs, Ebay, Washington, D.C.*

Ashlee Nekuza, *Interactive Media Planner, Tracy Locke, Dallas*

Jaime Onorofski, *IP Manager, Starlink Worldwide, Chicago*

Jenifer Putalavage, *Research Director, Nielsen BuzzMetrics, New York*

Randall Rothenberg, *President & CEO, Interactive Advertising Bureau, New York*

Annie Sarabia, *Media Planner, Crispin Porter + Bogusky, Miami*
Tracey Soledad, *Senior Media Planner, Fogarty Kline Monroe, Houston*
Terry Young, *Group Account & Interactive Director, Rapp Collins Worldwide*
Brian Wensel, *Media Search Coordinator, Razorfish, Philadelphia*

Production

Marni Beardsley, *Director of Art Buying, Wieden + Kennedy, Portland, Oregon*
Matt Blitz, *Broadcast Producer, Leo Burnett, Chicago*
Jeremy Boland, *Art Director, Borders Perrin Norrander, Portland, Oregon*
Regina Brizzolara, *Senior Vice President, Director of Broadcast Production,*
	McKinney, Durham, North Carolina
Nate Brown, *Associate Broadcast Producer, DDB, Chicago*
Marc Carter, *Senior Art Producer, The Martin Agency, Richmond, Virginia*
Char Eisner, *Group Supervisor for Art Production, Leo Burnett, Chicago*
Marissa Eller, *Art Producer, Bartle Bogle Hegarty, New York*
Amy Favat, *Senior Vice President, Executive Broadcast Producer, Arnold, Boston*
Chris Folkens, *Broadcast Production Assistant, Leo Burnett, Chicago*
Ken Gilberg, *Vice President, Senior Producer, Leo Burnett, Chicago*
Sebastian Gray, *Art Producer, Crispin Porter + Bogusky, Miami*
Cindy Hicks, *Senior Art Producer, The Martin Agency, Richmond, Virginia*
Jessica Hoffman, *Senior Integrated Art Producer, Crispin Porter + Bogusky,*
	Boulder, Colorado
Samantha Jaffoni, *Senior Art Producer, Publicis, New York*
Amy Jarvis, *Senior Art Production Manager, Leo Burnett, Chicago*
Alicia Kuna, *Art Producer, Wieden + Kennedy, Portland, Oregon*
Annalise Meyer, *Assistant Broadcast Producer, Wieden + Kennedy,*
	Portland, Oregon
Scott Mitchell, *Vice President, Director of Creative Broadcast Production,*
	DraftFCB, Chicago
Rebecca O'Neill, *Assistant Art Producer, Crispin Porter + Bogusky, Miami*
Andrea Ricker, *Art Producer, Arnold, Boston*
Molly Schaaf, *Broadcast Producer, The Martin Agency, Richmond, Virginia*
Jeff Selis, *Broadcast Producer, Wieden + Kennedy, Portland, Oregon*
Shawn Smith, *Director of Art Buying, Fallon, Minneapolis*
Kate Talbott, *Executive Broadcast Producer, Fallon, Minneapolis*
Eric Terchila, *Copywriter, Borders Perrin Norrander, Portland, Oregon*
Jackie Vidor, *Broadcast Producer, Secret Weapon, Los Angeles*
Jeff Yee, *Broadcast Producer, TBWA\Chiat\Day, Los Angeles*

About the Authors

Editor & Production Chapter
Brett Robbs is an associate professor in the School of Journalism and Mass Communication at the University of Colorado at Boulder. He has over 20 years of advertising experience, having served as a copywriter or creative director for numerous regional and national advertising agencies including DDB Needham and McCann-Erickson.

Editor & Creative Chapter
Deborah Morrison is University of Oregon's Chambers Distinguished Professor of Advertising and a member of The One Club Board of Directors. As creative mentor to young talent and consultant to advertising agencies, she's developed an international network of creative and strategic professionals.

Account Management Chapter
Carla Lloyd is an associate professor and Associate Dean of Scholarly and Creative Activity at the S. I. Newhouse School of Public Communications at Syracuse University where she teaches a variety of advertising and mass communications courses. Her research explores media planning and fashion and mediated beauty ideals.

Account Planning Chapter
Kendra Gale has more than 15 years of experience in consumer research and account planning largely focused on ethnographic and other qualitative approaches to understanding the symbolic aspects of consumption. She is an assistant professor at the University of Colorado at Boulder.

Media Chapter
Marian Azzaro is an associate professor of integrated marketing communications and head of IMC studies at Roosevelt University in Chicago. She enjoyed a 20-year career in the advertising media world, working on the agency side as a media supervisor for Foote Cone & Belding and on the client side for Kraft where she handled media planning.

Digital Media Chapter
Gene Kincaid developed the Texas Interactive program for The University of Texas at Austin, an international leader in digital media education. He is an entrepreneur, a marketing guru, and a national leader in digital media studies.

Résumé Expertise
Brad Karsh is the president and founder of JobBound and author of *Confessions of a Recruiting Director: The Insider's Guide to Landing Your First Job*. He was previously Vice President and Director of Talent Acquisition at Leo Burnett.

Acknowledgments

We'd like to thank all of those who helped in innumerable ways from assisting us in obtaining interviews to reading drafts of the manuscript to helping with editing. Of course, our special thanks to all of those who generously shared their insights with us in the interviews. They are listed in our Brain Trust section.

David Blaser
Jennifer Capshaw
Mindy Cheval
Kathy Cho
Tim Christy
Andy Dao
Leah Dieterich
Julie Erich
Teri Fildey
Liz Franko
Glenn Griffin
Jason Hoff
Rubin Hower
Dave Koranda
Karie Laubhan
Marci Miller
Jennie Piel
Jon Randazzo
Joel Redmount
Tim Rivera
Kim Sheehan
Brandon Sides
Ashley Sommardahl
Marty Stock
Kara Taylor
Bill Weintraub

And to The One Club:

Yash Egami *for editing and many hours of counseling,*
Jennah Synnesvedt *for a beautiful clean design,*
Maiko Shiratori *for leading the education bandwagon,*
Kevin Swanepoel *for inspiration,*
Mark Leger and Joni Davis *for organizational magic, and*
Mary Warlick *for nurturing the next generation of advertising professionals.*

Image Credits

Index